BIO/PICS

BIO/PICS

How Hollywood Constructed
Public History

GEORGE F. CUSTEN

■ ■ ■

RUTGERS UNIVERSITY PRESS   NEW BRUNSWICK, NEW JERSEY

Library of Congress Cataloging-in-Publication Data

Custen, George Frederick.
  Bio/Pics: how Hollywood constructed public history /
George F. Custen.
      p. cm.
  Includes bibliographical references and index.
  ISBN 0–8135–1754–0 (cloth)—ISBN 0–8135–1755–9 (pbk.)
  1. Biographical films—History and criticism. 2. Historical
films—History and criticism. 3. Motion picture industry—United
States—History. I. Title.
PN1995.9.B55C87 1992
791.43′658—dc20   91-26427
                                                                                          CIP

British Cataloging-in-Publication information available

For my family and for Phillip
and
in the memory of Lenore Frantz Custen
"To the world's markets I bring merchandise unique."

CONTENTS

List of Illustrations   ix
List of Tables   xiii
Acknowledgments   xv

Introduction: CLIO IN HOLLYWOOD   1
1   MAKING HISTORY   32
2   STOUT-HEARTED MEN   81
3   NIGHT AND DAY   110
4   REEL LIFE   148
5   CONFIGURING A LIFE   177
6   THE FRAME SHRINKS   214

Appendixes
    APPENDIX A: Methodology and Coding Sheet   235
    APPENDIX B: Purposive Sample (PS) of Biopics   240
    APPENDIX C: Biopics by Studio   242
    APPENDIX D: Biopics by Profession   247
Notes   259
References   283
Index   291

■ ■ ■

ILLUSTRATIONS

1. Commodity tie-ins: Pictorial Events Films exploitation kit for *A Dispatch from Reuters* 14

2. Young audiences: exploitation material for *Tennessee Johnson* 15

3. The personalization of history: the great man craves apple pie, and his wife obliges in *Edison, The Man* 20

4. Research as spectacle: discourses of reality—Florence Eldridge as Elizabeth I in *Mary of Scotland* and the portrait that inspired RKO's "accurate" costume 35

5. Research for research's sake: making 5,000 wigs—MGM's campaign book for *Marie Antoinette* 39

6-7. Greer Garson as Marie Curie; Marie Curie, model for Garson 40-41

8-9. Louise Randall Pierson arrives in New York for the premiere of her life story, *Roughly Speaking;* Rosalind Russell as Pierson 42-43

10. Star as self: Errol Flynn as John Barrymore in *Too Much Too Soon* 46

11. Popular art: Hollywood chronicles itself—S. Z. Sakall as Fred Fisher in *Oh, You Beautiful Doll,* with June Haver and Charlotte Greenwood 49

12. Imprimaturs of reality: Babe Ruth and his impersonator, William Bendix, in a publicity still for *The Babe Ruth Story.* Ruth died later that year. 57

13-14. Star acting: George Arliss in *Disraeli* . . .And acting like a star in *Voltaire* 62-63

15. Paul Muni, in costume, on the set of *The Life of Emile Zola* 64

16. In *Love Me or Leave Me,* Doris Day, as Ruth Etting, acts out the roles of both entertainer and paramour 65

17. "Churchill" and "Stalin" of *Mission to Moscow* with the real Joseph Davies, American ambassador to the Soviet Union   *100*

18. Gloss: Greta Garbo and John Gilbert in *Queen Christina*—the woman who loses all for love, in life and on the screen   *104*

19. The troubled company of *The Court-Martial of Billy Mitchell:* Gary Cooper, director Otto Preminger, and producer Milton Sperling *117*

20. *Night and Day:* the Hollywood code of biography recasts marginalized sexual behavior in the proper garb—Cary Grant and Alexis Smith as Cole and Linda Porter   *125*

21. Trial as metaphor: Miriam Hopkins as Caroline Carter at her divorce trial in *The Lady with Red Hair*   *127*

22. "A scientific person can be a strange bird."—Darryl Zanuck. Don Ameche as the inventor of the telephone in *The Story of Alexander Graham Bell*   *133*

23. Valorizing research: Twentieth Century-Fox models of Bell telephones, reconstructed for *The Story of Alexander Graham Bell*   *137*

24. Intertextuality: solving Joel McCrae and Maureen O'Hara's marital problems in *Buffalo Bill* by looking back at *Drums Along the Mohawk*   *145*

25. Deathbed valediction: In *Man of a Thousand Faces,* Lon Chaney (James Cagney) passes his makeup kit on to his son (Roger Smith). Note the addition of "Jr." to the label.   *154*

26. Acting as female strategy: Jean Simmons as the young Ruth Gordon (née Brown) with father Spencer Tracy in George Cukor's *The Actress*   *157*

27. Laying bare the device: George Jessel, as himself, articulating Zanuck's biopic credo to two writers of the film within the film in the Eva Tanguay biopic, *The I Don't Care Girl*   *174*

28. Henry Fonda as Bell's assistant, Watson: the star actor actualizes the historical figure with his specific attributes   *181*

29. Gramsci in Hollywood: Greer Garson as Emma Gladney faces opposition to her Illegitimacy Bill in *Blossoms in the Dust*   *189*

30. A different drum: Sister Elizabeth Kenny (Rosalind Russell) confronts the male, British medical establishment, with ally Dr. McDonnell (Alexander Knox)   *191*

31. Gender and fame: Henriette Desportes (Bette Davis), in *All This and Heaven Too,* left to her schoolchildren after love has failed   *194*

32. Revue as history: Mary Martin, playing herself, reprises her star turn "My Heart Belongs to Daddy," increasing the marquee value of *Night and Day*   *196*

33. The Ragman's Son as alienated genius: Kirk Douglas as Vincent Van Gogh in *Lust for Life*   *198*

34–35.   Star casting: Garbo as Queen Christina, and . . . A contemporary portrait of the Swedish monarch   *200–201*

36. Star couples: Walter Pidgeon and Greer Garson as the Gladneys in *Blossoms in the Dust,* one of six films they made together   *203*

37. Ad for *Madame Curie* with a focus on the star couple Garson and Pidgeon   204

Photo 1 courtesy of Warner Bros., Inc.; photos 2, 3, and 5 courtesy of Turner Entertainment, Inc.; photos 22, 23, and 28 courtesy of Twentieth Century Fox, a division of Twentieth Century Fox Film Corporation. All other photos courtesy of the Museum of Modern Art/Film Stills Archive.

■ ■ ■

TABLES

1	Biopics by Studio	*83*
2	Percentage Entertainer/Artist Biopics by Studio	*88*
3	Biopics by Historical Era and Country	*91*
4	Age of Character at Start of Biopic	*155*
5	Source Material for Biopics	*179*
6	Biopics by Gender and Network	*225*
7	Biopic Professions by Network	*229*
D.1	Biopics by Profession, 1927–1960	*248–255*
D.2	Biopic Professions by Studio	*256*
D.3	Female Biopic Professions	*257*

■ ■ ■

ACKNOWLEDGMENTS

There are many people who helped me construct this book. From the outset of this project in 1986 to the completion of the manuscript in 1991, a number of friends and colleagues read part or all of the manuscript. In all cases, their comments improved what were often ideas in a rough form. At one point, it seemed to me that a large part of the academic establishment on both coasts had read some part of the book, and I was fortunate to have such wonderfully patient friends. Particular thanks goes to my good friend Charles Affron, for his tough and fair (and repeated!) readings of this text. George Gerbner offered useful advice, as did Mirella Affron, Richard Barsam, Victor Caldarola, Richard Dyer, Larry Gross, Arnie Kantrowitz, David Marc, Carolyn Marvin, Ella Shohat, Amos Vogel, and Jim Woods. My friends in the Department of Performing and Creative Arts at The College of Staten Island—Joe Shiroky and Carlin Gasteyer—helped me with a number of critical details. Victor Mattfeld helped me prepare the daunting graphics of Appendix D.

During the summer of 1987, fellow participants at the National Endowment of Humanities Seminar on Theory and Interpretation in the Visual Arts discussed this project, and I remain indebted to Ludmilla Jordanova, Annabel Wharton, Michael Ann Holly, and Svetlana Alpers for their perceptive comments. The Research Foundation of the City University of New York provided me with funds for the bulk of the research for this book, and *Bio/Pics* would not have been possible without this generous assistance. Mike Gregory helped me prepare some of the photographs that appear in the book.

At various archives and libraries there were a number of helpful people: Ned Comstock at the Film/Television Library at the University of Southern California, Sam Gill at the Academy of Motion Picture Arts and Sciences Library, and Birgitta Kueppers at the Theatre Arts Library at UCLA were all helpful. At the Museum of Modern Art, Mary Corliss and Terry Geesken helped me select some of the stills in this book. Much of what is interesting in *Bio/Pics* could not have been included without the permissions granted by the studios and film corporations to publish heretofore private materials: thanks must go to Lorrayne R. Jurist of Twentieth Century-Fox Film Corporation, Diana R. Brown at the Turner Entertainment Co., and to Judith D. Noack at Warner Bros. A small legion of people complied with my requests to tape films for me, and I must thank Judy Glassman and Allen and Lenore Custen for abetting my obsession with the biopic.

My editor at Rutgers University Press, Leslie Mitchner, always had the good sense to tell me when to rewrite (she was usually correct); her support has been much valued. The outside reader of this manuscript, Daniel Czitrom of Mount Holyoke College, offered valuable insights into the connection between film and other media.

Last, I must give deep personal thanks to my lover, Phillip Kautz, who lived with me amidst mounds of videotape, innumerable folders, two computers, and endless talk about Hollywood and its particular ideas on history. I could not have written the book without his support.

BIO/PICS

■ ■ ■

INTRODUCTION
Clio in Hollywood

"I have often thought that there has rarely passed a life of which a judicious and faithful narrative would not be useful. We are all prompted by the same motives, all deceived by the same fallacies, all animated by hope, obstructed by dangers, entangled by desire, and seduced by pleasure."
—SAMUEL JOHNSON

"All history resolves itself very easily into the biography of a few stout and earnest persons."
—RALPH WALDO EMERSON

Richard Nixon, that most self-conscious of presidents, once remarked that he liked his movies "made in Hollywood." On the eve of one of the increasingly frequent escalations of the war in Vietnam, Nixon—who had built and sustained a career by attacking the ideological power of the media—sought reassurance for his decisions within the camp of the enemy. He screened Franklin Schaffner's 1970 biopic, *Patton,* nurturing his dream of war while sitting in a darkened White House theater. This image conjures up one of Walter Lippmann's most pessimistic scenarios about the pictures in our heads created out of the mediated "pseudo-environment" in which modern decision makers must dwell; even the president of the United States gets his scripts from Hollywood. Though the consequences of watching biopics are seldom so influential as they were in this instance for Nixon, most viewers, at least in part, see history through the lens of the film biography. In *Patton,* Nixon found a view of history that was congruent with his own. More importantly, Nixon's—and many Americans—views of the world have been shaped, in part, by a lifetime (and not merely a single) exposure to filmic representations of powerful individuals and the roles they played in history. A system of film production and distribution once upon a time created an environment in which film biographies were a common feature. This book is about those films, the system under which they were produced, and the place they held in the lives of their viewers.

Released with increasing regularity from the earliest days of the cinema to the end of the studio era, the biopic played a powerful part in creating and sustaining public history. In lieu of written materials, or first-hand exposure to events and persons, the biopic provided many viewers with the version of a life that they held to be the truth. The biopic reached its peak—at least numerically—in the 1950s during the dying days of the studio mode of production. From its cultural high-water mark in the William Dieterle/Paul Muni greatman cycle at Warners in the 1930s (the lives of Zola, Pasteur, and Juarez), the biopic seems, since the 1960s, to have faded away to a minor form. Today, it is seen most frequently on cable channels like AMC or TNT, in a rare contemporary form like *The Doors* (1991) or *Sweet Dreams* (1985), or in intriguing transmutations of made-for-TV movies that cultivate a very different ideology of fame from their cinematic counterparts.

What kind of lives did the biopic construct? Why did the biopic decrease in significance? What happened to the industry that nurtured this cultural form? What parts did these great lives on film play in shaping the audience's notion of the self? What kind of historical narratives were the studios attempting to fabricate in the production and distribution of the lives of the famous?

This book is an attempt to answer some of these questions. It has been suggested by François Truffaut and others that the Hollywood cinema was excessively obvious, and that the cultural significance of genres like the biopic stood out with the clarity of cartoons, texts to be effortlessly deconstructed. Yet, as the recent debate over cultural literacy versus multiculturalism shows, to a large extent the purported universality of culture is constructed rather than spontaneous.[1] In order to understand the importance of this genre, we must come to see the films as the product of an organized culture of production. The contribution of these films to public culture and film culture alike can best be seen not through the analysis of individual works, but through the constitution of a large body that forms a kind of supertext. Almost three hundred biopics were produced by the major studios during the classical period 1927–1960. This body forms a code with distinctive components. The films were shaped by industrial practices that no longer exist, were nurtured by a star system that limited the specific shapes a life could take, and were sold to a moviegoing public through diverse publicity machines that created specific contexts for the reception of the great lives.

Rather than being obvious, the overall configurations of this group of films are, in many instances, unknown. With this institutional approach, the "obvious" honor of *The Life of Emile Zola* (1937) or the strenuous patriotism of *Yankee Doodle Dandy* (1943) attain a significance beyond the particular histrionics of a Muni, or the unique charm of a James Cagney. The films form a tapestry whose narrative can be best appreciated by apprehending their place within the whole work. Through a close analysis of the machine that shaped the warp and woof by which the individual figures are woven, we are able to comprehend an identifiable historical pattern.

This book, then, is a study of how the Hollywood biographical film created public history. The biographical film (the "biopic") routinely integrates disparate historical episodes of selected individual lives into a nearly monochromatic "Hollywood view of history." One way this integration occurs is through the construction of a highly conventionalized view of fame. These films build a pattern of narrative that is selective in its attention to profession, differential in the role it assigns to gender, and limited in its historical settings. Another way the Hollywood view of history is integrated is through the studios' strategic use of star images in the creation of the stories of famous people. Because I am interested in the codes formed by the overall Hollywood construction of biography, I will examine these issues by looking at the patterns produced by all Hollywood biopics made during the studio era, 1927–1960.[2]

Prior to television, and along with newspapers, magazines, paperback books, and radio, it was the Hollywood film, attended with great regularity by a large part of the American people, that shaped the public's perception of issues and set the public agenda on topics both important and trivial. Although there have been several studies, from all segments of the ideological spectrum, of the film industry as a producer of culture, none has investigated the code of the biographical film, its construction, and the particular world view it creates when defining history.[3]

The film industry, as a manufacturer whose product is culture itself, has rarely been studied as an institution qua institution, one whose complex social organization possesses (and had to possess) rules for governing its seemingly naive cultural output. However, as Garth Jowett (1990:237) suggests, this previous trend—of slighting the institutional context of film production—has been changing. Movie corporations have made once-closed files available, and recent work by a number of scholars suggests that there is an increasing recognition in cinema studies, just as there is in communications, that texts must be studied as texts in action, in particular institutional settings, with specific audiences' responses.[4]

In the place of studies on how decisions were made to produce movies, anecdotal and mythological works bearing the imprint of the story lines of the films themselves functioned as a Hollywood substitute for a more historically grounded set of creation myths. Until recently, while there had been no shortage of glossy coffee-table books on the stars—of which the studios surely would have approved—there had been little serious scholarship on what anthropologist Hortense Powdermaker (1950) referred to as the "closed tribe" of Hollywood and its fascinating rituals.

One of the most interesting rituals to study is the construction of the Hollywood biographical film. In making the lives of the famous fit particular contours—and thereby controlling normative boundaries of actions and lives—these films cultivate the interests of their producers, presenting a world view that naturalizes certain lives and specific values over alternative ones. Biopics also created a view of history that was based on the cosmology of the movie industry; in this world, key historical figures became stars, and the producers of these films often filtered the content of a great life through the sieve of their own experiences, values, and personalities. In this view of history, the greatness of the individual figure becomes that set of qualities that made a producer great or powerful in Hollywood, rather than those traits that characterized the famous person in his or her own lifetime.

What Is a Biopic?

For my purposes here, a biographical film is one that depicts the life of a historical person, past or present. Biography is mediated through the creation of and competence in symbol systems, and the cinematic version of such mediation has antecedents long before there was a film industry or even the technology of film. While undoubtedly people recalled tales of ancestors and other previous significant figures in their lives, the creation of notation systems (written language, iconic representations) more than the performance of a life through dance, gesture, or music created a sense of biography that located it in a particular permanent form. Biography thus arguably became the basis of the earliest forms of literature, for one of the oldest human impulses is to record for posterity something of the lives of one's fellows. This expression is found on prehistoric slabs and scraps of papyrus, and even, as we know, on cave walls.

So, too, is it found in the earliest works on film. Historical films, or rather re-creations of real events from the past, almost certainly were among the earliest genres of the cinema. In 1895, one could watch *The Execution of Mary Queen of Scots*, or shortly after, in 1898, view J. Stuart Blackton and Albert E. Smith's *The Battle of Manila Bay* in a re-creation of this event that possibly was advertised as a record of the real thing. Sarah Bernhardt scored a major triumph in her 1912 performance of *Queen Elizabeth*. In Germany, Dimitri Buchowetski (*Danton* [1920] and *Peter der Grosse* [1922]) and Ernst Lubitsch (*Madame Du Barry* [1919] and *Anne Boleyn* [1920]) directed biopics of royalty, this focus being an early staple of the genre that would change by the 1930s. In France, Abel Gance commenced his film career acting in an early biopic, the 1909 production of *Molière*, and went on to direct the epic 1927 work, *Napoleon*, as well as the less startling 1936 *Un Grand Amour de Beethoven*. Sir Alexander Korda, whose erratic career encompassed the roles of producer, director, and Svengali, helped cement a tabloid-inspired view of biography with *The Private Life of Helen of Troy* (1927), and, with more prestige, the 1933 *Private Life of Henry VIII*. One of the Warners' earliest commercial successes came with a biopic of the

American ambassador to Germany, *My Four Years in Germany* (1918). The biopic, then, was a known commodity almost from film's beginning. Further, it had many variants—hagiography, psychological biography, autobiography—and was embroiled in the same controversies about truth, accuracy, and interpretation as its literary predecessors.[5]

Biography and the Recorded Image

In 1880, it became possible to reproduce halftone photographs, altering the content of newspapers as well as the picturing of the news. Readers, who heretofore had to content themselves with pen-and-ink drawings of the day's famous, could now see what such a person actually looked like. This expectation of seeing and not just reading about the famous certainly carried over into the cinema in two important ways. First, film with its added dimension of motion and its narratization of images created a most attractive forum for explaining the news, or explicating past events within present-day frames. Second, pictures and their use in popular journalism transformed the very concept of fame. Leo Braudy, in *The Frenzy of Renown* (1986), argues that the possibility of reproducing an actual photographic image shifted the focus from perennial, one might even say societally structural famous, like royalty and rulers, to a celebration of anyone in the news. As an early 1902 silent film, *The Capture of the Biddle Brothers* (later made, in 1984, as a romance called *Mrs. Soffel* with Diane Keaton and Mel Gibson), demonstrates, "headliners" from the print media became the subject matter of biopics, expanding the definition of this genre, which had previously centered on the doings of already famous, often lofty figures. In such a way, fame was democratized.

Sound film made possible another significant development in telling a life story; the broadening further still of biography, as the medium of mass entertainment finally had the ability to fully narrate its own history of entertainment. From the 1940s on, biography came to mean not just what Leo Lowenthal (1944) dubbed "Idols of Production," or headliners (good and bad), but also and even particularly came to be associated with the entertainers themselves.

A biopic, then, from its earliest days is minimally composed of the life, or the portion of a life, of a real person whose real name is used. Other than this trait, the definition of what constitutes a biopic—and with it, what counts as fame—shifts anew with each generation. It is not that each generation creates or discovers necessarily new forums for fame; rather, certain careers and types of people become the prime focus of public curiosity in each generation. Moreover, the ways in which their lives are explained shifts subtly, so that a life depicted in one way in 1930 might be a very different thing by the mid-1950s. Tracing a code for the biopic is an exercise in reconstructing a shifting public notion of fame.

Regardless of the surreal connotations with which Hollywood surrounded, say, Cleopatra, she was an actual living figure. Hercules or Salomé, regardless of their physiques or number of veils, are probably figures of fiction. The point of such analysis is not the limited question, "How 'realistic' is Hollywood biography?" The answer would surely be that Hollywood biography is to history what Caesar's Palace is to architectural history: an enormous, engaging distortion, which after a time convinces us of its own kind of authenticity. Hollywood biographies are real not because they are believable. Rather, one must treat them as real because despite the obvious distortions ranging from the minor to the outright camp, Hollywood films are believed to be real by many viewers. They represent, according to Hayden White, not a concrete illustration of history, a literal recapitulation of physical cause and effect, but rather types of behavior and explanation that comprise the category "history": "Demands for a verisimilitude in film that is impossible in any medium of representation, including that of written history, stem from the confusion of historical individuals with the kinds of 'characterization' of them required for discursive purposes, whether in verbal or in visual media" (1988:1198–1199).

While most biopics do not claim to be the definitive history of an individual or era, they are often the only source of information many people will ever have on a given historical subject. As John E. O'Connor notes, "However unfortunate, it appears likely that even well-educated Americans are learning most of their history from film and television" (1988a:1201). Even at the height of its popularity, Lytton Strachey's 1928 book, *Elizabeth and Essex: A Tragic History,* was read by fewer people than saw the Strachey-inspired Bette Davis/Errol Flynn film, *The Private Lives of Elizabeth and Essex* (1939). Although most biopics make only limited claims to be treated as the final word on their subject, neither are they meant to be ignored as useful historical materials. Unlike other films, almost all biopics are prefaced by written or spoken declarations that assert the realities of their narratives.[6]

In biopics, as I define them, the characters' real names are used. Thus romans—or films—à clef, such as *The Greek Tycoon* (1978), a thinly disguised story of the Callas/Onassis/Kennedy affair; *The Rose* (1979), based on the life of singer Janis Joplin; or Warners' 1935 headliner, *Black Fury,* a vehicle for Paul Muni based on the murder of labor organizer Mike Shemanski, although intriguing forms of creative bricolage, will not be considered here. The fact that real names are used in biographical films suggests an openness to historical scrutiny and an attempt to present the film as the official story of a life. And, while such openness may indeed be a pose by a film's producers, it nevertheless is publicly presented as a natural state of film narration: Hollywood biopics are the true versions of a life.

Searching for the overlooked patterns that reveal the social order hidden beneath the doings of those heralded entertainers, scientists, artists, writers, inventors, capitalists, statesman, politicians, and others, I also want to offer an explanation of why Hollywood, where the hero can have a thousand faces, should have constructed fame with such a limited, contorted profile. Following Emerson's dicta that all history "resolves itself very easily into the biographies of a few stout and earnest persons," the history of Hollywood has been reduced to the history of a few "great" (read, larger-than-life) men.[7] While this corridors-of-power approach to history might be compelling as any Warners biography of the 1930s, it is also ideologically self-serving. The family resemblance between the chronicled histories of the Hollywood industry's founders and the famous figures frozen in black-and-white, ninety-minute narratives produced by these men, the boilerplate tales of immigrant pluck rewarded by a benevolent America, is a tantalizing, but uncharted relationship, which forms part of this study.

Film and History

In focusing on the biopic as a kind of overlooked historical discourse, I am not claiming that the issues that adhere to film and its relations to history have not been considered. These issues are both large, and to an extent largely unsettled. Because of this, the scope of any project purporting to deal with film and history as discourses must first lay out the terms under which questions about film and history might be asked.

Hayden White suggests that one must make a distinction between *historiography,* the representation of history by verbal images and written discourses, and *historiophoty,* the "representation of history and our thoughts about it in visual images and written discourse" (1988:1193). For White, film and video as branches of visual praxis are constituted by discourses that are "capable of telling us things about its referents that are both different from what can be told in verbal discourse and also of a kind that can only be told by means of visual images" (1193).

Much discussion of the biopic, as a kind of historical artifact, hinges upon some issue of how true it is, and how the process of creating a film or video inevitably alters, in some way, the truth or accuracy of the telling of history.[8] Stated simply, one of the concerns of historians studying fiction film's relation to history is with what gets lost in the translation of the event from its verbal state to a visual/pictorial one; how condensation and narratization alter the facts deemed "not essential" to the narrative to fit both a medium and the conventions of genres (e.g., romance).[9]

This translatability problem—from event to its telling or describing—is unique neither to history as a kind of discourse nor to film as a medium. Since Plutarch, there has been an awareness that recorded or written history is a text that freezes the narrative in a particular, interested form. Biography, the isolation of a single life from the flow of history, can reduce the imputation of motive and the rendering of historical explanation to something even more facile. For the presumption that one can get inside the mind of another subject and mediate this incursion with a narrative explanation is a problem as old as literature itself. Reading the *Iliad* or the *Odyssey* illuminates how ancient a habit self-interested historical projection is; past generations, reconstructed by the present, are often seen as different, sometimes superior to the current crop of heroes. Homer, and writers ever since, have used tales of the past to score a point about the current inadequacies of a contemporary social group.

It is a particularly postmodern fixation, however, to be concerned with the processes of mediation as themselves being shapers of meaning worthy of a separate study. The processes used and the materials that constitute recorded history are found to be far from transparent or neutral ideologically, formally, and in other ways. Instead of asking what kind of clothing history's muse Clio wears, contemporary practice prefers to disrobe her, deconstructing the fabrics used to weave the cloth that previously made up her transparent dress.

The larger issue surrounding the accuracy of historical representation, then, is not built solely upon pillars of facticity, legality, or any other single issue. Rather, the problem of encoding the historical narrative can be profitably addressed from a vantage point that incorporates many of these issues into a larger pattern. Communications might frame the issue of biographical mediation as one of translation of information; those conditions created when information encoded in one set of symbol systems is translated into another, partially different set of signs.[10] Since the very acts of daily interaction themselves are full of gaps, of poor translations, of approximations of "information" from one telling to the next, to assume that history (written on a larger scale than the information exchanged as part of the average human dyad) could avoid these issues present at the microlevel is both incredibly naive and severely limiting. For to frame the issue of historical representation solely as one of accuracy or truth is to overlook the social functions that might be performed by differential structurings of the historical discourse.

Recent work by feminist historians as well as gay and lesbian archivists have suggested that the very point of view represented by conventional history eliminates the perspectives of a sizable portion of its own subjects. History's pose of accuracy, and its foregrounding of this issue as a litmus test in assessing different mediations of past events, empower some groups (and some symbolic forms) at the expense of others. Alan Berube's *Coming Out Under Fire* (1990), a study of gay and lesbian soldiers during World War II, is a recent example of a history that conventional chroniclers had banished. Such recent excavation—often, of necessity, self-excavation—suggests that history as a process of mediation is far from disinterested, or complete. Rather, some historians accommodated and even encouraged the repression of minorities by not raising problematic, nonmainstream perspectives as part of their narratives. The history of sexual minorities, as well as other groups, banished from conventional annals for many years, has only recently been recovered. To address history from the point of view of "accuracy" alone is to accept that such a condition exists, and that it is disinterested, rather than ideologically motivated.

There are those who would defend the position that research—historical or other—can get at the truth relatively untrammeled. Although anthropologist Margaret Mead believed that, given the proper training in observation, and with the use of certain techniques and equipment, an event could be filmed unaltered, there are few who would defend this essentialist position that the event, or its recording, exists in such a pure state. As White suggests,

> No history, visual or verbal, 'mirrors' all or even the greater parts of the events or scenes of which it purports to be an account, and this is true of even of the most narrowly restricted 'micro history.' Every written history is a product of processes of condensation, displacement, symbolization, and qualification exactly like those used in the production of filmed representation. It is only the medium that differs, not the way in which the messages are produced. (1988:1194)

All history, then, is a mediation, a set of discursive practices encoded in a time and often a place removed from their actual occurrence, and thus subject to some degree of restructuring. To suggest, as Ian Jarvie does, in "Seeing Through Movies" (1978), that film, biased toward description rather than analysis, lacks an adequate information load, in two hours, to do justice to most topics that can be done in print, is to miss the point entirely. Rather than ask the question, "How true is *I Wonder Who's Kissing Her Now* (1947) or *Wilson* (1944)?" one might ask, "What factors shape the construction of history in these particular mediations, and how are they similar to or different from other constructions of biography in film? In literature? In magazines?" The pattern of these lives, the narrative and other devices used to construct these lives as parts of an institutional machinery of making film narrative, are of greater interest than the distortion of a single film, book, or folk tale.

I suspect that professional historians and film scholars have different ideas on what constitutes history, and on the uses of film both as history and as a medium of communication. But there is a growing awareness that popular encodings of history—rather than those created for professional historians or film scholars—are powerful materials in building a consensus on what constitutes history, and on what kind of history shall be constituted. To an extent, the memory of history many of us carry—if there be such a portable item as a collective memory—is a mediated one. Thus, both the coverage of history, and its selective recovery, through textbooks, film, and other media, is an important project only just begun.

The Creation of Public History

"Public history" refers both to the product and to the process in which members of the mass public—the "public-at-large"—obtain their definitions of the symbolic universe from watching and talking about the communications media. Although the term is also used to refer to history written "from the bottom up," this related aspect will be less discussed than the idea that mass media texts, and not other forms of historical narrative, are significant sources of history for large segments of the American population. Movies today are not the prime media agent cultivating historical images that they once were. In many respects, the enculturation function of movies has been co-opted by other media, notably television. However, film still exerts a powerful influence on people's notions of what counts as history, what properly constitutes a life. Today, because of their still potent popularity and their apparent readability, films are an attractively persuasive source of information. The Hollywood biographical film created and still creates public history by declaring, through production and distribution, which lives are acceptable subjects. Part of this project, then, particularly in chapters four and five, will be an analysis of the kinds of stories films tell in reconstructing the lives of celebrated individuals.

In telling history through the individual life, Hollywood has had an enormous impact upon viewers' conceptions about the world. Sometimes this attempt at influence was intentional, as in campaign books studios distributed to exhibitors, exhorting them with a variety of strategies to exploit their audience before and after screenings. Biopics could be sold as educational, instructional materials. Some of this selling was actually sanctioned by various institutions with ties to educational systems. For many years study guides for selected Hollywood films were published by *Photoplay Studies* and other corporations for formal instruction in history, drama, or literature in different public school systems.

A company called "Pictorial Event Films," with the cooperation of the Warners studio, produced film-strips of selected Warners films (among them William Dieterle's *A Dispatch from Reuters* [1940]) for classroom and other showings, advertising "By special arrangement, Warner Bros. make available for the first time a practical pre-tested plan to exploit motion pictures in classrooms and at large groups through the medium of especially prepared Pictorial Events Films." Included in this package, along with maps and charts used to illustrate key background points on the state of Europe in Reuter's time, was a prewritten lecture for the teacher, with "Each shot . . . keyed by a number to a corresponding number on the text." These guides contained suggested lesson plans for the teacher to use after a film's screening; their focus ranged from cinematic questions to historical ones. And, by their use in classrooms, these films in particular, and film in general, were validated as legitimate carriers of the lessons of history or literature for viewers. These publications also contained information on the film's stars (though rarely on the screenplay's author), and this focus helped cultivate movie-going and star worship as lifelong habits.

Other forms of influence tied films in with other media in exploitation campaigns to maximize interest and attendance. Additionally, as Gaines and Herzog (1990) have noted, commodity tie-ins, in the form of clothing and cosmetics, helped exhibitors sell a film by keeping it in the public eye long after the duration of a screening. Thus, an exhibitor's campaign kit for MGM's *Tennessee Johnson* (1942) comes with a copy of a telegram endorsing the film from the publisher of the influential *Parents' Magazine*. Exhibitors were urged to "Get cooperation of local Parent-Teacher organization to endorse picture to its membership," or, "Offer prizes for best reviews of 'Tennessee Johnson' written by history-class students under sponsorship of department head." The perceived historical value of these films, then, became a bargaining chip in the lucrative educational market.[11]

In addition to organized campaigns to integrate film content into the lives of young viewers via education, information gleaned from

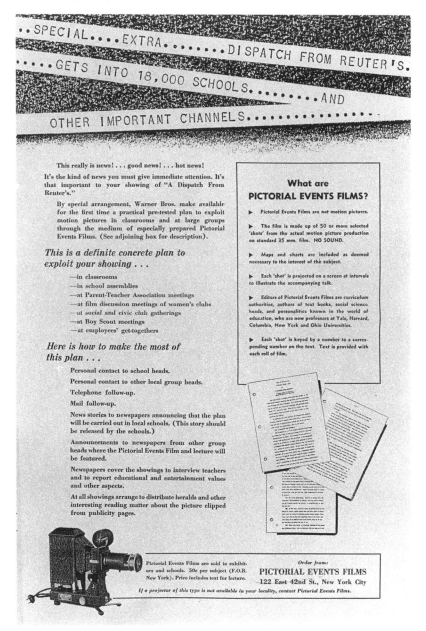

··SPECIAL····EXTRA········DISPATCH FROM REUTER'S.
·····GETS INTO 18,000 SCHOOLS.·········AND
OTHER IMPORTANT CHANNELS.·················

This really is news! . . . good news! . . . hot news!

It's the kind of news you must give immediate attention. It's that important to your showing of "A Dispatch From Reuter's."

By special arrangement, Warner Bros. make available for the first time a practical pre-tested plan to exploit motion pictures in classrooms and at large groups through the medium of especially prepared Pictorial Events Films. (See adjoining box for description).

This is a definite concrete plan to exploit your showing . . .

—in classrooms
—in school assemblies
—at Parent-Teacher Association meetings
—at film discussion meetings of women's clubs
—at social and civic club gatherings
—at Boy Scout meetings
—at employees' get-togethers

Here is how to make the most of this plan . . .

Personal contact to school heads.

Personal contact to other local group heads.

Telephone follow-up.

Mail follow-up.

News stories to newspapers announcing that the plan will be carried out in local schools. (This story should be released by the schools.)

Announcements to newspapers from other group heads where the Pictorial Events Film and lecture will be featured.

Newspapers cover the showings to interview teachers and to report educational and entertainment values and other aspects.

At all showings arrange to distribute heralds and other interesting reading matter about the picture clipped from publicity pages.

What are PICTORIAL EVENTS FILMS?

▶ Pictorial Events Films are not motion pictures.

▶ The film is made up of 50 or more selected 'shots' from the actual motion picture production on standard 35 mm. film. NO SOUND.

▶ Maps and charts are included as deemed necessary to the interest of the subject.

▶ Each 'shot' is projected on a screen at intervals to illustrate the accompanying talk.

▶ Editors of Pictorial Events Films are curriculum authorities, authors of text books, social science heads, and personalities known in the world of education, who are now professors at Yale, Harvard, Columbia, New York and Ohio Universities.

▶ Each 'shot' is keyed by a number to a corresponding number on the text. Text is provided with each roll of film.

Pictorial Events Films are sold to exhibitors and schools. 50c per subject (F.O.B. New York). Price includes text for lecture.

Order from:
PICTORIAL EVENTS FILMS
122 East 42nd St., New York City

If a projector of this type is not available in your locality, contact Pictorial Events Films.

1. Commodity tie-ins: Pictorial Events Films exploitation kit for *A Dispatch from Reuters*

2. Young audiences: exploitation material for *Tennessee Johnson*

films by viewers finds its way into people's daily conversations after screenings. Such conversation has the general function of what Peter Berger and Thomas Luckman, in *The Social Construction of Reality* (1967), refer to as "reality maintenance," as topics initially raised by a film are broached in familiar settings in daily, non-aesthetic conversations with others. In *The Tacit Dimension* (1967), Michael Polanyi noted that with this kind of "tacit" knowledge, while eventually you could be conscious that you knew a thing to be true, you are nevertheless unable to trace the initial source of such knowledge. For example, although it is possible that people's constructions about slavery were based on interpersonal communication, or books like *Roll, Jordan, Roll* or *Time on the Cross,* or a combination of interaction among different media and channels of communication, it is more likely that *Gone With the Wind* (1939) or *Roots* (1977), or even Ken Burns's recent PBS documentary *The Civil War* (1990) were the sources of this information. Eventually, knowledge from different sources becomes merely what we know; the initial contact is indistinctly remembered, or even falsely attributed to another experience. Such tacit effects of biopics certainly influenced audiences as much as organized attempts to market, like some university in a frame, the films as valuable civics lessons.[12]

Film and Social Order

As George Gerbner and others, notably members of the Frankfurt School and more recently critical theorists, have observed, television, film, and earlier mass communications systems cultivate the perspectives of the social order from which they spring. While much of the biographical doings in Hollywood films seem, from the professional historian's perspective, to constitute a slightly deranged form of Dadaism, these films undoubtedly cultivated, for many viewers, images of what the life of, say, Madame Curie was really like. Not only did films order and in some instances create history, they also virtually defined for uninitiated viewers entire realms of endeavor and ways of being. For, as John O'Connor notes, "since the 1930s, film and television have become major factors in politics and culture. . . . some of the most important events of the past century took place before newsreel or television cameras" (1988a:1201). In many cases, in seeing biopics, filmgoers were witnessing the first visual attempt to re-create a narrative that they knew of only from reports in school texts or newspapers. The re-creation becomes, de facto, the only version of history they will ever see.

While the obvious impact of *Madame Curie* (1943) may have been to tell viewers the story of the great scientist who discovered radium, it also posited a vision of what a scientist should be, how the experimental method is applied to scientific discovery, and how a scientist should behave if the scientist was also a woman. Ex nihilo, these films told the tales of history's actors; yet, they also symbolically annihilated much of history by selectively eliminating certain activities, actors, and behaviors from the scripts of history. *Night and Day* (1946), the story of Cole Porter, is particularly instructive in creating a false history that systematically eliminates "problematic" aspects of a life from public consciousness. Porter's marriage of convenience to an older woman covers the fact of his homosexuality. By glossing over this critical aspect of Porter's life, sexual preferences other than those sanctioned by society and approved by the Hays Office are relegated to public oblivion, though, as often is the case, private channels arose to deal with what mainstream channels would not validate. Instead of proposing a subversive construction of marriage and sexual relations, *Night and Day*, with the full cooperation of the Porters, presents the myth of the devoted, supportive spouse of the (quasi)-isolated composer or artist, a human being presented as so special, he or she can only be nurtured by one person who understands the nature of genius-awaiting-discovery. At another level, the distortion in Porter's life on film also naturalizes heterosexual marriage as the norm by eliminating other possible forms of relationship in the life of the artist. As I will suggest later, this attempt to "normalize" genius is a critical part of the construction of the well-adjusted, successful biopic hero. Each instance of biographical selection has this dual function: it both proclaims an episode as true while, as part of a larger pattern of a body of other films, valorizing it as natural. In this world of created history, all acts of selection are value-laden.

It is apt that Hollywood should give public figures the star treatment. Like figures in some festive holiday parades altered to fit this year's celebrity fashion, the set of filmic lives selectively unveiled before the public are changing spectacles which are, in the long run, observable. There is a finite, repeated set of myths about what it means—signifies—to be, say, a statesman (but not a politician), a female entertainer—suffering through four reels of liquor and unfaithful men only, perhaps, to triumph at the end—or merely a famous person. It is possible that the model all professions conform to is one of fame and its relation to the ordinary individual. That is, what is operating in biographical films is the star system speaking of itself through its own contained, controlled means, animating its own values through the figures of a parallel world of stars. Here we have a world where we see history as the film industry, great men as the star system.[13]

Was the Great Man Created by Great Men?

In Hollywood, where all unique stories must be presentable in a short form for conference discussion, the incredible rearrangements and substitutions of the lives of the famous are strategies for rendering these different lives predictable and therefore mass producible. Such control is an attempt to make each new film, though filled with a novel and unpredictable combination of variables, conventional enough to be as successful as the previous studio or industry incarnation it had in part been based upon. The very novelty that makes a celebrated person famous, different from the viewer, must be packaged in a guise familiar to many viewers.

Darryl F. Zanuck, who was a writer at Warners before he was a studio head at Fox, stated this formulation clearly. In a blistering memo of September 29, 1945, to producer George Jessel concerning the script for *I Wonder Who's Kissing Her Now* (the story of composer Joe Howard), Zanuck growled that the script was the "most frustrated conglomeration that it has been my misfortune to spend my time on." An irritated Zanuck felt the treatment as developed broke his cardinal rule of all biopics, and possibly all films: that there was, in his words, no "rooting interest" for the viewer in the life of the famous person. No matter how alienating the character's actual life, it had to be told in terms congruent with audiences' own experiences and expectations about how the famous conducted their lives or lived. A Zanuck famous person had to have clear motivation for the decisions that brought him or her greatness. Actions had to be communicated to the audience in a telegraphic scene or two which served as an explanation of the forces that drove the person to achieve his or her unusual destiny.

This strategy of clearly foregrounding the motivation for the character's actions is evident in Zanuck memos on two films made almost five years apart, *Cardinal Richelieu* (1935) and *The Story of Alexander Graham Bell* (1939). In story conferences for both films, writers were urged to provide explanations for Richelieu's and Bell's fame. At Zanuck's urging, Cardinal Richelieu is shown being impressed at an early age by a specific incident he observes. His past specifically motivates his future. This scene, in which the young Richelieu witnesses the military defeat of France, shows that his entry into the clergy had a particular, personal motivation. Similarly, the opening titles of *Bell,* penned by Lamar Trotti at Zanuck's insistence, inform the viewer that Alexander Graham Bell invented hearing-related devices to make his wife's deafness more bearable. From Zanuck's practiced perspective, it was such personalizing of history that made the great man, or woman, a figure to root for in some cosmic contest. Personal narratives of the famous rendered them understandable to the average viewer, though the construct "understandable" most often meant the producer's notion of what a viewer would understand. Ironically, while Zanuck opted for portraying the genius as having a normal home life and love of family and children, the viewer was meant to treat the achievements of genius with reverence. Thus, the cinematic great were constructed so we could have it both ways: the viewer could relate to the "normal" aspects of private life (a love interest for Marie Curie, a home life for Alexander Graham Bell, simple cravings for apple pie for genius inventor Thomas Edison) while venerating their unusual achievements. The endings of MGM's *Edison, The Man* (1940), a montage of Edison's gifts-to-humanity-in-the-form-of-patents; or Fox's *Young Mr. Lincoln* (1939), in which we see Lincoln enshrined in marble and hear on the soundtrack "The Battle Hymn of the Republic"; or the utopian march of the world's people to a city on the hill that ends Warners' *Mission to Moscow* (1943); or Sister Kenny's ovation from the children she has struggled for, are all typical closing signatures that end the great life with a flourish of grateful homage, a reminder to viewers of how fortunate we have been to be beneficiaries of this great person.

3. The personalization of history: the great man craves apple pie, and his wife obliges in *Edison, The Man*

In memo after memo on a score of biopics, Zanuck drives home the related points of motivation and rooting interest. All cinematic lives had to be understandable in terms that viewers would find congruent with their own experiences. Thus, the cliché-ridden draft of the Joe Howard story (originally titled "Hello My Baby") insults the intelligence (of Zanuck's idea) of what the audience wished to see and would find comprehensible. Zanuck informed producer Jessel that "as the pages turn and the contrived complications increase, he [Howard] becomes more and more idiotic, and then you have the audacity in the last few episodes to try and make an audience feel sorry for or root for this impossible person" (3). Both Thomas Schatz (in *The Genius of the System*, 1988) and Ethan Mordden (in *The Hollywood Studios*, 1988) note that Zanuck exercised an unbelievably thorough control over every aspect of production, often roaming the sets, emphatically making his point about a script, performance, or a costume by whacking his hand with a sawed-off polo mallet. He had definite ideas on the crossroads at which the average audience member would encounter the great man. Through his lengthy memos that often rewrote entire sections of a script, he made sure that he, and not some actor, director, or writer, would be the animus behind the Fox version of cinematic greatness, and that he would cast the mold into which all greatness would be poured.[14]

Studies such as Robert Carringer's 1985 analysis of the production of *Citizen Kane* (1941) suggest that American commercial filmmaking is almost always a collaborative process. It is thus difficult for the analyst of film to assign credit to any one figure for what appears on a screen. But as a perusal of production correspondence suggests—even with a notoriously independent director like Alfred Hitchcock, with whom Zanuck worked on *Lifeboat* (1944)—quite often a strong producer like Zanuck made certain he had the last word on most details. As organizational flow charts show, the buck often did have to stop at a certain point, whether film production was organized with a central producer system (Samuel Goldwyn) or else used the producer-unit system (most film studios after 1931). More often than not, at most studios there were only one, two, or three repositories for intellectual currency.

By highlighting the part played by Zanuck and other film personnel in shaping the life on the screen, it is not my intention to create a parallel narrative of my own that explains biopics by extolling the great men of Hollywood as the ultimate authors of the lives of the famous. However, to overlook data, in the form of production correspondence, or censorship and legal correspondence, which suggest the enormous leverage a Hal Wallis or a Zanuck had on a typical studio product, would be to overcompensate for the past sins, imagined and real, of the auteurists. Rather than seeing the input of a producer as the characteristic signature of an auteur, I prefer to frame a Zanuck and a Wallis, at their respective studios, as men wielding power that was limited or increased within institutional contexts that had rules for their role in the production of films. While both men did their best to help shape these rules (so they might in turn benefit by such a constitution), their input on a film was one organized way of dealing with the production of work. The same system that enabled them to wield extensive power over many aspects of a film's production also made it possible, as I suggest in chapter three, for many collective and individual members of the production team to have a hearing, to exercise real input in the making of a film, and for others to check any undue extensions of power.

Controlling Difference

Although producers could exert an enormous amount of leverage in constructing film lives, they were constrained by factors outside their own hubris and desires. For example, legal considerations were a factor controlling a biopic life. Studios often had to consider the (highly contestable) rights of surviving relatives of the recently deceased famous person as well as laws of privacy adhering to the picturing of actual living individuals. Although under American law a dead person can neither be defamed nor libelled, surviving relatives could halt production with a variety of causes (e.g., injury to reputation), or, if powerfully placed, could make it difficult to obtain favorable publicity for a film they felt cast an unfavorable light on their famous ancestor.[15] A conventional, and profitable route of dealing with the family of the famous person was to hire them as paid consultants, or to obtain their approval. MGM made certain, in publicity materials for its two Edison films, that Edison's surviving daughter, Mrs. Madeleine Sloane, was photographed on the set of the film, and that Spencer Tracy visited Edison's widow, Mrs. Mina M. Edison Hughes, in West Orange, New Jersey (Press Preview Program for *Edison, The Man,* at Grauman's Chinese Theatre, Los Angeles, May 16, 1940). Twentieth Century-Fox used the same strategy with their sensational biopic of Evelyn Nesbit, *The Girl in the Red Velvet Swing* (1955), hiring the reclusive, aging artist's model as a consultant, thus providing her stamp of approval on events that had transpired fifty years before, a lifetime ago.[16]

The studios tried to control, through various means, the attempts of others to shape their making of history. They accomplished this—in part for reasons of efficiency, in part for ideological purposes—through standardization of the great man narrative, through ritualized use of certain actors in certain parts, through control of publicity, and through adherence to legal standards of what things could be pictured about the famous, living and dead; although historically accurate, certain events have been elided from films for fear of legal action.

As a method of understanding the significance of the Hollywood life on film, content analysis alone could never show all the ironies and burlesque of the construction of the Hollywood film biography.

Film and Communication

This book attempts to fill a gap in the literature on film history, as well as to add dimensions to sociological studies of film. It has been written for students of film, communications, American studies, and cultural studies, but I hope it is also interesting to a general readership that follows the movies, or that is interested in the role media play in creating key social constructs. In particular, I have tried to unite research methods not commonly used in studying film as mass communication in order to place the richness of individual works within the context of their larger manufacture and dissemination. In utilizing the techniques and methods of the social sciences, and applying them as a sociologically relevant set of questions, this study could unite two sets of methodological and epistemological assumptions about film, viewers, and history, into a single project that treats texts as dynamic, multifunctional, and polysemic. And, while I recognize that all research methods are themselves social constructions embedded with their own biases, I presume that this book's sample will be less biased than previous genre studies because it was selected using methods other than the presumed good "taste" of the researcher.[17]

The approaches used here emphasize different orders of data, from production memoranda of actual films, to censorship correspondence between individual studios and the Motion Picture Producers and Distributors of America (MPPDA). These multimethodological approaches suggest that as pieces of complex social behavior that are activated through a text, the meanings of a film should include the analysis of diverse, and sometimes unexpected materials surrounding a text, like film publicity campaigns, production data, star interviews, product tie-ins, the routines of celebrity impersonators, and the like.[18]

Although the genre of literary biography has been studied by scholars from Georg Lukács to Lytton Strachey, there have been no systematic studies of the biographical film. There are individual pilot works germane to this theme (Dyer, 1979; Elsaesser, 1986; Flinn, 1975; Freeman, 1941; Hanson, 1988; Miller, 1983). Part of the reason for this absence of research, as I have noted elsewhere, is that social science and film have the longest courtship on record without a proposal (Custen, 1986). The methods of the various social sciences have only sporadically been brought to bear upon Hollywood. Further, a formulation of film as art, with an accompanying focus on texts as sites of meaning to be mined and remined until all precious material has been extracted, tends to lead toward one set of priorities and methods and away from another. There is, however, a body of literature that supports the rather long-standing (but rarely grounded) applied theoretical assumptions of this study, namely that films as a form of mass media reflect the social orders from which they emerge.

This last point is problematic. Different models of scholarship define evidence and data quite differently. Further, a problem that is often the focus in cinema studies—imputing individual agency or authorship—is, in a collective enterprise like film, even more difficult. Thus, attempting to specify a film's relation to its era of production, distribution, and exhibition is far from a simple task. The question of how broadly one can take this film-as-tea-leaves-to-read-an-era approach is at the heart of much of recent work with film as cultural data. While films are, of course, a part of a society, an indexical, point-to-point reading of film and contemporary history can be misleading. Often films are scripted and conceived in one time, shot and released in another. Which era, then, can the film be said to reflect, if reflection is even the appropriate metaphor for the relations of film to history? This use of film-as-popular-culture is a common approach, and perhaps it is time to reformulate some of the issues adhering to the use of film as cultural and historical data.

More than forty years ago Margaret Mead and her collaborators in *The Study of Culture at a Distance* (1953) asked how loosely one could connect films to the cultural settings in which they were found. Mead and her colleagues, strongly influenced by the methods of structural and descriptive linguistics just coming into their own, came up with the answer that one should exercise great caution in using film as cultural data, drawing conclusions about the film's relations to culture only after explicit description of the film's content had been accomplished. More recently, Michael Baxandall, an art historian, in his *Patterns of Intention* (1985), notes that while undoubtedly painters (and here, filmmakers) are not social idiots, and thus would have incorporated the ideas and values of their time and culture in their work, the precise degree to which we can state that the ideas of an era find expression in a work is problematic. As I wonder here with this corpus of films, Baxandall asks of paintings, "can one move from a vague sense of affinity towards something critically useful and historically sustainable? And does one move through critically interesting terrain when one does?" (75).

Among significant early works in the descriptive tradition, Leo Lowenthal's landmark study of magazine biographies, first published in 1944, presented a content analysis of a sample of biographies in popular magazines from the period 1901–1941. His now famous observation that a change in the subject matter of these profiles signalled a cultural value shift from "idols of production" to "idols of consumption" will be similarly applied to biographical film. Gerbner and Gross (1976), in a series of studies carried on since the 1970s, have looked at the impact television programs have on viewers' perceptions of the world. We study media effects not by observing a viewer's subsequent modified behavior, or a single program, but by observing how people think about the real world after prolonged exposure to a large body of mediated fare.

The varied literature on the concept of media fame, from Daniel Boorstin's historical approach to Leo Braudy's recent philosophical probes, is also relevant, as are cultural theories of the construction of meaning through narrative exemplified in the work of Hayden White and Clifford Geertz. Additionally, in recent years, work in history has increasingly focused on "public history" and "collective memory," as historians recognize the roles mass media play in shaping public's notion of historical events.[19]

Thus, while a content analysis of a large number of films might tell us what is the same about biographical films, it is not the only method of investigating something as rich as popular narrative film. For, within the Hollywood celebration of the individuality of the great man or woman, an enormous, unexamined irony is present. While proclaiming the greatness of individuals by honoring them with a showcase about the uniqueness of their lives, Hollywood film really reduces individuals to part of a set of almost Proppian moves, a mass-tailored contour for fame in which greatness is generic and difference has controllable boundaries.

As François Truffaut noted of Hollywood films, what impressed him the most was not their differences, but their resemblances. While this bit of mandarin French apercu is almost zen in its simplicity, there is much truth in his shrewd observation that despite the critical focus we place on a given film, popular individual works are still best appreciated as part of a system of mass-produced, quality-controlled art.

I am also concerned with, though not primarily focused upon, the processes by which film communication—particularly cultivation and socialization—might occur. In stating conclusions about what the patterns of the corpus of biopics mean, I am not suggesting that this is the level at which these ideas were received by viewers of different eras. Reconstructing an historical audience is a terribly difficult task, and the best cinema studies and communications seems able to do is to take a particular discourse—the writings of critics— as one level of data suggestive of how films were received in their era of first release. Several recent studies, however, have reshaped the definition of reception, using real responses of lay audience members to test how viewers interact with a particular event in a given medium.[20] Thus, many of my statements about what individual films or parts of films might mean are enormous leaps of faith into a world where my reading might be presumed to be like those of many other audience members. This is why, in part, the bulk of the statements about the significance of the biopic as a genre are made about the pattern formed by the whole sample of known films rather than my own experiences as an eager viewer with these films; I just do not have faith that any one individual's perceptions about the meaning of a narrative should, as a form of criticism, be privileged beyond being his or her own peculiar interaction with a text. As with many individual readings of texts, the reading of a biopic should be compared alongside other, alternative readings to chart the larger constellation of the category response. Before leaping to any conclusions about what these films did for their audiences, an adequate description of their content is a useful beginning in understanding their significance.

Sampling Film

In general, there are few grounded analyses in film studies that use large systematically selected samples of films. Although there are numerous studies on large bodies of films, most studies either privilege the established canon, or help create auxiliary ones in their analyses of a given genre. In a model borrowed from art history and literature—but surely descended from the practice of making commentaries on difficult points of interpretation of religious and philosophical texts—the film scholar's task is seen as discovering or reexamining masterworks and explicating their meanings. Thus, previous models of scholarship would suggest that in studying the biographical film, the texts that would illuminate the distinctive features of this genre are obvious, having been written about before; such a commonsensical approach would dictate that I select *The Pride of the Yankees* (1942), *The Story of Louis Pasteur* (1936), *I Want to Live!* (1958), and other exemplary products of Hollywood. While the films discussed might be old established exemplars of their type (the canon), what I would say would be presumably new. This approach, while perhaps touching upon shared audience tastes through the illumination of familiar major films, ignores less familiar, perhaps inferior films. Nevertheless, since I am interested in the patterns formed by the machine of Hollywood biography, the formulation "major" or "minor" attached to a film is misleading, guiding one into the realm of analysis cum axiology rather than analysis through description. David Howard's *Daniel Boone*, made at RKO in 1936, while arguably less entertaining than *Mary of Scotland*, released by the same studio in that year, is just as important a piece of the overall pattern formed by the social construction called film biography as the better-known film, which contains two major stars (Katharine Hepburn and Fredric March) under the direction of a fellow luminary, John Ford. We reframe masterworks at the expense of overlooking richly informative, minor efforts. If conventional scholarship had its way, *The Mighty Barnum* (1934), with Wallace Beery, or *The Great Awakening*, a k a *New Wine* (1941), the story of Franz Schubert, or *The Bonnie Parker Story* (1959), with TV's Dorothy Provine, would not, as relatively unknown works, take their places as objects of study beside better known works of famous directors or the performances of major stars.

An analysis of a majority of these films, therefore, will compare Hollywood's idea of history within many members of its own family, not just a select, perhaps ideosyncratic few. It will also enable us to chart, over time, the shifting contours of fame through biography, giving credence to Leo Braudy's observation that, as a social category, fame is constructed anew each generation; "time and the evolution of human societies have their effect most clearly on the arena available for personal distinction, just as the modes of communication available in a period indelibly mark what is communicated" (1986:18).

Because previous work focused so much attention on the individual text and so little on the industrial practices that made possible their production, the method I have selected becomes critical in addressing the significance of the biopic. This book is, therefore, at some level, as much concerned with methods of scholarship as it is focused on their product. That is to say, I am concerned with how I selected the research methods used here, and how these shape the conclusions I am able to draw. The degree to which I am able to be self-conscious about my methods will inform the degree to which I can say that my results represent "all" biopics, or merely reflect those collected for my sample.

In film, this self-consciousness about method is a particularly daunting task, for method or reflection upon method as such has never been a topic of great interest to the extent that such an approach has characterized other disciplines, like anthropology. Much film history has been autotelic, as if the mere existence of a research topic vitiates questioning the appropriateness of the way the topic has been framed or data collected. In fact, many studies are amazingly unquestioning about first concepts: what counts as data, what standards of proof are acceptable, and so on. In the recent past, there were studies that accepted the studio's own biographies of stars as accurate, building auteurist or other arguments on the biographical facts contained in these useful and self-serving fabrications.[21] However, as I suggested earlier, recently, this kind of ungrounded work has ceded the territory of scholarship to more empirical studies that approach the study of the film text from a variety of vantage points, and studies focusing on the institutional, reception, and industrial and business practices of film have replaced the model of connoiseurship that once dominated the field.[22]

Classical Hollywood

Bordwell, Staiger, and Thompson, in *The Classical Hollywood Cinema* (1985), argue forcefully that 1960 was the "end" of the studio system mode of production that had produced many classic texts like the biographical films. The dates that form the boundaries of this study, then, are based upon their data about the contexts of production of studio films.

In many ways, the biopics made during the studio era represent the last of an American culture shaped by the world before World War II. The absences in this body of films are as telling as the distinctive shape afforded the lives represented. The films of the studio era present a world in which minority groups are largely ignored or else were deeply submerged in menial roles within the textures of a world dominated by white males.[23] Almost every enormous shift that characterized the world after World War II—the rise of nuclear energy, the move to the suburbs, the postwar black migration north, the articulation of oppositions to the patriarchal system by the feminist, black, and gay and lesbian movements—is absent in most studio-era biopics. It took at least two generations for the cultural content of the world outside the frame to catch up with the biopic. Well into the 1960s, when other genres had adjusted their stance to a new postwar social order, the biopic continued to articulate an ideology of fame that presented a vanished world of values. Long past the time (1968) when the studio mode of production was in good operating order, Hollywood still produced major hits (like *Funny Girl* [1968]) that drew upon this "old" culture. But, more often than not, the formulaic reflexivity of star biopics that characterized the postwar era failed to find a public in the post-studio era, and a series of disasterous attempts to continue the ideology of the 1940s into the 1960s (as was the case with the biopic of Gertrude Lawrence, *Star!*, in 1968) suggested that the ability to shape public history had, with rare exception, been passed on to television. The cultural initiative once held by film had been seized by television, and the smaller screen constructed the self with a very different image than film.

Ironically, the preeminence of television, and cable TV, as purveyors and creators of public history has not banished the brand of public history cultivated by movies to archives. The rise of cable systems has meant that the public can get a second look at many of these biopics produced during the studio era, as superstations (like Ted Turner's TNT Network) open the vaults and screen the holdings of MGM, Warners, and RKO. Once again Muni, Arliss, Garson, and Davis visit, figures in black and white (or ersatz color), ghosts from the past whose history lessons seem quaint, madly heroic, and certainly out of step with today's tabloid ideology of fame. Yet, even though their tales have been told, the echo of these scripts continues to haunt us in the behavior of the leaders who came of age with these studio era norms, and internalized them as barometers of public value. To hear Ronald Reagan, or George Bush, or Mario Cuomo speak out on public issues is to hear the cadences once written for the cinematic scenes of public triumph of the biopic great man. The meters and metaphors of the biopic have become part of the vernacular of public debate. Even as the narratives that spawned them have lost favor with the movie-going public, the ideas of script construction that form the heart of the biopic are incorporated into the public rhetoric of a culture.

The shape of the remainder of the book is as follows: Chapter one, "Making History" discusses the role the studios played in making public history, and presents several key content categories, like the prevalence of explanatory titles in almost all biopics. Chapter two, "Stout-Hearted Men" discusses the bulk of the numeric data in the study. Since my conclusions are based on the patterns formed by the whole sample of biopics, these data are templates that will be used throughout the book. Discussions center on nationality, time, and place, and house style as variables in biopic production. Chapter three, "Night and Day," looks at the machinery of biographical research in the film industry. The role of publicity for biopics, how the historiocity of a film was sold as a consumer commodity, will be discussed. Chapter four, "Reel Life," discusses the cinematic construction of fame. Here, I look at the moves that constitute the creation of fame and the events in its aftermath. Since the famous person of the biopic has fellow actors sharing the screen of history, the role of family and friends in his or her life will be examined. Particularly, I will discuss an odd characteristic of the biopic which seemingly places it on the margins of other mainstream Hollywood narratives: the idea that the family is a force of resistance to, rather than supportive of, the behavior that secures the fame of the hero or heroine. The cultural explanatory mechanisms for fame—the temporal and physical boundaries in which fame is placed—are also discussed. Chapter five, "Configuring a Life," looks at the rhetoric of fame as mediated by the formal conventions of the narrative film. Further, the role of the star image as a context for biography is assessed. Last, chapter six, "The Frame Shrinks," looks at the decline of the biopic in the seventies, eighties, and nineties, and the subsequent rise of the docu-drama and the made-for-TV movie that have, in many respects, gerrymandered the cultural territory once occupied by the cinematic biography.

1

■ ■ ■

Making History

"It is personalities, not principles, that move the age."
—OSCAR WILDE

In 1944 Leo Lowenthal, a member of the Frankfurt School, published his now famous article "Biographies in Popular Magazines." In it, he proclaimed that twentieth-century capitalism had created a new set of myths—what he called "mass culture." Rather than being indigenously produced by a people, mass culture was instead manufactured for audiences by organizations we now refer to as mass media of communication. These myths—in this particular instance, a set of biographical sketches of famous men and women published in mass circulation magazines—were manufactured like the commodities of other industries that had come to dominate the American landscape; story form and content, like items on any assembly line, were standardized for easy consumption. Readers could thus peruse the pages of *Collier's* or *The Saturday Evening Post* and in the tales of the life of a Henry Ford and Ronald Reagan (when he was only a movie star) receive a kind of pseudo-education, one that reduced history to organized gossip.

In seeking to discern in these magazine biographies patterns over time, Lowenthal noted a shift both in the subjects of biography and in the explanations proffered for why a particular life was meritorious. His content analysis of 1,003 issues of *Collier's* and *The Sat-*

urday Evening Post, covering sixteen sample years, found that while magazines of the first decades of the century had focused their attention on the biographies of what he called "idols of production" (captains of industry, the military, and other members of conventional ruling elites), later magazines, inspired by the new media, radio and the motion picture, chose to highlight what Lowenthal called "idols of consumption." In this change from idols of production to idols of consumption, he detected a shift in American values and a shift in the morality lessons—"lessons of history"—that readers might derive from these magazines. Power through the making of the world had been replaced by power through ownership of its coveted items. Consumerism had replaced community as a way of life. This new power was attained through the appropriation of a proper and glamorous appearance. In this world, Andrew Carnegie was replaced by Hattie Carnegie as a figure to be admired.

Lowenthal shared with other members of the Frankfurt School (notably Theodore Adorno, Walter Benjamin, and Max Horkheimer) a fearful contempt for the products of the mass media which, according to his view, increasingly manipulated audience members into an authoritarian view of history cum popular entertainment. Fearing that the simplifications found in items like biographies in popular magazines, when not downright harmful, were "corrupting the educational conscience by delivering goods which bear an educational trademark but are not the genuine article" (134), Lowenthal felt that biographies performed another, more powerful function. In particular, biographies, like the earlier "Lives of the Saints," helped prepare average people to accept their place in the social structure by valorizing a common, distant, and elevated set of lives that readers could hope to emulate. More than examples of entertaining education, these biographical sketches were also propaganda that prepared readers for acquiescence in a status quo; in this world of biography, there would always be readers on the outside and those figures inside the covers whose lives were read about, admired, and emulated.

If he feared the impact of magazines (with their relatively modest circulations) as agents of socialization, one wonders what Lowenthal made of the infinitely more glamorous biographies manufactured and released by the Hollywood studios. For just as biographies in popular magazines played some part in socializing readers into a particular vision of America and the lived American life, movies, with their attractive stars, swelling, emotionally manipulative musical scores, and powerful publicity engines were rival sources of information about the lives of the famous. Movie biographies offered the public the possibility of connecting concretely with a glamorous image of a famous historical person in the guise of a contemporary movie star. One could admire the past life depicted while worshipping the very real current incarnation of this life on the screen, and off the screen, in publicity materials.

Movies created a rhetoric of fame that was essentially different from that of print. In movies, the actor portraying the eminent figure had an actual, corporeal existence outside the narrative frame of a particular biographical life that may or may not have been congruent with the figure depicted; in print, there was no such double life, except to the extent that print biographies, sanitized and censored as their movie equivalents, were as far removed from the real life as any film.[1] Stated another way, movie biographies presented a double level of the articulation of fame. At the first level, one was absorbed by the narrative constructed about selected episodes in the life of the subject. At the second level, one encountered the famous figure in other filmic contexts as well as through repeated exposure to publicity materials. Combined, these two levels of image created the facets of what Richard Dyer perceptively refers to as the polysemic star image. Here, the moviegoer is drawn to resonant aspects of the impersonator as well as the life impersonated. In this light, perhaps one admires Queen Elizabeth I for her statecraft but also because she is Bette Davis.[2]

Marketing Research

Biopics were often sold to the public as accessible versions of history. Credits within the film and publicity for the films made sure to highlight this research angle. For example, a title credit for Fox's *Stanley and Livingstone* (1939) acknowledged the researchers for the film as well as the director, producer, and screenwriters. The intensity of the research effort expended on a project was part of the publicity campaigns for many biopics. Bordwell, Staiger, and Thompson, in *The Classical Hollywood Cinema* (1985), have noted that both the spectacular and novel aspects of a film were commonly used to differentiate one product from the next. Extravagant research

4. Research as spectacle: discourses of reality—Florence Eldridge as Elizabeth I in *Mary of Scotland* and the portrait that inspired RKO's "accurate" costume

efforts became, for the biopic, a way of reassuring consumers that every effort had been expended to bring them true history in the guise of spectacle, as well as suggesting that the research for each film was, for the first time, bringing to the screen a true portrait, or at least a singularly true version or the accurate characterization of a person.

In part, the focus Hollywood accorded biopic research was like Leonardo's aging painting of *The Last Supper:* parts of the fresco were vividly drawn, with the most minute detail given emphasis. In other places, the image lacked clarity. With the full awareness of some of the personnel on a film, the most outrageous misrepresentations sometimes passed as the norm. In part, research for a biopic was shaped by particular expectations regarding what historical errors audience members and critics might catch, and what they were likely to overlook. Such slippage had to be avoided at all costs, for it could suggest that the product had been accorded less than the deluxe treatment.

The studios files are full of letters from fans who wrote gleefully to point out real or imagined mistakes. For example, Cpl. Maurice G. Smith, an RAF pilot, wrote Warners Research Department on October 30, 1946, that some of the personnel in a hospital scene in the Cole Porter biopic, *Night and Day,* were wearing inappropriate decorations. Hetta George, of Warners Research, defended the accuracy of the costumes: "Our uniform expert, however, who incidentally is an ex-Royal Navy Officer, assures us that the ribbon worn by the British Medical Officer in our picture was carefully checked by him and is absolutely correct" (Warners Collection, University of Southern California). Similarly, a preview card from MGM's *Parnell* (1937), in May 1937, contained a query from an audience member about the accuracy of the film's narrative. Although praising one of the film's stars ("Anything with Myrna Loy suits me"), the anonymous viewer noted, "Also, I thought Parnell and O'Shea were married after her divorce" (USC, John Stahl Collection). From its earliest days, film audiences seemed to demand a loose code of realism in certain cinematic contexts. Kevin Brownlow writes:

> The alibi, 'The audience will never notice' was given lie early in *Photoplay's* 'Why Do They Do It?' column— which was entirely devoted to blunders made in movies. . . .
> Audiences spotted every conceivable error, and specialists in various subjects had a field day when films appeared dealing with their favorite topic. (Brownlow 1968:276)

He suggests that both the demand for accuracy on the part of the audience, and the studios' means of satisfying that demand, were in existence by the 1920s.

Particularly because biopics were films differentiated from other narratives by dint of their historical nature, the studios maintained a watchful eye upon their use of facts. While most critics were willing to accept a certain amount of poetic license in biopics and other historical narratives, a film that wandered too far into biofantasy inevitably drew sarcastic critical comment. Thus, H. T. Jordan, a critic from the *Cincinnati Times-Star,* under a review for Fox's *Cardinal Richelieu* titled "Bad History," lectured:

> In the motion picture *Cardinal Richelieu* featuring George Arliss, there is an incident which is so contrary to truth and so palpably a distortion of historical facts that the entire production, despite its extravagent beauty of setting, is rendered distasteful to any well-informed person.
>
> It is realized that a writer of motion picture plots is permitted some freedom with historical facts, but when one of the greatest characters in history is introduced wantonly and unnecessarily into the plot structure and in a manner derogatory and despicable, the occasion gives rise to protest.

The critic refers to the depiction of King Gustafus Adolphus of Sweden as a kind of drunken lout, a portrayal that drew a protest from the Swedish government. Geoffrey Shurlock, of the MPPDA, took note of the protest, and suggested to Fox that such an error "serves to remind us how very careful we will have to be with regard to these historical pictures" (Academy of Motion Pictures Arts and Sciences, MPPDA Collection, *Cardinal Richelieu* file). Fox, in an unusual capitulation, eliminated the offensive scenes.

For the biopic of the Brontës, *Devotion* (1946), the anonymous critic for the *New York World Telegram* noted that while "the picture can look forward to the popularity that goes to all slickly produced tear jerkers these days," the creators of the wildly inaccurate narrative of the Brontë family "should have their knuckles rapped for making up such fibs about their elders" (AMPAS, MPPDA Collection, *Devotion* file).

Although some critics and viewers lay in wait to catch the slightest slip, the attitude of most audience members, as well as producers, seemed to be that unless the error was particularly outrageous, or the events were so recent that many patrons would recall the facts, an odd mixture of careful research, of compromised whimsy, and of outright fabrication characterized the sets, the costumes, the characters, manners and mores, and the narratives of most biopics. As Darryl Zanuck, in a memorandum of August 12, 1950, notes of some of the fabrications of the life of Ben Hogan, *Follow the Sun* (1951), "No one, in my opinion, will ever pin us down to dates except the later dates in the past two or three years which are clearly remembered." Zanuck believed if the film were entertaining enough, no one would attend to a minor glitch or two. When Kenneth MacGowan, the associate producer of a Zanuck favorite, *Lloyds of London* (1936), complained that some of the depictions of financial operations of nineteenth-century insurance companies were inaccurate, Zanuck, in a memo dated July 28, 1936, lectured film neophyte MacGowan on what audiences would and would not accept as film history:

> Technicalities of this type never cause any trouble. In *Rothschild* I made Rothschild an English Baron and there never was a Rothschild a Baron. I had the King of England give him the honor, and at this time there was no King of England as the king was in the insane asylum— and the Regent had the gout and couldn't stand up, but I used Lumsden Hare and the picture in England got the same wonderful reviews it received in America and no one ever mentioned these technical discrepancies. (UCLA, MacGowan Collection)

Research and historical accuracy were woven among the threads of narrative demands, producer's taste, and the marketing strategy in which a film could be exploited for its "spectacular" research.

We see this approach to exploiting research in the road show and souvenir books printed by each studio for the premieres of important films. Typical of these efforts is MGM's booklet for their prestige production of *Marie Antoinette* (1938). The campaign book for the film is filled with numerical data, informing exhibitors that "during the four years in which the picture was in preparation, 59,277 . . . questions were answered. This required compiling a bibliography of 1,538 volumes, gathering 10,615 photographs, paintings and sketches, and mimeographing 5,000 pages of manuscript containing more than 3,000,000 words" (USC, *Marie Antoinette* Campaign Book). It seems that Metro could now boast that they had more researchers, as well as more stars, than in heaven, for no detail was too small to demand attention. According to the *Antoinette* campaign book, sharp-eyed director W. S. Van Dyke spotted one extra, amid a crowd of 250, wearing anachronistic and inappropriate pants; he would not shoot the scene before this minuscule detail was rectified.

5. Research for research's sake: making 5,000 wigs—MGM's campaign book for *Marie Antoinette*

6. Greer Garson as Marie Curie

Selling the film as historically accurate, as an epic of research, was key in differentiating the biopic genre from other studio fare. Thus, MGM's book for the West Coast premiere of *Madame Curie* suggests that

> The research task to achieve authentic realism was one of the most thorough ever attempted for a motion picture. Fortunately, many photographs of the Curies, of their lab-

7. Marie Curie, model for Garson

oratories and of Paris during the turn of the century were available. A treasure of Curie photographs was obtained from Mlle. Curie. They furnished accurate guides for make-up, costuming and sets. . . . Whenever possible, these photographs were brought to life. . . . Miss Garson's make-up as Marie in her later years, of Pidgeon as Pierre, Travers as Dr. Eugene Curie and Dame Whitty as Mme. Curie, were carefully matched to family portraits.

Sometimes, producers attempted to attain the active participation of the surviving family members of the great man or woman. Their imprimaturs were valuable publicity commodities, though only occasionally were their contributions more than symbolic. Producer Sidney Franklin even tried to get Marie Curie's daughter, Eve, whose book, *Madame Curie,* was the source material for the Paul

8. Louise Randall Pierson arrives in New York for the premiere of her life story, *Roughly Speaking*

Osborn and Paul Rameau script, to speak the opening narration, noting in a draft of a letter to Eve Curie that, "Since the words are yours, it seems to us it would be most fitting that the voice should be yours, also" (USC, Lewin Collection). Eve Curie demurred, and the poetic opening was spoken in classic dulcet narrator tones by Cambridge-educated novelist James Hilton who had, earlier, written the screen-

9. Rosalind Russell as Pierson

play for another Greer Garson/Walter Pidgeon hit, *Mrs. Miniver* (1942).

Similarly, the program for the press preview of MGM's *Edison, The Man,* which took place at Grauman's Chinese Theatre on May 16, 1940, avers how research aided Spencer Tracy in his portrayal.

> Before the picture, Spencer Tracy visited Edison laboratory in Greenfield Village, talked with Henry Ford, who has collected the Edisoniana, and visited Mrs. Mina M. Edison Hughes, widow of the inventor. . . . During production, Mrs. Madeleine Sloane, Edison's daughter, watched many scenes during a trip to Hollywood.

Further, copious newsreel footage of Edison was assembled by the research department, and "Tracy studied them many times to capture the inventor's mannerisms and actions."

Never one to be outdone in the serious business of ballyhoo and promotion, Cecil B. DeMille claimed, in the souvenir book for the West Coast premiere of Paramount's 1938 Jean Lafitte biopic, *The Buccaneer* (1938), that he was descended from the governor of Tennessee who financed the War of 1812. DeMille, the master showman, thus connected himself in a deeply personal way with the narrative; it became a tale of his own ancestor, as well as a reconstruction of history. RKO claimed a similar genealogical link for Katharine Hepburn to a character she portrayed, Mary Queen of Scots.

Publicity campaigns, then, asserted that the film seen by the viewer was the end product of copious research efforts on sets and costumes, in verification of historical chronology, and in accuracy of mannerisms. These prodigious efforts to bring the authentic life to the screen were overseen by surviving relatives or experts whose presence, in addition to providing valued publicity, also served as a guarantee of authenticity.

This issue of authenticity, stressed in every road show publicity book for every biopic, could be reframed as the question, "To what extent did studios consciously attempt to cultivate a sense of accurate history in film biographies?" Here, I am interested in the kinds of research that went into narratives about the famous, and in a general way, the kind of history Hollywood producers felt they were creating for viewers. Was Warners' effort on *Juarez* (1939) typical of Hollywood's approach to understanding biography? For this film, the vice consul of Mexico acted as a technical advisor while the producer, star, and director toured and studied their way through a six-week trip to Mexico to acclimate themselves to Juarez's milieu. The final product of this jaunt seemed to be neutralized by other Hollywood conventions, notably the demand for heterosexual love; the film canted the frame of history more toward the romance of Maximillian and Carlotta than toward the struggle of Benito Juarez. The luxury of a six-week tour of Mexico was not a common agenda item for the Warners research department. However, every biopic, and many nonbiographical films, made extensive use of the studio's own in-house research departments at every stage of film production.

Research came into play before a script was written, during actual shooting, and for publicity purposes prior to release. The kinds of questions asked of the research departments as well as the use to which such findings were put in film production are important signposts on the road to Hollywood history.

Star Actors

While there may be large, overarching structures formed by the corpus of biographical films, individual factors, like the personality of the star, are also significant features of the biopic. To an extent, every famous figure, from Henry Fonda's Lincoln to Barbara Stanwyck's Annie Oakley, is filtered through the persona of the star image in two ways: inside the frame by the tradition of the actor's performance, and outside the film by publicity and public relations materials. Because events outside the film (the life depicted) interact with our responses to the actor inside the film, the meaning of this body of films is both multivalent and interactive. Chapter five, "Configuring a Life," deals with this more in depth, but a brief mention of the role of the star persona and its impact on the life depicted is in order.

The very real strengths and limitations of the actors under contract to any particular studio at a given time influence the life selected for depiction and its manner of enactment. While Paramount had Betty Hutton under contract, they cast her in films that presumably used the attributes that made her enormously popular. Thus a Betty Hutton film featured the singing, dancing, and above all the vibrant, at times abrasive energy that made her a top box office draw of the 1940s. After she scored a major hit in Preston Sturges's *The Miracle of Morgan's Creek* (1944), she appeared in three biopics in the 1940s, culminating in 1950 with a starring role, as a replacement for an ailing Judy Garland, in MGM's *Annie Get Your Gun*. Hutton could only play tough, heart-of-gold types and the lowest of physical comedy. Producers, realizing this, cast her exclusively within this type. Thus, her Pearl White, in *The Perils of Pauline* (1947), is constantly played off against the high-art manners of Shakespearean actor Michael Farrington (John Lund) and the good-natured grand dame gestures of her companion, Miss Julia Gibbs (Constance Collier). When audiences heard Pearl White referred to, in the film, as too kinetic for Shakespeare but just perfect for the silent movies,

10. Star as self: Errol Flynn as John Barrymore in *Too Much Too Soon*

they knew the line referred as much to the so-called Blonde Bomb-
shell's performance style as to the historically created character of
silent movie queen White. This illustrates what Dyer (1979) has suggested as one dichotomy of the star: star-as-star/star-as-actor. Betty
Hutton, actress, seems incapable of acting like anything but the star
Betty Hutton. The Pearl White biopic trades on our realization
of this: when Pearl is allowed to "be herself" she succeeds; forced
by her high-toned love interest to be some other personality, she
fails.

On the other hand, there is some difference between the performance characteristics of stars and their personal history outside the
frame. For the part of the dissolute John Barrymore in *Too Much,
Too Soon* (1958), the producers cast Errol Flynn, whose own fading

career (he made but two more films) and declining health (he died, at fifty, less than a year after completing the film) were used as palpable hooks for the viewer. As they watched the story of John Barrymore, they knew they were also watching Flynn perform in his own cautionary tale. Here we have what Dyer refers to as a dichotomy in which star-as-self/star-as-role interact. These individual factors, and their patterned deployment, are part of the code of the biopic. They are as significant a determinant of the film biography as any sense of ideological history producers or other film personnel may have had.

Studios as Sites of Production

In addition to looking at a body of films as constituting a code of biography, and the star as a set of lenses through which the life is rendered meaningful, biopics can also be studied as in-house reflections of the community of producers, in the way, say, that Muriel Cantor, in *The Hollywood TV Producer* (1971), studied the culture of production of American popular television. George Jessel's production of six biographies for Zanuck at Fox—*The Dolly Sisters* (1945), *I Wonder Who's Kissing Her Now, Oh, You Beautiful Doll* (1949), *Golden Girl* (1951), *The I Don't Care Girl, Tonight We Sing* (1953), and for Paramount *Beau James* (1957)—all placed vaudeville at the center of the universe. These films might be seen less as an example of house style than as reflections of Fox's available talent pool of Betty Grable, Mitzi Gaynor, and company, including Jessel's own, highly limited skills. Producer Jessel, in preserving this crepuscular form, created a mythology: that vaudeville was the only legitimate form of entertainment, and that the era of vaudeville was a privileged, halcyon time. This perspective of biopics as a product of a culture of producers suggests that, in addition to the studio's own house-style ideologies asserted by these films, each studio was also shaping biography based on the talent pool available under contract, both above and below the line.

House style might include not just the studio personnel and their repeated, conventional deployment, but also an ideology of biography. It seems that in a general way, studios had different class attitudes toward their biographical materials. Studios selected careers they opted to use as film materials (see Table D.2), with certain studios showcasing common people who performed feats uncommonly well. Even given common material (say, entertainer biopics), studios manifested significantly different attitudes toward a life. Fox tended to showcase vaudeville stars and stars of the stage, luminaries from popular entertainment, while MGM opted for headliners from high culture, with films of Enrico Caruso (Mario Lanza), Jenny Lind (diva Grace Moore), Clara Schumann (Katharine Hepburn), and the like.

In fact, the differences between conventional formulations of high and popular culture are themes of the performer and entertainer biopics. This distinction is at the heart of the movies picturing themselves. One of the stranger biopics in the sample—it is the only starring vehicle for that mainstay character actor S. Z. "Cuddles" Sakall—*Oh, You Beautiful Doll* clearly illustrates this tension. Sakall plays Fred Fisher, composer of hugely popular songs "Chicago," "Peg o' My Heart," and the title number. Alfred Breitenbach, though trained as a classical composer, shamefacedly moonlights under the name of Fisher to support his family (daughter June Haver and "Mama" Charlotte Greenwood). Unable to support himself or his family as a serious artist, though hugely successful as a popular balladeer, he flees his home after denouncing his family as being Fishers (popular artists) interested only in money rather than Breitenbachs (serious artists) whose only interest is art. Fisher/Breitenbach tells his family, "Money, what is money, but the vulgar implement to tempt man's soul." By making him ridiculous—his character is a portly figure whose malapropisms and spoonerisms are the stuff of good-natured humor—the film suggests that his artist's point of view is also, like the befuddled Fisher/Sakall, silly, if somewhat endearing.

A key scene in the film illustrates this high art/popular art formulation, and articulates Hollywood's own attitude toward movies as a cultural form torn between pretensions of high art and the lure of popular acceptance. Fisher has gone to his (popular) music publisher, Ted Harris, an amiably tone-deaf capitalist, to get out of his contract. They argue, and Fisher asks how he, the publisher, who admits to knowing nothing of music, can predict when a song will be a hit, when Fisher himself, a trained classical musician, is unable to predict such a thing. The publisher replies, "Because it's my business to make it a hit. Tin Pan Alley is just a huge company to make

11. Popular art: Hollywood chronicles itself—S. Z. Sakall as Fred Fisher in *Oh, You Beautiful Doll,* with June Haver and Charlotte Greenwood

people listen. Get them so used to it, they like it. Then, they buy it. Good or bad, it's our job to make it a hit, anyway." This justification of selling music as a commodity rings with the tone of self-justification. Earlier, even Fisher's future son-in-law, a resourceful song plugger, compares the peddling of Fisher's operas turned into ragtime to selling groceries, or to serving leftover meat reheated with the horseradish of syncopation. In the end, it is the popular Fisher, and not the classical composer of serious classical works like *Der Finstervald,* who triumphs as a composer, as Mama and others have secretly schemed to have his music played at a concert at Mayolian (sic) Hall. And, while the name announced in the program is Breitenbach, the orchestra, arrangements, and the conductor are classical, the music is popular, like the Boston Pops's dreadful, bloated renditions of Beatles songs. Breitenbach is resolved to being Fisher, as Mama, always the voice of common sense, tells him, "You see,

Papa, good music is good music. Some people like it played slower, some people like it played faster." Fisher has lived out Adorno's nightmare of how popular music impoverishes the classical. In the movie view of the world, Breitenbach embraces Fisher with enthusiasm, or *con brio*.

These attitudes reflect, in part, the attitudes of the production heads toward what constitutes culture, including what kind of culture Hollywood itself constitutes. Zanuck at Fox repeatedly voiced his democratic leanings, his feeling that film should be in accord with audience tastes and desires. Mayer, at MGM, had a somewhat variant view of movies as morally uplifting; it was his duty, in selected films, to bring culture and taste, in the form of enlightenment, to the masses. These differences suggest that each studio signed up the talents they deemed fit to carry the studio colors at the box office. If you signed up photogenic and lively soprano Grace Moore, and if she made a biopic, it would have to be one that showcased her talent, singing. It is difficult to imagine Betty Hutton, say, as Jenny Lind or Marie Curie; her robust personality was better suited to brash nightclub hostess Texas Guinan or physically active Pearl White.

Thus, if the 1950s saw a dominance of biographies about performing artists (28 percent of all biopics made in this time) this curious fact could be seen as the swan song of producers' ideas of "good entertainment" in a world where vaudeville and the live stage was being usurped by Elvis, the LP record, and television. One could also see these films as products utilizing an available—and predictable—pool of talent at each studio in a highly conventionalized way, a way that controlled for the unpredictability of different content with the ritualistic and repeated use of certain stars and producers in successful star/genre formulations. That is, in this loose application of principles derived from the sociology of work, singers under contract make biopics about singers, George Arliss portrays great statesmen of a certain age, and James Stewart, once he passed the age deemed suitable for romantic leads, and once, as a freelance artist, he could select his own roles, can portray anything from aviators (Charles Lindbergh) to wounded athletes (Monty Stratton). The universe of figures on film we have come to accept as great or important are venerated equally for the morality of their deeds and the convenience and availability of their talent.

Formal Elements

Given all the possible variables—star casting and available personnel, censorship, the power of some producer's point of view, legal considerations—that can influence the shape of a life on film, how do these films situate themselves as historical narratives? Unlike most films, almost every biopic opens with title cards that place the piece in context or with a voice-over narration that historically "sets up" the film. For example, *The Stratton Story* (1949), the biopic of Monty Stratton, who overcame a crippling shotgun wound to continue pitching in baseball, opens with the title "This is the TRUE story of a young American—Monty Stratton—and it starts one fall afternoon near Wagner, Texas." The title here serves the function of avowing that the film that follows is true. This convention of the biopic, the introductory assertion of the truth, serves as a reminder of a fact so obvious that we might overlook it: that most films made in Hollywood are not supposed to be taken as true. This use of the title sets up one of the genre's distinctive qualities, a claim to truth.[3]

The title also sets up the moment of a life when we can witness the birth of a particular talent—seldom the character's literal birth. *The Stratton Story* opens, *in medias res,* at the jumping-off point of Stratton's fame, on the eve of his being discovered by a scout. Similarly *The Pride of the Yankees* opens with young Lou Gehrig demonstrating his ability, as a juvenile, to hit the long ball for which he would become famous as a New York Yankee. Many film lives selectively highlight a part of a life so well known that a portion of it bears closer scrutiny (*Young Mr. Lincoln, Young Tom Edison* (1940), *Young Daniel Boone* (1950), *Young Bess* (1952), and *Young Jesse James* (1960). The formulation "young" in a film's title performs several functions. It seemingly permits the viewer to be present at the creation, witnessing the birth or the first display of the traits that will make the older version of the biographee famous. Second, it also suggests that fame is often largely a genetic predisposition, present from a very early age. Thus, "young" Mr. Lincoln, although only a moderately successful lawyer in Springfield, Illinois (at least in John Ford's version of history), nevertheless possesses the keen judgment, the ability to "balance" two sides of an issue, which will become his hallmarks as a senatorial candidate and, later, president.

"Young" Tom Edison displays the persistence needed to struggle through many false starts as well as the ingenuity that are the core of cinematic inventor's trial and error.[4]

Some films eschew the opening written word for the spoken word. Director William Wellman's *Buffalo Bill* (1944) opens with a rather long narration by an omniscient, anonymous narrator who informs us that

> In 1877, a young man rode out of the West and overnight his name became a household word. He was not a great general, or great statesman, or a great scientist. Yet, even now more than sixty years later, the legends which surround him are as vivid as they were then. His name was William Frederick Cody. But to the young and old, rich and poor, king and commoner, he's known as Buffalo Bill. This is the story of his life.

From the outset the film is set up in contrast to one of Lowenthal's biographies, with a kind of self-consciousness that its subject is not one of the conventional great men about whom movies might be made. Throughout the film that follows, Bill Cody will be presented as a link to the common audience member, as the champion of the authentic, of the West versus the East, of the rights of Indians to live on their own terms and not the Indian Bureau's, and as a proponent of entertainment as education. In Wellman's vision, Cody's "Wild West Show" is created to give the American people a true image of the West. Wellman's version of Cody's life may well be a displacement, in which Cody is Wellman himself and the Wild West Show is Hollywood. If Cody could make the truth a popular hit, so can Wellman.

Even in the very rare cases in which the biopic starts without an assertion of truth, some signifier of the "facticity" of the film is present. For example, *The Actress* (1953) opens with a family photo album, suggesting that the drama will be an intimate domestic tale based on a photographic re-creation of a life. Similarly, *Madame Du Barry* (1934) opens with a series of oil portraits of the historical figures in the film. Cleverly, these portraits, created by the art department of Warners, made certain that Louis XV looked like his filmic impersonator Reginald Owen, and that other royal figures were painted as the actors who portray them. The opening shot of *Roughly Speaking* (1945) tracks into an engraved funeral invitation for the leading figure's father, setting the stage for the life of Louise Randall Pierson, a woman who was able to make her way, from the title on, independent of male dominance. *The Left-Handed Gun* (1958), Arthur Penn's revisionist history of Billy the Kid, opens, self-consciously, with a ballad that intones a series of questions about Billy's motivations in his short life. The film is thus located as a piece of (pseudo) folklore, attempting to narrate a life of one of America's folk bandits in the appropriate musical genre. It is the rare film, for example, *My Wild Irish Rose* (1947) or *Shine On, Harvest Moon* (1944), that dispenses with an opening claim of veracity, and moves directly into the story. Presented thus with an assertion of truth, viewers are given the limited option—which they may or may not take—of believing that what they see is, in fact, true.

The introductory titles of biopics thus help to prepare at the outset the conditions under which the film will operate. Rather than being a mere formula, the phatic "Once upon a time . . ." that assures us that the storytelling machine is in order and operating, titles can give us a key to what will follow. Much the same way Orson Welles's voiceover opening ode signals his somewhat ironic nostalgia for the vanished magnificence of the age of the Ambersons, the adjectives used to describe time and place in the first biopic titles set the tone for and assert the value of their subjects.

Warners' *Pride of the Marines* (1945) illustrates this setting of the ideological stage with the correct props through writer Albert Maltz's judicious title. The film is the story of a marine, Al Schmidt, who loses his sight during a battle. The film focuses on his coping with this disability, and his subsequent readjustment to his new life, aided by a sympathetic fiancée. John Garfield, as Schmidt, speaks the introduction.

> This is Philadelphia, 1941. Everybody's got a home town. My name is Schmidt, Al Schmidt. Maybe you've heard of me, maybe not. Anyhow, one way or another, what I've got to tell you started here in Philly. I grew up here. . . . But it could have begun anywhere. It could have begun in your hometown, maybe. And what happened to me might have happened to you.

Although we see the sights of Philadelphia—Independence Hall, the Betsy Ross House—the stage, as the voice-over suggests, could be anytown. Philadelphia is really Schmidt's hometown, but it is also rife with symbols connecting the current struggle of World War II to past struggles, specifically the founding of the American republic. Schmidt is a rare famous person in Hollywood in that he was unknown before a misfortune singled him out. Thus, the goal of the film seems to be to connect "regular guy" Schmidt to every member of the audience. Unlike other ordinary men—Audie Murphy, Alvin York—who perform heroic feats during the war, the focus in this film is on the social readjustment Schmidt must accomplish if he is to be reintegrated into postwar society. Made in 1945, as the war was winding down, the film situates itself as an instructional text for family and friends of the wounded serviceman.

It is interesting to note the strength of the title convention in the biopic, for it is definitely not a convention of most other sound-era films. Bordwell, Staiger, and Thompson (1985) note that title credits were a staple of silent film, and were used to "announce the salient feature of the narration. In the sound era, other film techniques take on this role of foregrounding the narration" (26). Titles or introductory voice-overs were also conventions of documentaries of the period and it is likely they were appropriated by biopics as a recognizable signal that the film was true. Luis Buñuel, in *Land Without Bread* (1932) and, later, Woody Allen in *Zelig* (1983) would, in different ways, acknowledge the ironical function such verbal framing devices can perform in fiction films purporting to be true. But films that purport to be true seldom use this device ironically.

Avowals of the truth of the film can take other forms. John Sturges's *The Magnificent Yankee* (1950), the biography of jurist Oliver Wendell Holmes, opens with an aural narration by an actor playing the writer Owen Wister (author of the popular, much-filmed novel *The Virginian*) who informs us, "You might have read one of my books, *The Virginian*. It was fiction, but this story is true." We have in *Yankee* a clever bit of disingenuous conjuring; one mediated form (the novel) is used, in its ficticity, to create the fiction of truth for another mediated form, a film. "Wister's" preface serves as a kind of pseudo-celebrity endorsement of the veracity of the film's content. Nevertheless, this endorsement is rendered ironic because it is an actor whose voice informs us that he knew about the events that were about to unfold, and not the actual writer who witnessed them.

Occasionally, if they are still living, the filmed subjects themselves lend ultimate credibility to a film. In several films in the purposive sample, the signed endorsements of the actual figures appear, attesting to the truth value of the film. *Somebody Up There Likes Me* (1956), directed by Robert Wise for MGM, opens with a title card that assures us, "This is the way I remember it, definitely" and this characteristic assertion, which we will hear repeatedly in the film that follows, is signed by Rocky Graziano, the former middleweight boxing champion.[5]

Another example of the function of the opening credit with its verbal or written avowal of truth is Delbert Mann's *I'll Cry Tomorrow* (1955). It opens with the poignant but enigmatic inscription that makes sense only after the film is over. The inscription, "My life was never my own. It was charted before I was born," is more of a teaser for the viewer than a helpful piece of information. Signed by singer Lillian Roth, whose battles with her possessive stage mother and (her own) subsequent alcoholism the film chronicles, it serves neither as validation of truth nor as temporal marker. Instead, it functions as a kind of leitmotif in an overture, one whose variations will be specifically spelled out in the work to follow. A later film, Robert Wise's *I Want to Live!*, for which Susan Hayward won her only Oscar, is signed at both the beginning and end by the journalist whose stories inspired the film treatment. The appearance of his signature, without any sound on the soundtrack (a pseudo-documentary marker in a film using an otherwise obtrusive cool jazz score that reminds us of the seedy, nighttime world Barbara inhabits), as well as a magnificent gray scale and a plethora of newspaper headlines all signal the film as factual.

In-Person Avowals of Truth

Rarer still is the biographee who plays him or herself. In the complete sample, only seven films, RKO's *The Flying Irishman* (1939), the story of Douglas "Wrong Way" Corrigan; *Harmon of Michigan* (1941) with the gridiron star impersonating himself for Columbia; Columbia's 1943 *Is Everybody Happy?*, the biopic of entertainer Ted Lewis, in which Jolson impersonator Larry Parks, anticipating his stardom in *The Jolson Story* (1946), plays a role; United Artists' *The Fabulous Dorseys* (1947); *The Jackie Robinson Story* (1950); Allied Artists' *The Bob Mathias Story* (1954); and Universal's *To Hell and*

Back (1955), the story of war hero Audie Murphy meet this criterion.

Of the seven films, only Murphy's and Corrigan's efforts stands out as truly extraordinary. Lewis and the Dorseys are professional entertainers, and Harmon, Robinson, and Mathias are athletes, all used to performing in public. In the case of athletes, it may have been felt that only the athletes could realistically duplicate—or simulate—the feats for which they were well known. This solution of having professional athletes portray themselves in movies may have been inspired by the case of Gary Cooper who, playing Lou Gehrig in *The Pride of the Yankees,* had to be taught how to play baseball. Cooper, already forty-one when filming began, had never played America's national pastime. Although he learned enough of the fundamentals to approximate a baseball player, he was not able to master Gehrig's left-handed batting stance. Since it was unthinkable that audiences would not notice this—Gehrig, who had died only one year earlier, had been one of the most famous ballplayers of that era—producer Sam Goldwyn had a major difficulty to resolve. A. Scott Berg, in his 1989 biography of Goldwyn, says that the editor of the film, Danny Mandell, came up with an ingenious solution to the problem: Cooper batted right-handed, with a specially designed uniform that reversed the New York Yankee letters and numbers, and ran toward third base. The negative was flopped in the printing, and Cooper appeared to be batting left-handed and running in the right direction. Thus, through a trick of the film laboratory, the guise of authenticity was created.

Often, in the stories of athletes in which they do not play themselves, long shots of action key the film as "real," even though the knowledgeable spectator realizes that an overage William Bendix did not remotely resemble Babe Ruth, or that Errol Flynn only passably imitated James J. Corbett's boxing style. The dislocation viewers might feel when confronted with a fictive portrayer simulating real physical feats is compensated for by having actual athletes populate the film in cameo parts, playing themselves.

Nor is this strategy limited to athletes. *The Perils of Pauline* convinces us that it is an accurate picture of the early days of silent films (even though it is not) by having an enormous cast of old-timers appear as themselves alongside Pearl White/Betty Hutton, and *The Great Caruso* (1951), although showcasing the talents of quasi-

12. Imprimaturs of reality: Babe Ruth and his impersonator, William Bendix, in a publicity still for *The Babe Ruth Story*. Ruth died later that year.

operatic tenor Mario Lanza as the great Caruso, provides him with genuine opera stars Dorothy Kirsten, Blanche Thebom, and Jarmila Novotna as partners in various ensembles. At the far end of some spectrum of performance verisimilitude are the biopics of pianists—like *A Song to Remember* (1945)—in which inserts of the hands of real pianists (there, José Iturbi) fill in for the star, who is most often filmed from in front of the piano, with the full view of his or her hands blocked.

Short of having famous persons play themselves, the mixture of actors and actual professionals provides an odd bricolage of truth for biopics. But Murphy and Corrigan were not actors, and since neither war hero nor misdirected flyer were performers like musicians and athletes are, it must have caused a sense of dislocation to be playing oneself against actors standing in for family members, friends, and the like. Perhaps the very awkwardness of such performances is meant to be read as sincerity, an attempt to convince us that such people are only playing themselves, and not acting.

Often, participation of the subject of the biography is limited to and credited as "technical advice," as in the Joe Howard biopic *I Wonder Who's Kissing Her Now?* and *The Jolson Story* and its sequel. The case of Jolson is unusual, for although Columbia's publicity for the film suggested Jolson himself trained Parks in performing his routines, this was not the case.[6] Jolson had desperately wanted to play himself in his own life story. But at sixty, he was deemed, even by Harry Cohn, his most worshipful admirer, as too old to pull off this stunt. In actuality Jolson's input into his life story took, for this figure most in need of public approval, an uncharacteristic form; in addition to recording the musical vocal track for the film (a false vocal Jolson would be unimaginable) he appeared in the film, unbilled, and unknown to the movie audience, in long shot, doing his inimitable dance on a theater runway. Like "Jolson" in the film, Jolson couldn't keep away from an audience or duck out on an opportunity to entertain. Only, in *The Jolson Story,* he appears, for once, unbilled and anonymous.

If starring impersonations by the actual subjects of the biography are, for reasons of unavailability or advanced age, rare, as I suggested earlier, cameo appearances by celebrities are fairly common. Sophie Tucker, with an enormous leap of faith into a time warp, plays her 1930s self in the 1957 *The Joker Is Wild* (1957), and Babe Ruth, Sam Snead, and other athletes play themselves in cameos in a number of films. Athletes, in particular, are often used in bit parts in sports films, adding authentic physical business to proceedings the viewer knows are otherwise largely staged. Similarly show business folk often appear in cameos, frequently in comic moments where, breaking the narrative frame created by a film, they are recognized as themselves or in brief performance in benefit revues that increase the entertainment value of a package by adding famous names to the marquee. We see this variation on reality casting when Fanny Brice, later to be impersonated by Barbra Streisand in her own story, *Funny Girl* and *Funny Lady* (1975), playing "Fanny Brice," does a couple of songs in MGM's *The Great Ziegfeld* (1936), performing alongside fictional portrayers of her actual co-stars, like Anna Held (Luise Rainer).

A last level of use of stars playing themselves in biopics is the use of a star associated with a historical personality in one film to play that life as a bit part in someone else's life story. Since, as Chapters three and four suggest, much of the biopic strategy is based on inter-textuality, such self-referential casting asserts the validity of past film triumphs. Thus, James Cagney, whose memorable 1942 inter-pretation of the then-living George M. Cohan in *Yankee Doodle Dandy* drew favorable comparisons with the real thing, plays Cohan, some thirteen years later, as a cameo to the leading character of Bob Hope's Eddie Foy in *The Seven Little Foys* (1955). Eddie Foy, Jr., himself a performer in vaudeville and on Broadway, made a minor movie career out of portraying his own father (as in *Yankee Doodle Dandy*) complete with his trademark lisp. Wallace Beery earlier por-trayed P. T. Barnum as a supporting part in *A Lady's Morals* (1930), the Jenny Lind biopic, before assaying the great impresario as a lead-ing figure in *The Mighty Barnum*. Charles Laughton played the lead as Henry VIII in the 1933 British *Private Life of Henry VIII* and reprised this character, as a supporting player, twenty years later in *Young Bess*. Raymond Massey, who played Lincoln on stage, trans-ferred the Robert Sherwood *Abe Lincoln in Illinois* (1940) to film, and then played a cameo of Lincoln in the 1963 *How the West Was Won*. He also impersonated a figure linked to Lincoln's history, the abolitionist John Brown, two times: first in *Santa Fe Trail* (1940), and again in *Seven Angry Men* (1955). Bette Davis is unique in her biopic roles, as in so many other aspects of her career, for she is the only female film actor to portray the same leading character (some sixteen years apart), playing the aging Elizabeth I of England in *The Private Lives of Elizabeth and Essex* and later playing the yet older Elizabeth in *The Virgin Queen* (1955). In both cases, the later inter-pretations of Davis and Laughton seemed mannered, over-madeup versions of earlier performances of great originality, as if merely reappearing as the figure would rouse the collective cinematic memory of the moviegoer without the benefit of a strong script or a well-thought-out performance.

Last, film can establish the realism of its casting by other forms of self-reference. In *Somebody Up There Likes Me,* Rocky Graziano's crusty manager, Cohen (Everett Sloane), tells a young fighter, "Either you wanna be a fighter, or you wanna have fun like Errol Flynn," a reference to Flynn's performance as boxer James J. Corbett in *Gentleman Jim,* and a veiled suggestion that while the 1942 Raoul Walsh film is pure "Hollywood," Wise's film is authentic.

The use of either the actual biographee to play himself, or the repeated use of an actor to play the same historical figure, are both strategies film studios used to anchor the factual fiction of biopics in an undeniable authenticity of casting.

Biography as Differentiation

If the truth value is a distinctive feature of the biopic as a film genre, such a characteristic does more than taxonomize bodies of film. One might argue that in addition to functioning as a framing device that sets up audience and producer expectations for biopics, this feature (the assertion of truth) is yet another strategy used to differentiate a product, be it film genre or star, in a highly competitive consumer market. Warner Brothers seemed aware of this, and as Thomas Elsaesser notes, "Distinctive about the publicity for Warner's biopics was the emphasis on historical accuracy, on the quality of the research materials, the extensive inspection of original locations and the quality of the professional consultancy" (1986:23). As I will show in chapter three on film research, "Night and Day," one attribute all studios, not just Warners, often foregrounded in publicity for biopics was the historicity of the film. The extravagant effort put into research becomes another example or manifestation of spectacle the studios used to frame their films as marketable commodities.

If we view this truth as a significant selling point of these films, we might see the distinction certain actors associated with the genre attained in another, peculiar light. For example, George Arliss was already sixty-one when he made his first sound film, *Disraeli* (1929). He attained stardom in films by transferring his stage successes to the screen, perhaps lending the new sound medium a patina of

Broadway and West End theatrical respectability (as well as providing an example of the great man who speaks with a Mayfair accent). Seeing Arliss as the definitive biopic actor (*Disraeli, Voltaire* [1933], *Alexander Hamilton* [1931], *House of Rothschild* [1934], *Cardinal Richelieu*, and, in England, *The Iron Duke* [1934]) misses the point; the use of Arliss to play film biographies by both Warners and later Fox is, I think, more significant than the contribution made by his portrayals, for it suggested that film biography was serious, making a contribution to public culture comparable to theater or books.

Producer Darryl Zanuck worked with Arliss at Warners (*Disraeli, Alexander Hamilton, Voltaire*) and later shanghaied the actor to his own studio Twentieth Century-Fox (*House of Rothschild* and *Cardinal Richelieu*). Zanuck was well aware of the public's expectation of how Arliss should be cast. In fact, after the initial strong impression he made in *Disraeli*, which, after all, he had played both on the stage and in silent film, Arliss's great men became, except for a new wig here, and a change of scenery there, remarkably interchangeable. Index finger pointing aloft in justified rage, fists clenched in anger, a benign smile creasing his homely face, the Arliss great man was a kind of crafty favorite uncle, always ready to help young lovers and uphold the honor of the country in which he happens to live. So firmly established was the Arliss biopic persona after his triumph in *Disraeli* that Zanuck permitted the actor to attend story conferences, actually listening to his suggestions on how best to manage the Arliss character. The best judge of the Arliss great man persona was its keeper, Arliss himself.

Zanuck, too, was aware of how entrenched was the Arliss persona, and what kind of narrative could best show it off. In a story conference of January 7, 1935, for *Cardinal Richelieu*, Zanuck urges the writers to come up with a scene like an earlier episode in *Disraeli*, where Disraeli, to show support for young love and to outsmart the French, sends a character on a daring mission. Arliss, present at the conference, concurred and even made suggestions for lines of dialogue (USC-Fox Collection). Thus Zanuck had a definite idea how Arliss should be used as a great man; this idea was based on what audiences had come to expect through previous, successful use of Arliss.

Biography presented a category in which actors who did not fit other acting types could be utilized. This might be said of Paul

13. Star acting: George Arliss in *Disraeli* . . .

Muni—*The Story of Louis Pasteur, The Life of Emile Zola* (1937), *Juarez, I Am a Fugitive from a Chain Gang* (1932), and as mentor to Cornell Wilde's Chopin in *A Song to Remember*. After Arliss, he is a candidate for the representative biopic actor. Muni was a star of the Yiddish theater whose triumphant film appearances were largely in serious dramatic parts. Biopics gave him an opportunity to display his trademark conscientious preparation in accents, dress, and the re-creation of historical figures. As Thomas Elsaesser has noted, Muni's prestige as an actor could be used to create publicity for the film, just as MGM would invoke Spencer Tracy's two Academy Awards when exploiting *Edison, The Man*. A trailer for Warners' *Juarez* links the film to other serious artistic portrayals by Muni, and attempts to convince viewers that they are participating in an educational, even uplifting endeavor. Biopics gave actors with certain,

14. And acting like a star in *Voltaire*

perhaps difficult qualities a niche in which to excel and offered an attractive strategy for marketing film and actor as culturally valuable commodities.

Of course, having succeeded with Muni and Arliss, studios would try the biopic strategy with other performers after they had attained fame in a biopic role. This was the case with Don Ameche, who made *Swanee River* (1939) (Stephen Foster) and *So Goes My Love* (1946) (inventor Hiram Maxin) after his success in *The Story of Alexander Graham Bell*. Paramount would try this formula, too, with Betty Hutton, placing her in three biopics about vaudevillians and other entertainers after she established her credentials with a portrayal of Texas Guinan in *Incendiary Blonde* (1945). But product differentiation as a strategy to market films and actors was like other Hollywood strategies; it worked some of the time and not at others.

15. Paul Muni, in costume, on the set of *The Life of Emile Zola*

Interestingly, female stars are not usually associated with a series of biopics, though Susan Hayward (*I Want to Live!*, *With a Song in My Heart* [1952], *I'll Cry Tomorrow,* and *The President's Lady* [1953], and, in a supporting role, *Jack London* [1943]) and Doris Day (*Young Man with a Horn* [1950], *I'll See You in My Dreams* [1951], *The Winning Team* [1952], *Calamity Jane* [1953], and *Love Me or Leave Me* [1955]) each made five. Betty Hutton (*Incendiary Blonde, The Perils of Pauline, Annie Get Your Gun,* and as vaudevillian Blossom Seeley in *Somebody Loves Me* [1952]) made four, and Bette Davis performed in four (the two Elizabeth biopics, *Juarez,* and the 1940 *All This and Heaven Too*), doing a fifth role, a cameo of Catherine the Great, in *John Paul Jones* (1959). This relative absence is in contrast to a number of male stars who were prolific performers in biopics: Jimmy Stewart (4) (*The Stratton Story, Carbine*

16. In *Love Me or Leave Me*, Doris Day, as Ruth Etting, acts out the roles of both entertainer and paramour

Williams [1952], *The Glenn Miller Story* [1954], *The Spirit of St. Louis* [1957]); Gary Cooper (5) (*The Adventures of Marco Polo* [1938], *Sergeant York* [1941], *The Pride of the Yankees, The Story of Dr. Wassell* [1944], and *The Court-Martial of Billy Mitchell* [1955]); James Cagney (4) (*Yankee Doodle Dandy, Love Me or Leave Me, Man of a Thousand Faces* [1957], and *The Gallant Hours* [1960]); Spencer Tracy (4) (*Boys Town* [1938], *Stanley and Livingstone, Edison, The Man, The Actress*); and Henry Fonda (5) with two leads (*Young Mr. Lincoln* and *The Return of Frank James* [1940]) and three supporting roles (*The Story of Alexander Graham Bell, Jesse James* [1939], and *Lillian Russell* [1940]).

Such an unequal distribution has to do, I think, with the overall configuration of biography by gender. (See Table D.3 for this breakdown.) There are almost two and a half times as many male biographies as female biographies. Moreover, the bulk of female biographies are of entertainers and paramours. There is thus a strong chance that the cinematicly famous woman depicted must be able to sing, and further must be conventionally beautiful in the paramour mode. Hayward fit these qualifications, or rather historical figures who presumably had these qualities fit Hayward's talent. All of Hayward's impersonations were headstrong, colorful women, marked in some way by tragedy. And, as this was one of Hayward's characteristics as a star—she suffered with sublime intensity—the biopic was a niche into which her talents could be fitted. Chapters four, "Reel Life" and six, "The Frame Shrinks," discuss gender and fame more fully. Here I might note that, in general, the distribution of power in society is mirrored by the distribution and limitation of the lives women are allowed to depict. The male shape to biography is further a reflection of the talent Hollywood validated. If stardom is a sign of elevation within the society at large, stars playing great men or women are metaphors that signal the domination of both Hollywood and the larger world by men.

Although biopics were used as a way of differentiating both genres and their stars, only one director has been closely associated with the life on film. William Dieterle was Warners' leading biopic director. Born in Germany in 1893, he studied with theater director Max Reinhardt. Initially his career in Germany was that of an actor, but in 1923 he started to direct. Dieterle came to Hollywood in 1930 at the urging of producer Henry Blanke, who felt he might be able to make German-language films for its lucrative European markets. He was successful in a variety of genres before scoring an enormous triumph, in 1936, with *The Story of Louis Pasteur.* He became one of the few directors in 1930s Hollywood to exercise complete control on a film. Publicity for his pictures inevitably stressed his link to the stories of principle he guided. An article in the January 1940 issue of *Coast* magazine stressed his devotion to ideals and principles ("above all he is the one director in Hollywood who has repeatedly risked his reputation on what are roughly, very roughly, termed 'artistic pictures' "). Dieterle, a man who directed wearing white gloves, was held up as the standard-bearer of Warners' culture and idealism. The films he made at Warners bear a remarkable structural affinity to one another, with a great man (or woman) scorned by an establishment only to be vindicated in a scene of public acceptance.

Dieterle himself appears to have taken his own public image seriously, rarely granting interviews, and, when speaking at all, offering weighty opinions like, "I believe that a picture's basic idea is more important than the story that is told. A story can be trivial" (Joseph, 1940:8). He guided six great man or woman films at Warners (*The Story of Louis Pasteur, The White Angel* [1936], *The Life of Emile Zola, Juarez, Dr. Ehrlich's Magic Bullet* [1940], and *A Dispatch from Reuters*) and was signed by that hoarder of prestige, Louis B. Mayer, to direct *Tennessee Johnson* for MGM. He later followed former Warners production head turned independent producer Hal Wallis to Paramount, ending his American career on a low note in 1957 with *Omar Khayyam*. While many major director worked at least once in the biopic genre (George Cukor, John Ford, Vincente Minnelli, Raoul Walsh, Billy Wilder, William Wyler), few established their reputations largely with film biography. Dieterle stands out as the lone exception to the dictum of director as product differentiation, and Warners used public recognition of his association with the genre as a way of generating publicity.[7]

Narrative Components: Elements of the Life

Just as the patterned use of one kind of formal element—title cards—characterizes the biopic as a unique film genre, the way the narrative of a life is constructed is also characteristic. For example, the point in the life when the film starts shapes differing discourses about the role of family in the life of the valorized figure. Many films commence just at the point of the narrative where protagonists display the talent or behavior that will make them famous. Other films, however, like *The Great Caruso,* start literally at the character's birth, to show that the gift that would bring the hero fame was present in some embryonic form at life's debut. These questions—at what point does a biography commence, and how does the film account for unusual gifts—are central to understanding the construction of biography. Fame is presented quite differently if it is seen as a biological predisposition (a gift) or if it is, after a series of trials, earned through hard work and apprenticeship. Either explanatory schemata is often used as an argument supporting genetic or environmental theories of character. The implications of presenting either a biologically based or a socially constituted theory of fame lie at the heart of a culture's ideas concerning social stratification; a road to fame based on the "accident" of heredity provides marginalized members of a society a different path to travel upon than one based on the gospel of hard work. Those films that seem to support the nature route can be seen, in part, to support a theory of society that argues for stability in the form of a caste system.

Family

What part does family play in the hero's life? Are they supportive of a career? Are they divided in their support? In *Interrupted Melody* (1955), soprano Marjorie Lawrence's family is shown viewing her singing voice as a proverbial gift from God; they support the divine mandate, if not the career. While her father leads the family in a prayer accepting Marjorie-as-God's-tool (after she has won a singing contest), brother Cyril (a young Roger Moore) is much more excited; he will become Marjorie's manager and, leaving Australia, travel the world with her, profiting from her talent. His support is differently motivated from the rest of the family and, not having a pure interest in his sister's welfare, only in the state of her voice, his support waivers when Marjorie is struck down by polio.

In *The Jolson Story,* Asa's parents, particularly his father, are initially shown opposing his entry into show business. Later, his father (played as a generic Hollywood version of an Eastern European by Austrian Ludwig Donath), more than reconciled to having a jazz singer in the family, will closely follow his career, reading Asa's notices in *Variety* to the befuddled, but proud, Mama Yoelson. A similar formulation of parental support is seen in *The Pride of the Yankees.* Mama Gehrig wants Lou to be an engineer, like her adored brother Otto, whose portrait on the wall is a constant reminder of Papa Gehrig's lowly status (he is a janitor) as well as Mama's strong urge for upward mobility. Resistant at first to Lou's career (and his marriage), once Lou is established as a well-paid hero, the Gehrig parents become experts at baseball, attending games regularly, and, comfortably using baseball slang, knowledgeably analyze the game. Uncle Otto, his portrait turned to the wall by a triumphant Papa Gehrig, is forgotten.

Chopin's family in *A Song to Remember* support his musical career, but they dream only of his obtaining a post at the local conservatory. As Norman Maine might say, their dream is not wrong; it's simply not big enough. More cosmopolitan dreams—a future triumph in Paris—are the province of someone outside the family, Frédéric's teacher, Professor Elsner. Paul Muni plays this fictional creation, Frédéric's artistic and social conscience, and his presence allows the Polish liberation theme to be showcased at a time when Poland was under Nazi oppression, and contemporary classical musicians from war-torn countries (like Italy's Arturo Toscanini and Poland's Artur Rubinstein) were mixing music and Allied propaganda in their public performances.

In Lowenthal's work, the family is a key explanatory frame that provides the appropriate environment for fostering the growth of the future famous person. Here, we will consider the family as the source of support or opposition. We will also see if family members change their minds, as, overwhelmed by their relative's gift, they are forced to become just another member of the public and to admire the prodigal. In *Somebody Up There Likes Me*, Rocky Graziano's father only acknowledges his son's gifts at the end of the film; his hatred and jealousy of his own son have, to an extent, been presented as the motivating force behind Rocky's rage to fight. In *Somebody,* we have fame framed with a Freudian explanation. Compare this to a similar film made three decades later, Martin Scorsese's *Raging Bull* (1980), where little in the way of family environment is specifically offered as an explanation for Jake LaMotta's rage; it exists, pure and unmotivated, in a state of its own.

If You're Ever Down a Well . . . : Close Friends and Guides

Does the hero have a close friend who supports him or her in the quest for fame? Often, the famous figure shown in a negative light is one who has lost touch with the neighborhood and old friends. Old friends are often touchstones, reminding heroes, living in some stratosphere, that they generally came from a less exalted sphere.[8]

The presence of an older figure, the bearer of conventional (sometimes limited) wisdom is a staple of many cinematic biographies. Frank Morgan's old baseball player who discovers the young protégé, Monty Stratton, who will one day outshine him; Jolson's fictional companion Steve Martin (William Demerest), a cellist whose small talent has left him "at liberty" until Jolson puts him on the payroll as a permanent friend in attendance; and Alfredo Brazzi (Ludwig Donath in one of his last performances before being blacklisted), Enrico Caruso's washed-up tenor friend who becomes a kind of combination secretary/conscience are all examples of this figure. In Caruso's case, his faded tenor companion serves also as a reminder of the fleeting nature of fame. Alfredo Brazzi's ruined career and lost voice are cinematic *memento mori,* reminders—like an ex-pug reminds the champion boxer at the top—that one's gifts can vanish in a flash, and that a life lived badly now can later destroy any talent.

Occasionally a peer of the hero aids him or her in attaining fame. In *A Song to Remember* we see Franz Liszt (later the focus of a 1960 biopic *Song Without End*), the reigning piano virtuoso of his day, champion the cause of the unknown Chopin after Pleyel, the leading impresario of the day, refuses even to hear the unknown artist. Although his province is art, his métier is business; Pleyel is still a bureaucrat tied to conventional notions of beauty and novelty in art as well as a conservative sense of social decorum in recognizing who can and cannot play in his salon. Liszt, an accepted star, can; Chopin, an unknown, cannot. Liszt and Chopin, while sharing the same salon with Pleyel, inhabit different spheres from their impresario. With their dramatic long hair and tempestuous natures, they display this movie's as well as the overall cinematic artist's code of (rather tame) contempt for bourgeois notions of propriety. Artists, they speak another language than that spoken unctuously by Pleyel.

The two pianists meet in the salon, and Liszt's curiosity over the unusual sheet music he sees on the piano (Chopin's) prompts a career-saving introduction for the young Chopin. They are introduced while playing a four-handed arrangement of the "Grande Polonaise" (Liszt sight-reads the notoriously difficult piece), exchanging handshakes and names in an orchestrated contrapuntal greeting that both introduces the artists to one another and presents Chopin's music in a favorable light to tastemaker Pleyel. Liszt is presented as secure enough in his talent to recognize fellow genius, and we have here a classical illustration of three motifs that will play a role in performer biopics: resistance by the establishment of the field, advice from an older colleague and a dramatic breakthrough, a lucky break—often in the nick of time—for the novice.[9]

Liszt is also shown playing this benefactor role to Robert Schumann in *Song of Love* (1947). His motives, there, are less pure. Smitten with the married Clara Schumann (Katharine Hepburn), he champions her husband's music to gain favor with her. He is rebuffed in the brusque Hepburn manner.

The examples above are older figures who were involved in the same field as the famous person. However, older advisors can at times be a civilian. Living thus outside the odd world of celebrity, they can offer solicited and unsolicited down-to-earth advice. Thelma Ritter often specialized in parts such as these, and can be seen doing this turn in *With a Song in My Heart*. As Clancy, the Brooklyn-born nurse with a sharp tongue and inevitable heart of gold, she dispenses gutsy common sense along with medicine to the beleaguered Jane Froman (Susan Hayward), injured in a plane crash at the height of her singing career. Because they are not part of the world of the celebrated person, figures such as Clancy have little to gain in the way of professional advancement, and are freer to give advice the hero does not want to hear, but must be told. Their very outspokenness, in a world populated by toadies, is their value to the star.

If the biographee is too old to receive advice from one yet older, then the biopic will show the great person as a kind of master advice-giver, one wise to the world after repeated encounters with treachery, avarice, and the like. George Arliss plays this part—the crafty older statesman—in *Disraeli, Cardinal Richelieu, House of Rothschild,* and *Voltaire*. Because Arliss was already rather old (sixty-one) when he made his first biopic, another actor would have to portray him as a young (and even middle-aged) man. And, unless his youthful incarnation was part of the narrative, the potential situations for receiving advice were rather limited. Besides, this was the point: Arliss, with his monacle and long career, had earned wisdom.

Public Reception of Talent

Often the celebrity is shown attempting the undoable, performing the unconventional, and presuming the impossible. Performing artists (like Lon Chaney, George M. Cohan, Al Jolson, and Marjorie Lawrence) are constantly being told their performance technique is too radical, but it is this violation of performance norms that establishes their unique greatness. In science and medicine, it is a commonplace occurrence in the world of biopics to have all members of a scientific community (save our hero), march to the tune of an outmoded and outdated drum. *The Story of Louis Pasteur, Dr. Ehrlich's Magic Bullet, Madame Curie,* and *Sister Kenny* (1946) all show central characters who must buck both a vituperative scientific establishment as well as impediments to knowledge before they discover the procedures for which they are famous. Such a struggle is not limited to medicine, science, or the performing arts. Henry Stanley (*Stanley and Livingstone*) must overcome prejudice against his professional affiliation and his adopted nationality (American, though born British) before he can convince the Society of British Geographers (led by a bloodthirsty and xenophobic Charles Coburn as British newspaper magnate Tyce) that the maps he presented to them were actually drawn by the "lost" Dr. Livingstone.

A central conflict of the biopic, then, is the hero's antagonistic relations with members of a given community. One might even go so far as to postulate that in this conflict, the hero is attempting to reformulate the boundaries of a given community, to create a Kuhnian paradigm in an already constituted field. As Brecht noted, "The element of conflict in these bourgeois biographies derives from the opposition between the hero and the dominant opinion, which is to say the opinion of those who dominate" (quoted in Elsaesser, 1986:24). It is often in such reactionary poses that tradition is represented. This is an irony worth discussing, and chapter four, "Reel Life" will discuss it more fully. We are told in countless films that Hollywood, as a branch of show business, venerates tradition. Entire songs ("There's No Business Like Show Business" and "Be a Clown," to name two) celebrate this inheritance of the performing artists. Yet, film biography perhaps venerates the star who creates a dramatic new tradition far more than it respects the old. It is both the continuation of a lineage ("the tradition") as well as its reformulation ("uniqueness") that forms the Hollywood code of biography.

For example, Babe Ruth, in *The Babe Ruth Story* (1948), first revolutionizes the game by adding the drama of sudden shifts in the score with his prodigious home runs. In his hitting skills and in his public persona, he is an original. As such, he has run-ins with his tradition-bound manager, Miller Huggins, who presents a contrast to the image of Ruth in both his lifestyle and physique. However, as Ruth's career wanes, the one-time innovator becomes the upholder of a tradition he helped to shape and which in turn shaped the more desirable aspects of his personality. His skills fading, Ruth is shown retiring with extraordinary grace, giving his place on the ballfield to the very rookie who had, earlier, scorned him.

BABE: Run for me, kid. Play for me, too. You've got a steady job.

ROOKIE: Babe, I'm sorry for everything. If I can . . .

BABE: Forget it. Be good to the game, kid. Give it everything you've got. Baseball'll be good to you. Come on, get goin'.

Similarly, in *Gentleman Jim* (1942), the soundly defeated heavyweight champion, John L. Sullivan, comes to the victory celebration of the man who vanquished him, James J. Corbett, to acknowledge that a new style of boxing, and a new more refined style of life, is acceding with Corbett's victory.

We see this transition, from one performance style to another, in *The Great Caruso* and *My Wild Irish Rose,* where Jean de Rezske and Billy Scanlon, respectively, acknowledge the arrival of new kings Enrico Caruso and Chauncey Olcott in their domains of singing. Frequently, a physical token completes the ritual of passing the torch, as where Sullivan gives Corbett his championship belt, and Olcott receives a watch given to Scanlon by the Prince of Wales. These graceful transitions—from one era to another—mask the fierce competitiveness that is part of many professions. Any sour grapes over the arrival of newcomers are dealt with by giving the most hostile lines to second-rate talents, whose bitterness is explained by their obvious envy of the newcomers. Thus, the feud between Babe Ruth and Lou Gehrig is glossed over in both the Ruth and the Gehrig biopics, and Cohan's hostile relations with many of his peers (as suggested in Mast 1987:34) is relegated to mere high spirits rather than Cohan's fierce competitive drive or his opposition, as a producer, to any form of theatrical unionization. Sentimentalizing the competition of many professions—suggesting they consist of sororities or fraternities of good will—is a way of eliding the real work, the struggle that might show the world as a place where not all men and women are created equal, and where injustice and influence often go unchecked. From the point of view of Hollywood as a producer of upbeat images of the world, it is often better, or more economical, to show such struggle through the attenuated means of montage, where reversals of fate can be dealt with in a newspaper headline or two. The romanticization of most professions also throws heroic light on the professions that comprise the motion picture business, sanitizing a Darwinian view of the world by presenting it as a Disneyland. Work is transformed into play, and those who perform these transformations are rendered heroic.

Innovation

What part does innovation play in the construction of fame? Innovation may be the most vaunted quality sold through biopics, whether it is in vaudeville or microbiology. The veneration of innovation is at odds with Hollywood's own marked conservatism in modes of production, where, as Bordwell, Staiger, and Thompson (1985) note, innovation is typically slow and occurs within controlled contours. The symbolic function served by innovations in the biopic will be discussed as a kind of homeostatic device to insure not greatness but ordinariness. The public is meant to take innovation-as-deviation as the price of greatness, a price too high for the average spectator to accept and still be a member of the community. One way of dealing with innovation in work is to make the famous person relentlessly normal in other spheres. Chapters four and five will discuss this process of normalizing genius.

The Price of Being Different: Retribution

Does the famous person achieve a sense of vindication over those who opposed their innovations? In *A Song to Remember,* the pompous critic who first denigrated Chopin's talent is later shown as a desperate toady who, once the establishment figure Liszt has given his imprimatur to the young Chopin, will stop at nothing to praise the newcomer.

The degree to which the figure is vindicated suggests a public acceptance of his or her gift; its absence is often tied to tragedy, and tragedy is framed as the lack of fame, as in *The Magic Box* (1951) where the British inventor of the cinema camera, William Friese-Greene, having failed to attain public recognition for his work, dies alone and, except for the existence of the testimonial film, unacknowledged.

Most intriguingly, if the subject of the film is living at the time of its release, vindication can come in the form of the production of the film itself. Thus a celebrity who has passed the time of public visibility, or a figure whose deeds have faded from memory can see, through the public reception of a film, a career revived or witness in the poignant limelight of the projected image the reestablishment of a reputation. Upon the release of *The Jolson Story,* Al Jolson, unhappy in a bitter semi-retirement, experienced one last burst of fame as a result of renewed public interest in his performance: his record sales increased, his radio show received high ratings, and he headlined one last time, entertaining American troops in Korea before his death, from a heart attack, in 1950.

Fortune and Misfortune

To what extent are success and misfortune corollated in biopics? Is such corollation linked to gender, nationality, or other variables? What part does misfortune play in molding the life or in shaping the gift?

Part of any mythology of fame consists of the biographee coping with the misfortune that can level any elevation. Is the hero the agent of his or her own suffering, or merely the recipient of blows from Olympus? The way fame is linked to misfortune and, in turn, happiness, is one of the most powerful instructive lessons biopics display. This is readily apparent in the gender coding of suffering, where women who seek fame are dogged by foiled romance and the specter of life alone in a way their male counterparts—when there are any—are not. Chapter six, "The Frame Shrinks," deals with this disparity, which is more apparent in movies made for TV than in theatrical films.

The lesson one learns from biopic vicissitudes, at least on the surface, is quite simple: with an unusual gift comes unusual suffering. As Lowenthal and Adorno suggested of other popular forms of narrative, the audience member viewing a misfortune in a popular film is reassured that a normal, obscure life is perhaps preferable to the proverbial price of fame; life as it is, not life as the movies show it, should be cherished.[10] However, this is far too simple an understanding to take away from a complex body of films. While suffering is often the lot of the famous, it is not distributed evenly throughout the biopic populations.

Thus, more than a rhetoric of suffering, I will try to create a taxonomy of suffering as shown through the biopic. In most cases, no matter how one suffers, salvation is just around the corner in the form of the very institutions that the famous share with most members of the audience: family, community, and home. It is in these tensions—between home and public, between opposing communities, and between definitions of family—that the lessons of fame are created. As Lillian Russell, the already arrived star, tells Chauncey Olcott, the ambitious hopeful, in *My Wild Irish Rose,* "We of the theater live apart from the outside world. We never open our mouths to speak, or our lips to kiss but to further our careers." But, she tells Olcott, who has a "nice girl" waiting for him at home until he gives up the foolishness of the theater, "I'd give the theater away a lot of times if I could do that [have a normal home life]." Although the solution is at hand, and the famous person often articulates his or her desire for the normal life, at times the price of fame is the renouncement of these institutions, though not the values they represent.

In *The Five Pennies* (1959), jazz musician Red Nichols is too obsessed with his career to devote any time to his adoring daughter. When she is stricken with polio, he tosses his cornet from a bridge, only taking up music after a decade of silence when his daughter, now adjusted to walking with a brace, gives him the same pep talk he had earlier given her. It seems that Nichols's success caused his daughter's illness; left alone at a boarding school by a father too busy touring to visit her, she stays out in the rain for hours, contracting the illness shortly after. Several films in my sample question the possibility that the entertainer, seized by the muse, can carry on any relations other than professional ones. This abandonment of family is a harsh price to pay in a culture that venerates family and parenthood.

Historical Era Depicted

There is a tendency in Hollywood to limit the presentation of history to a few periods. While there is no shortage of films set on the American frontier, there are very few films concerning the American Revolution and its heroes. George Arliss's impersonation of Alexander Hamilton in a film of the same title is the lone exception, though figures from the post-Revolutionary era like Dolley Madison appear in historical romances like *Magnificent Doll* (1946), and the Jean Lafitte biopic, *The Buccaneer*. An analysis of the historical eras depicted will give us an image of Hollywood history. The distribution also suggests that certain eras were more important than others in the formation of the American character. For example, one of the great absences in biopics is the late nineteenth and early twentieth century entrepreneur. Such symbolic annihilation of Henry Ford, Andrew Carnegie, and Henry Frick is all the more significant because written materials of this same period—magazines and newspapers—sang the praises of these men with great frequency. Substituted for the portrayal of capitalists as shrewd and crafty predators was Hollywood's biopic image of the capitalist as a colorful figure who, thwarted in love, has only the domain of finance in which to exercise his energy. Edward Arnold twice portrayed this image of the capitalist as frustrated lover in *Diamond Jim* (1935) as Diamond Jim Brady, and in 1937 in *The Toast of New York* as Jubilee Jim Fisk. Similarly, Hetty Green, the famous pathologically stingy millionaire, was depicted as possessing abundant gold, but little personal emotional wealth in *You Can't Buy Everything* (1934). Other businessmen and women are reframed with nonbusiness references, or else figure prominently in fictive contexts where the figure of the capitalist can either be painted in benign strokes, as in Charles Coburn's depiction in *The Devil and Miss Jones* (1941), or else can be constructed as a threat to all that is decent, as in Edward Arnold's impersonation in *Meet John Doe* (1941). Edison and Bell are framed as inventors, donors of fabulous inventions to the public welfare, and thus are sanitized as capitalists. These absences, as much as what is present, constitute a state of symbolic annihilation (to borrow a term from George Gerbner), in which a sanitized view of history is constructed eliminating problematic areas from public perusal. One needs neither a Ferdinand Saussure nor a Jacques Lacan to tell us that the patterns formed by both presences and absences help cultivate assumptions about history, preserving certain versions of history rather than others.

Character Demographics and Ethnicity

The map of world history via Hollywood is even more inequitable than the Mercator projection. In my analysis, biopics are broken down by key demographic variables to see how the great of the world have been allocated. The degree to which white, North American, or European males of the twentieth century have dominated this canon is staggering, and the exact dimensions of this profile will be discussed looking at content categories such as occupation, nationality, sex, marital status, and the historical era in which a life is set.

Since it is a truism that Hollywood is the land of the beautiful and bland, the treatment of ethnicity in biography is problematic; quite often, ethnicity in a film is only dimly alluded to, or else ignored. Presumably, one of the reasons for ignoring ethnicity is that it represents alternative traditions to the mainstream realities represented by all Hollywood films. Ethnicity, in short, could be a threat. One way of dealing with this was to limit ethnic representation to certain stereotypes, even in animated films. Another strategy was to eliminate any reference to ethnic origins and traditions, as if all Americans sprang fully socialized from a small town in the Midwest. Lastly, films sometimes showcased ethnicity, proudly pointing to certain traits and achievements (e.g., patriotism for the Irish Americans in *Yankee Doodle Dandy*) that helped, isomorphically, define groups in the melting pot.

Ethnicity is an issue larger than its mere representation in a script. As Ella Shohat notes, "ethnicity is culturally ubiquitous and textually submerged, thus challenging the widespread approach to ethnicity as limited to 'content' analysis" (1990:225). Where a character's ethnicity was alluded to, or indeterminate, the actor portraying the character often had few options but to submit to a kind of ethnic drycleaning. A. Scott Berg describes this process with Brooklyn-born Jewish actor Danny Kaye: "Some people suggested he looked too 'sinister,' a euphemism for Jewish. The uninhibited Harry Cohn said he had not signed Danny Kaye because 'he looked like a mountains comic' " (1989:382). Goldwyn, who signed Kaye to a contract, came up with the solution of dying the former David Kaminski's hair blond, thus altering the purported ethnic way he photographed. Ethnicity, then, is a key component of biography, and in addition to its presence or absence, we will see the role, if any, it plays in explaining the rise of a character to fame.

Social Class

From what social class does the famous person come? Are talent and genius qualities that are class coded, or are such traits evenly distributed throughout a culture? One of the tensions of modern American life, resolved in part by the lessons taught by the media, is the contradiction between drives that emphasize individualism (stardom, fame, etc.) versus drives that encourage community, and lack of individualism. Different social classes emphasize one trait rather than another, either encouraging individualism or fostering community. Thus, in Warners' *My Wild Irish Rose,* Chauncey Olcott, with his "Irish charm," singing voice, and strong ambition, wishes to be more than the tugboat worker he is presumably, by class restrictions, destined to be. His class-bound friend Joe Brennan, taking note of Chauncey's desire to associate with the powerful and famous (Lillian Russell) tells the upwardly mobile Chauncey (who sits in the balcony dressed as a movie capitalist is, with top hat, cape, and cane), "Let's go home. We don't belong here, Chauncey. We're tugboat people and you've got to get on to yourself." But of course, the famous person, or soon-to-be famous person, will not be held back by conventions, class or otherwise. The class origin of the famous, as well as their families' attitudes toward pursuing a career that will remove their son or daughter from his or her rank, are indicators of Hollywood's attitude toward class, mobility, and innate versus developmental aspects of fame. In Olcott's case, his wise mother (Sara Allgood) resolves the individual/community dichotomy by suggesting Chauncey's voice is heaven-sent, and that "I guess it becomes his duty to share it with the whole world." A mandate, higher than ethnic boundaries or social class, thus frees Chauncey to abandon his community, pursuing his destiny.

The contours of biographical fame will flesh out Hayden White's notion that the construction of history depends not merely on which events are covered. Biography is also shaped by rhetoric. As Leo Braudy (1986) argues, fame is not so much a person, but a *story* about a person. Different modes of depiction of the same life constitute different tales. Several of the figures in the sample have had multiple films made about their lives (Billy the Kid, Catherine the Great, Madame Du Barry, Disraeli, Thomas Edison, Elizabeth I, Jesse James, Lincoln, Annie Oakley, Queen Victoria, and François Villon to name a few). The stories they tell, while sharing certain elements in common, are also notable for their differences. These differences suggest that the texts that present fame can also illuminate the processes used in constructing difference. As Hayden White has noted of narrative's role in fabricating history, a filmmaker (similarly) selects plots and orders lives with "choice of the plot structure that he considers most appropriate for ordering events into a comprehensible story" (1978:84). Although the creation of fame is heavily reliant upon a text that helps to establish the famous person, fame is not solely a textual activity. But an analysis of fame's texts will yield much that is significant about public attitudes toward the famous.

2

■ ■ ■

Stout-Hearted Men

"This, too, is probable, according to that saying of Agathon: 'It is part of probability that many improbable things will happen.'"

ARISTOTLE, *POETICS*

The eight major film studios (Columbia, Twentieth Century-Fox, MGM, Paramount, RKO, United Artists, Universal, and Warner Brothers) produced 277 biopics in the thirty-three-year period of this study. Additionally, minor studios, like Republic, or independent production companies, like Monogram or its prestige subsidiary Allied Artists, produced fourteen biopics during this same era. Five aspects of the complete sample of 291 films will be discussed in this chapter: the allocation of biopics by each studio, the predominance of one profession or vocation over others, the distribution of biopics within each decade of the study, the historical settings of the biopics, and, last, the distribution of occupation by gender and nationality.

House Styles and Biography

Much has been written of the "house styles" of the major film studios during the period when all of the studios, except for Columbia and United Artists, integrated, in differing degrees, the three functions of the integrated film corporation: production, distribution, and exhibition.[1] This issue of house style, of course, is a particular manifestation of a larger issue: What organizing principle informs the rules for membership in any given group? We are already presuming, perhaps, a great deal, in suggesting that biographical films are, a priori, such a grouping. Further, despite statements from well-known directors that each studio had a discernible house style (the product, presumably, of either a formal or informal conventionalization of a mode of production in the hands of stable set of personnel as well as the existence of communication channels necessary to pass diverse information on) little convincing evidence other than these anecdotal testimonials has been offered to prove this point. Nevertheless, this frame has continued to be both a powerful and popular way of conceptualizing differentiation in the thousands of films produced in this period. Books like Ethan Mordden's *The Hollywood Studios* (1988) still promulgate a view of Hollywood as a factory town characterized by individual "plants" that turned out different models of film, each one easily distinguishable from the production line objects of the competition at other studios the way one distinguished a Reo from a Ford.

If we accept the construct biopic as a frame of varying elasticity that different communities use to "interpret" the meaning of film (producers used it to structure a film, viewers as a preparatory set guiding expectations about what they would see, and exhibitors use it to sell tickets differentiating the biopic from other fare, etc.), then we can also presume that within each frame, as part of each community formed by a studio, there might be looser frames yet that informed the house style of a particular genre within that studio. Each studio might structure biopics according to similar general contours caused by specific differences in intramural production practices, although intertextual references made by producers in constructing films show that films made at other studios affected biopic conventions. While Darryl Zanuck would urge his writers to treat the narrative of *The Story of Alexander Graham Bell* like a previous Fox film, *The Country Doctor* (1936), as "drama overlaid with comedy," he also referred his writers to another studio's construction of biography, MGM's *Boys Town,* as a model for mixing fact with fiction, of transmuting data into entertainment. Thus "house style" might suggest what is unique about a studio's production practices, but at the same time, it places such differentiation firmly within the structure of Hollywood conventions. Certainly the question of house

TABLE 1
BIOPICS BY STUDIOS

| Studio | Total Films | Biopics | | % of All Biopics |
		No.	% of Studio Output	
Warners	1,371	61	4.44	21
Fox	1,458	63	4.32	22
MGM	1,292	47	3.63	16
Paramount	1,374	31	2.25	11
United Artists	890	30	3.37	10
Universal	1,346	17	1.26	6
RKO	1,003	14	1.39	5
Columbia	1,487	14	0.94	5
All Majors	10,221	277	2.67	96
Other*	—	14	—	4
Total	—	291	—	100

SOURCE: Finler 1988: 280.
*Includes studios such as Monogram, Republic, Allied Artists, etc. See Appendix
C for a full listing of biopics by studio.

style in the biopic is worth testing, in a minimal quantitative sense, to see if studios differed in the content and subject matter of their biopics.

Less than 3 percent of all films made by the major studios were biopics. Table 1 shows that as a percentage of total studio output, Warners and Fox were the leading producers, releasing almost four times as many biopics as trailing Columbia and RKO. Previous conventional wisdom suggested that Warners was the leading biopic producer: First, because of Arliss's much-praised performances at Warners, starting with *Disraeli;* second, because of the high visibility and prestige the Dieterle/Muni/Wallis cycle was accorded in Hollywood (Muni won an Oscar for his portrayal of Pasteur, and *Zola* won the Best Picture award of 1937); and last, because Warners, in previous histories of Hollywood, has often been associated with the biopic.[2]

However, the data suggest that Fox, rather than Warners, was marginally the numerically leading producer of biopics. There were essentially four tiers to production. At the first tier, Fox and Warners displayed a commitment to the biopic at a higher level than the second grouping that includes MGM, Paramount, and United Artists. Below this level, Universal, RKO, and Columbia produced barely one-fourth the number of biopics as the leaders did. In particular, though Columbia did not produce its first biopic, *Harmon of Michigan*, until 1941, its entry *The Jolson Story,* one of the top grossing films of 1946, was tremendously influential in spurring a cycle of "vaudeville veneration" at other studios. Last, a small number of independent studios like Monogram (*Dillinger,* 1945) or Republic (*I Dream of Jeannie,* 1952) also produced a small body of biographical films, though the bulk of these concerned either frontier figures or outlaws and gangsters, a possible response, in turn, to the tremendous popularity of 1950s TV genres (the western), individual TV series like *The Untouchables,* or the currency of the Disney Studio's Davy Crockett fad.[3]

Biopic production was bounded by cultural epochs, as shifting conditions both within and outside the studios impinged upon the subject matter of films. Until World War II, Warners (N = 19), Fox (N = 20), and MGM (N = 18) evenly divided biopic production among themselves. Once the war started, and until 1960 with the decline of the studio system, Fox and Warners were the leading producers. MGM seems after 1940 to have lessened its emphasis on this genre.

The two eras of biopic production, determined by observing marked shifts in filmic subject matter, are divided by the Second World War. The first era (1927–1940) was dominated jointly by Warners, Fox, and MGM. Biopics produced in this prewar world took as subjects Lowenthal's "conventional" elites, with all studios producing films emphasizing royalty (N = 12) and government and political leaders (N = 10). In content, movies seemed on the same cultural wavelength as magazines. Prestige accrued to "great man" biopics first at Warners, when Arliss won the 1929–30 Oscar for Best Actor for his portrayal of Disraeli, and later, at other studios, like MGM, whose *The Great Ziegfeld* won the Best Picture Oscar of 1936. During this era (1927–1940), entertainers and artists (N = 9, each) were not the leading figures they would be in the following period.

The second era of biopic production, from 1941 to 1960, was dominated by a new kind of elite. The entertainer rather than the political leader became the paradigmatic famous figure; a quarter of all films made during this period focused on entertainers or artists. Fox, with its extensive use of color and its stable of mildly talented but photogenic performers, produced the largest number of entertainer biopics (N = 14), followed by MGM (N = 13) with its powerful musical units headed by Arthur Freed, Joe Pasternak (formerly Deanna Durbin's producer at Universal), and Jack Cummings. At MGM, the musical and its offspring the musical biopic were a deeply ingrained part of the studio's tradition. As Thomas Schatz has noted, "Metro's commitment to musical production remained its most distinctive feature throughout the post-war decade" (1988:447). Not to be outdone by the prestige-conscious Metro, Fox, under Zanuck's guidance, was committed to both biopics and musicals, notably its Jessel-produced "vaudeville" cycle. Shot in Technicolor—which Zanuck had, early on, used to differentiate his product from other studios—the Fox entertainer biopics signalled a shift in values from earlier times. The great man as a tragic or grand royal figure or the famous statesman, popular before World War II, had been replaced by the great man as a giant of some branch of the entertainment industry. While military figures and gangsters would be honored equally with biopics, particularly during the 1950s, the era of the biopic of the statesman vanished with the close of the war. Having fought two wars on a global scale, the idea of glorifying statecraft seemed oddly out of place once the war had been won. Instead of films glorifying a vanishing culture of statecraft, Hollywood, in its postwar entertainer biopics, turned to recording its own history, and the history of the larger family of entertainment in which it had membership.

If we extrapolate Lowenthal's findings—that the biographies of such figures constituted a culture of consumption rather than one of production—we note that the athlete, another new figure, makes a first appearance in the post-1940 period. While two early biopics of the period 1931–1940 had showcased boxer Henry Armstrong (the 1937 entry *Keep Punching*) and football coach Knute Rockne (*Knute Rockne, All American* [1940]), the cinematic appearance of solo stars in sports—from Babe Ruth to Ben Hogan—added further weight to the recasting of the model of great figure as entertainer. Like the tales of entertainers, Hollywood wrought tales of athletes are full of dramatic moments, incidents where these figures win over fickle fans, uniting a community of audience into the accord of adulation. Just as there is always the scene in an entertainer biopic where the chrysalis is shed and talent becomes greatness, so sports films are full of moments when the hero rises to an impossible occasion, tops the untoppable, pushes himself further than (even he) felt was possible. Biopic films witness Ben Hogan's "impossible" comeback after an auto accident, Bob Mathias's incredible feat of winning the Olympic Decathalon while still in high school (and then repeating the feat four years later), or James J. Corbett's upset win over the invincible John L. Sullivan.

Although Fox produced the largest number of biopics in the postwar era, Columbia (54%), Paramount (52%), Warners (31%), and notably MGM (41%) had higher percentages of their total biopic output devoted to performers than did Fox (29%); entertainment can be said to have characterized these studios' notions of biography. That is, all the studios saw their singing, dancing contract personnel as potentially profitable famous biographees. The musical biography could combine two genres, the musical and the biopic, and could be a showcase for either an individual talent (say, Betty Hutton) or a group (*The Fabulous Dorseys*). It could showcase dancers—Fred Astaire and Ginger Rogers in *The Story of Vernon and Irene Castle* (1939)—originally called "Castles in the Air"—or singers—Doris Day as Ruth Etting in *Love Me or Leave Me*. And, while the actors were often convincing when performing as famous actors or entertainers, in the way many divas are able to convincingly portray Tosca, they were often less than credible when cast as nonperforming artists. Thus, Cagney is superb as George M. Cohan, while Robert Walker is awkward as Brahms. Casting performers known for singing and dancing as painters and composers robbed them of these distinctive qualities; after all, how do you show a painter "performing" his or her work? Too often, a Hollywood display of the behavior that brought a painter or composer recognition often took the form of an exaggerated mime of the actor thrashing about over a tempestuous score or, as in *Song of Love* and *A Song to Remember,* famous music is narratized by linking it, isomorphically, to specific dramatic moments in the script. Thus Schumann's "Traumerei" becomes the leitmotif of his tragic love of Clara, just as Chopin's "Heroic Polonaise," in the Columbia version of his life, underscores his rejection of his frivolous love for George Sand ("Etude in E") and signals his recognition of his duty to Poland. Cole Porter composes "Night and

Day" longing for his love interest Linda (Alexis Smith) amid the drip drip drip of rainy World War I France, at least fifteen years before its actual composition in 1932.

The musical units at each studio already were "in gear," the personnel under contract, to produce slick, often profitable films with singing and dancing. To do so with the added twist of telling a life story presented little new in the way of technical challenge. Thus, one reason performer biopics flourished after the war was to take advantage of the contract personnel—both above and below the line—available. A Zanuck memo of 1950 suggests this money-saving motivation for the biopic of vaudevillian Lotte Crabtree, *Golden Girl* (originally titled "The Belle of San Francisco" and later, "I Wish Tonight"). He urges that the film be shot using sets from an already produced western starring Gregory Peck, *The Gunfighter* (1950), songs in the public domain, and low-paid contract personnel rather than a highly paid star, for "each number will be spotted and designed to fit into a production plan which will take advantage of the talents of players whom we cast in the picture." By casting new discovery Mitzi Gaynor in the title role, and contract player Dennis Day in a supporting part, Zanuck could produce a film tailored to the talents of players already under contract using sets made for another film. In addition, the presence of vaudevillian Jessel as producer (and omniscient narrator in one version of the script) would guarantee a certain authenticity to the proceedings.

One way, then, to utilize on-board talent was to create a biography that could showcase their marketable performing skills. Musicals about performing artists could do this; biopics, where painters fumed and composers were inspired, more often than not, were beyond the abilities of the scriptwriters and performers to bring to life. In any case, the public "expected" Judy Garland to sing, but did not have the same expectation that Katharine Hepburn should play the piano, or Fredric March dance.

In light of the above, merely stating, then, that Fox produced slightly more biopics than Warners, and that the two studios produced almost half of all biopics, still does not tell us what we want to know about house style, though in a general way it suggests that biography was one mode of channeling the latent message of Americanism to which the studios seemed committed. Since this book is not focusing on style at the level of film's formal characteristics, the

TABLE 2

PERCENTAGE ENTERTAINER/ARTIST BIOPICS BY STUDIO

Studio	% Entertainer Artist Biopic
Columbia	64 (N = 14)
Paramount	55 (N = 31)
MGM	40 (N = 47)
Warners	34 (N = 61)
UA	30 (N = 30)
Fox	30 (N = 63)
RKO	21 (N = 14)
Universal	17 (N = 29)
Other	14 (N = 14)

question worth attending to about house style is "What content areas characterized each studio?" or "What professions, if any, did each studio seem to favor in its output?"

When we look at these data in Table D.2, the distribution of biopic professions by studio, the allocation of fame, if not the reasons for it, is a bit clearer. Based on these data, the "rule" for biopic production can be stated as follows: all studios with a substantial output placed a disproportionate production emphasis on biopics of either entertainers or artists, this shift to "fame as entertainment" occurring in the period after the start of World War II. When we combine these two "artistic/entertainer" categories (as Lowenthal did) for each studio, the breakdown of biopics released by each studio as a percentage studio's biopic output reveals a significant pattern (Table 2). In seven out of the eight major studios (RKO with its focus on royalty being the exception) fame is largely tailored to the contours of the careers of artists and entertainers. Thus, "fame" or the "famous person" through biography is, in a sense, a kind of reflexive operation in which the studios used stars in the performing arena to depict "headliners" in a parallel universe outside Hollywood; to Hollywood, the famous person is a reflection of the attainment of stardom in movies themselves.

There is a certain sense in which this outcome is teleological; after all, by weighting the universe of fame so that it is numerically biased in favor of fame in the performing or creative fields, the movies justify their own system, lending credibility to idols of consumption rather than idols of production. In short, the dominance of performer biopics is a grand justification for the legitimacy of popular entertainment.

After glorifying their own communities, individual studios, though, still favored other arenas of fame. Warners, after entertainers and artists, made biopics about government and political figures and gangsters or lawbreakers. Like television content in the 1950s, Warners' equal focus on lawbreakers and law enforcers is a neat balancing act that shows the machine of public order in good running condition. Here their glorification of the workings of democracy attest to the "social consciousness" book after book tells us was their characteristic house style.

One of the more interesting profiles is that of United Artists, "the studio founded by the stars" (D. W. Griffith, Douglas Fairbanks, Mary Pickford, and Charlie Chaplin). Here, almost a quarter of all biopic output was about "creative" artists, and not just entertainers. Just as all the studios created a metalevel of commentary on their own profession with their emphasis on entertainment as fame, United Artists self-consciously salutes its roots as a family of entertainers: art is in the mastery over material, in the creation of art in the genetic sense, not merely in its re-creation through performing. It is also possible that United Artists profile is explainable by its distinctive organization as a studio. For, having no large tribe of actors under long-term contract, United Artists depended not on star/genre formulations (as did other studios), but instead gravitated toward properties suggested by strong, outside producers. With the exceptions of the Goldwyn-originated (and financially disasterous) *The Adventures of Marco Polo,* starring Gary Cooper, the studio's roster of famous biographees was not star-oriented, but project-oriented, the result of a producer's vision without the lens of the star image.

Not to be outdone by the "studio founded by the stars," MGM, the studio whose unofficial motto was "more stars than there are in heaven," seemed to take seriously its Howard Deitz-inspired motto "Art for Art's Sake"; fully 21 percent of its output was about creative artists, while 19 percent was centered on the performing arts. Thus, MGM, which in the eyes of many historians was the studio that most epitomized Hollywood in its high period, in addition to being, for many years, the most profitable studio, was the studio that, in its biopics, created a portrait of fame that was most like its own lineage. Without being reductive, it seems that MGM, while making films to entertain viewers, did so by making films about entertainment. Even when some of its alumnae, like James Stewart, became, after World War II, independent star/producers, they still spotlighted themselves as "performers"; Stewart's *The Glenn Miller Story* and *The Stratton Story* are tales about public performers who, in order to continue enjoying their status as performers, courageously overcome personal tragedy. In a sense, he was being true to his alma mater.

The World Is an American Stage

If the entertainer became the paradigmatic figure of cinematic fame, it is not surprising that the stage upon which the performers are presented is predominantly an American one. Table 3 shows the distribution of biography by both the historical era and setting in which a film takes place. Two-thirds of all biopics are either about Americans or set in America.

This distinction between Americans of native birth and immigrants to America is an important one. For, almost inevitably, films that open outside of the United States but are set largely in this country use the categories (and settings) American and non-American as barometers of success and failure. *The Great Caruso* is a good case in point. Although the first portion of the film transpires in Italy, and Caruso (broadly played by Mario Lanza of Philadelphia) has come to represent "Italian tenor" to most listeners, it is noticeable that "Caruso" as a social figure is not Italian, but Italian-American. That is, in cinematically constructed Italy, with its "tradition" (such as arranged marriages), Caruso, born of a humble family, cannot make his mark as an entertainer, a profession the movie presents as being looked down upon by the mercantile, bourgeois classes. Instead, he is a flour merchant because his fiancée's wealthy father feels this is a more stable profession for his future son-in-law. It is social convention, and not a lack of faith in his talent, that prevents flour merchant Caruso from becoming Enrico Caruso, tenor. In America, at the Metropolitan Opera, Caruso acquires fame, as well as an aristocratic American wife who, unlike his Italian fiancée, supports his artistic career. In America, Caruso, tenor of the people, is "invented" by the poorer people in the gallery after he is scorned by the philistine

TABLE 3
BIOPICS BY HISTORICAL ERA AND COUNTRY

Country	Century						
	20th	19th	18th	17th	16th	Other	Total
THE AMERICAS							
United States	116	81	1	0	0	0	198
Mexico	3	2	0	0	0	0	5
Canada	3	0	0	0	0	0	3
Caribbean	0	0	1	0	0	0	1
EUROPE							
France	3	13	5	1	1	4	27
Britain	1	15	0	2	4	1	23
Russia	2	3	3	0	0	0	8
Germany	1	5	0	0	0	0	6
Italy	0	1	1	0	0	2	4
Holland	1	1	0	0	0	0	2
Sweden	0	1	0	1	0	0	2
Austria	0	1	0	0	0	0	1
Denmark	0	1	0	0	0	0	1
Hungary	0	1	0	0	0	0	1
Ireland	0	1	0	0	0	0	1
Norway	0	0	0	0	0	1	1
Poland	0	1	0	0	0	0	1
Spain	0	1	0	0	0	0	1
ASIA							
Siam	0	2	0	0	0	0	2
China	0	0	0	0	0	1	1
India	0	1	0	0	0	0	1
Japan	0	1	0	0	0	0	1
Persia	0	0	0	0	0	1	1
AFRICA	0	0	0	0	0	1	1
Egypt	0	1	0	0	0	2	3
Belgian Congo	0	1	0	0	0	0	1
AUSTRALIA	3	0	0	0	0	0	3
TOTAL*	133	134	11	4	5	13	300

*The Total for Table 3 is more than the total number of biopics in the complete sample (291) because some films (like The Great Caruso) are set in more than one country.

boxholders at the Diamond Horseshoe. America, with its myths of opportunity and mobility, thus dominates the biographical stage, even in spheres that are quintessentially associated with other countries.

After the United States, Europe appears to be the center of the biographical universe, with 22 percent of films set there. If we combine the American and European totals, we see that 89 percent of all famous people are either American or European. Within Europe, America's traditional allies, Great Britain (33 percent) and France (38.5 percent), account for the bulk of non-American biopics. Germany (8.5 percent), Italy (6 percent), Holland and Sweden (3 percent), and Spain, Poland, Norway, Hungary, Ireland, Denmark, and Austria (1 percent) each account for a small portion of the famous of Europe.

Asia and Africa account for only 3 percent of all biopics. Moreover, the specific contexts of the films set in the "Third World" leave little doubt which world is really the focus of power. Two of these films are set in ancient Egypt (*Cleopatra* [1934] and *The Ten Commandments* [1956]), in effect relegating its achievement to the past while annihilating the (then) current division of that country into colonial empires ruled by France and Britain. Other films are set in the Belgian Congo (*Stanley and Livingstone*), India (*Clive of India* [1935]) or Siam (*Anna and the King* [1946] and *The King and I* [1956]). Of the latter films, it is significant to note that these settings are not presented as the birthplaces of great individuals. Rather, they are colonial possessions where white English or Americans go to create empire or attain heroism, native stages where non-natives star. In each of the modern Third World films, European figures come as teachers to educate the "natives" in the advanced ways of the world, importing a colonialist discourse masquerading as education, trade, or religion. The natives, after some resistance, and a certain amount of recidivism, embrace European culture, naturalizing the colonization of their own lands, suggesting that opposition to colonialism came from only a handful of truly uncivilized "savages" unwilling to let their people be helped.

In their projection of biography onto a world map, Hollywood created a distorted view of accomplishment that sustained an image of history that, painting most portraits with American faces, made it appear that entire domains of achievement had been invented by Americans. Neil Gabler, quoting Isaiah Berlin in another context, framed this issue of distortion clearly. The Hollywood vision of America, created by immigrants who longed to belong to the "inner circles" of power, exhibited "an over-intense admiration or indeed worship for the majority" that manifested itself, in Berlin's words, in a "neurotic distortion of the facts" (1988:2). Hollywood invented an America from the outside. Had the people who founded the film industry been more insiders to the arenas of power, it is doubtful whether the films they made of America would have displayed a kind of never-never land that sanitized most behavior and moralized individual lives at the expense of their own heritage. What is remarkable about a Hollywood view of the world created by the early studio heads is not its contours; in fact, the shape of fame was remarkably like the shape of fame in other media, like magazines. Berlin's term—"a neurotic distortion of the facts"—suggests that the movies they made were neurotic precisely because these men internalized norms that excluded them from the realm of the symbolic through acts of self-censorship.[4]

In this invention came the hope that the inventors themselves, barred from wielding social power, could in their creation of the portrait of America through film become the guardians of this image as a form of power, creating their own parallel power structure based on illusion. Denied entrance into politics and influential social circles, the men who created Hollywood, rather than criticizing this world, instead created a universe that extolled it. This empire of a fantasy America was one where they were kings. It was also, as Hortense Powdermaker (1950) noted, an insular world. This combination of insularity, self-absorbtion, and an obsessional yearning to belong may explain, in part, the distorted intertextuality formed by the near-xenophobic American world Hollywood pictured.[5]

The Time Frame

Since American history is often presented as beginning in the late eighteenth century with the events surrounding the American Revolution, the rest of the world in Hollywood's vision follows suit. Thus, 59 percent of all films set in the United States take place in the twentieth century, 39 percent in the nineteenth century, and only 2 percent in the seventeenth century. This is in contrast to Europe, where only 8.5 percent of all films are set in the twentieth century.

This timeline suggests that the images of the two entities, America and Europe, represent different social forces. America is the place of modernity, Europe of "tradition"; America is electricity and the automobile, Europe is gaslight and carriages, plumed helmets and Empire dresses. In short, this time bias suggests that the "antique," the quaint, might come from overseas, but its perfection and improvement is an American invention. When one thinks of stereotypic modes of dress and behavior of Europeans versus Americans, we see how this time frame creates America as a kind of Darwinian illustration of the branch of civilization that forged ahead, leaving behind, in a kind of cinematic amber, nonadaptive European ancestors. Non-European ancestors were, of course, unthinkable, and were numerically rare, framed as exotic.

Last, the time frame of biography creates a sense of history out of context; rather than presenting opportunities to see connections between other times and our own, Hollywood biography suggests a world where humanity and its discoveries are constantly, *ex nihilo*, being reinvented. Looking at the total sample, biographies of those before the Renaissance are rare indeed (4 percent), and limited to charismatic biblical figures or Egyptian or Greek royalty.

Part of this bias, of course, has to do with who the films are about; since a large portion are about entertainers (or later, athletes), they are set either in the "preferred" Hollywood era, the turn-of-the-century, or the twentieth century itself, where modern entertainment forms were invented alongside Hollywood.

It is interesting to hypothesize why so many of the films about entertainment are set in these two eras. More than 80 percent of all entertainment biopics are set in the eighty years between 1880 and 1960. Of these entertainer biopics, almost a third are about vaudevillians, while a handful (11 percent) are about figures whose main arena of fame was the movies (Buster Keaton, Pearl White, Diana Barrymore, Jeanne Eagels, Lon Chaney, and Rudolph Valentino). We might look to the producers of these films and their culture of production for a partial explanation as to why entertainment seems stuck in a time warp about the turn of the century. The ages of the producers of these films and the heads of the studios themselves, in conjunction with the age of ticket buyers, may explain this skewed vision of fame as entertainment, and entertainment as either vaudeville-based or clustered about the cusp of the twentieth century. Each generation finds favor in particular popular forms of amusement. The recapitulation of these forms can be more than nostalgic; along with the presumption of a shared taste communicated and created by these films, the producers of vaudeville films could have been trying to capture the audiences for these amusements. In a Proustian way, we are imprinted with the memory of these chosen entertainment forms even as, growing older, we adopt new ones or lose interest in once cherished modes of amusement.[6]

The founders of the film industry would have been young men, in their twenties and thirties, when they witnessed these entertainment forms at the turn of the century. Moreover, many of these men were socialized into notions of entertainment in the audiences of vaudeville, most first as patrons, some later as programmers. As Neal Gabler, in *An Empire of Their Own* (1988), has noted, few of the early movie producers and studio heads were formally educated; fewer still had an abiding interest in the "official" high culture of this era, though this did not prevent them from importing it to Hollywood if it carried with it profit, prestige, or both. Yet, one form of entertainment that mediated between the high art of the symphony and opera and the folk art of an indigenous group was vaudeville. Here, as Robert Allen (1980) has noted, a diverse range of acts, including many from concert stages, mixed with other artists in the variety format. It was socially acceptable to attend vaudeville; immigrants were not closed out of vaudeville audiences the way pricing and other factors excluded them from so-called high art of the period. It is not too far-fetched to imagine that these forms, these peculiarly American forms, suggested "entertainment" to the young men of the movies. Further, vaudeville and related forms may have defined popular entertainment, democratic entertainment, in a way that opera, theater, or the symphony could not. These forms were imprinted on the minds of producers and film executives the way Americans today set internal barometers via television content and various media incarnations of popular music. The films they would make were both an unconscious and conscious way of paying homage to their youth. In some ways, vaudeville was a rehearsal for the movies, where (some) of the disenfranchised would have a utopian stage upon which to arrange tableaux of an idealized America frozen in time in much the same way that Walt Disney would, in the "Main Street" in his own kingdom, Disneyland, create a never-never-land permanently set in Middle America at the turn of the century.

Conspicuously absent from the imagery of this "Main Street" were the newly arrived immigrants who made the other streets in the rest of Hollywood, outside Disney's domain, their own kingdom.

Other Limitations: Time and Place

The limitations placed on biography took temporal, geographic, and occupational forms. Hollywood's limited view of history created national stereotypes and, in part, helped foster a naive, uninformed view of the rest of the world that fit well with the provincialism Sinclair Lewis and a host of other native writers complained of in America in the first part of the twentieth century.

To gain a clearer pattern of national groups other than our own memories of the countless Europeans played by S. Z. Sakall, or the pillars of the Empire played by C. Aubrey Smith, or the sharp-tongued, shrieking Irishwomen played by Una O' Connor, we must look at the occupations or spheres of endeavor in which non-Americans were allowed to excel in biographies.

If you were German-speaking, chances are you lived in the nineteenth century (the "good" Germany) and composed music (Schumann, Schubert, Brahms, Strauss) or were a scientist (Ehrlich), or a humanitarian entrepreneur whose fondest wish was for "one world" (Julius Reuter). Interestingly, this image of the German speaker as a superior being of great achievement created a kind of "ubermensch" in cultural and scientific spheres, which would be ominously re-framed solely in military terms once World War II intervened.

If you were French, you lived in the nineteenth century, or were either an intensely romantic eighteenth-century female (Madame Du Barry, Marie Antoinette, etc.) or an intensely political writer (Zola), statesman, and military figure (Napoleon), or, in the case of Louis Pasteur, a man dedicated almost equally to the advancement of science and the honor of France. One of the compelling facts about the representation of the famous foreigner (the "other") in film, is that they are shown as childishly chauvinistic in a way Americans rarely are. The honor of these countries seems perpetually to be at stake in the form of political or scientific scandals (coded anti-Semitism in *Zola* and *Ehrlich,* Chopin's patriotism in *A Song to Remember*), as if suggesting that "honor" outside America is a tenuous thing salvaged from destruction, every ten years or so, by some great man in a given field. These films, like *A Song to Remember,* also stoked the wartime fires of patriotism, drawing parallels between historically oppressed peoples, reminding viewers that the contemporary Poland, like the biopic Poland of Chopin, was under foreign siege. The viewer was thus reminded that each of these noble foreign figures represented allies worth fighting for.[7]

The French line, then, is an intensely nationalistic one obsessed with the foundation of a country on the proper terms and, later, its maintenance through vigilance in a number of fields. This emotion-laden image, one filled with political upheaval and ferment, is in contrast to the competent German who, despite struggles to establish supremacy in a field, nevertheless has a phantom nation in which to do this. The lack of a united Germany is seldom presented as a backdrop for accomplishment the way France-in-tumult is a typification of French cinematic biography. Hollywood may have felt more secure presenting any democracy struggling to remain one (and succeeding) rather than democracy failing to survive. This lesson of democracy's failure in Germany would be relegated to the years surrounding World War II. And, just as Chopin was a stalking horse for the modern, suffering peoples of Poland, Paul Ehrlich, the scientist who discovered a treatment for syphilis, was consciously selected as a subject for a biopic because he was both German and a Jew. As Warners story editor Finlay McDermid explained to Will Hays (who was concerned with the explicitness of the "syphilis" angle in *Ehrlich*), "the reason for picking Ehrlich as a protagonist had very little to do with syphilis and its cure. Ehrlich happened to be a great humanitarian and a German Jew" (quoted in Behlmer, 1985:105). In biopics, beautiful music and powerful science were made with a wary eye turned toward contemporary events, but in a Germany devoid of its own history. Once Germany became the enemy, anti-German references could become part of the discourse on what it meant to be a German national. Thus, Darryl Zanuck suggests that, in *Wilson,* his writers retain an anti-German remark that alludes to the falseness of the very cultural superiority Hollywood had been packaging as ineluctably linked to Germany: "Mr. Zanuck wishes to retain the lines, 'All in the name of your discredited German Kultur and race superiority" (UCLA, Fox Collection, Box FX-PRS-445, story conference of October 6–7, 1943).

Noticeably underrepresented, of course, is America's modern

rival, the U.S.S.R., as well as uncolonized Asia. These enormous voids represent a kind of cinematic equivalent to isolationism, a willful ignoring of entire nations whose ethnicity, race, ideology, or, dangerously, all three prevented them from gaining the credentials needed for entering biographyland.

Certainly the idea of using nonwhite males as role models would, in the time frame covered in this study, be unthinkable. There were only twelve films (4%) made about nonwhite North Americans— *The Joe Louis Story* (1953), *Jim Thorpe—All American* (1951), *The Jackie Robinson Story, Keep Punching, St. Louis Blues* (1958), *Juarez, Viva Villa!* (1934), *Villa!* (1958), *Viva Zapata!* (1952), *Geronimo* (1939), *Chief Crazy Horse* (1955), and *Sitting Bull* (1954). Only two professions, athlete and professional entertainer, are associated with black Americans, representing in a simplistic way many people's perceptions of the limited careers open to blacks. Native Americans are represented largely as defeated warriors, victims of superior white military strength.

While blacks are shown "fitting in" to white culture, rather than possessing a rich culture of their own, Native Americans cling to their traditions. But the Hollywood discourse suggests that such tenacity is inappropriate. Surviving means surviving in the modern world, the colonial world. In *Walk the Proud Land* (1956), a Native American woman, Tianay (Anne Bancroft), is shown falling in love with the missionarylike Indian agent sent to rescue her people. In the end, John Clum (Audie Murphy), the subject of the biopic, convinces Tianay that the two races are better separated than united, that *Brown* v. *the Board of Education of Topeka* was still years in the future; separate and unequal cultures are the norm. The Native Americans, and Tianay, accept all of Clum's ideas on how to define culture, but in abandoning their heritage, Tianay and her people are shown enacting an impoverished version of the superior dominant social order. This portrayal of "natives" is no different from that depicted in *Stanley and Livingstone,* where the good Christian missionary, David Livingstone, teaches Martin Luther's hymn of colonialism, "Onward Christian Soldiers," to a group of Africans who shape it to their own "limited" performance style, with Livingstone joyfully conducting a grotesque singalong that somehow impresses nonbeliever Henry Stanley of the goodness of the Christian mission in Africa. Mexicans, with the exception of the revered

Benito Juarez and Emiliano Zapata—who are shown fighting wars of liberation modeled on the principles Hollywood suggests are part of the American Revolution (Juarez is shown reverently reading a letter from Lincoln)—are suggested by the duplicitous Pancho Villa (two films), the escapades of the latter balanced by the saintliness and self-sacrifice of the former.

Films set in Japan and China (less than 1 percent) take place either in the long ago past (*The Adventures of Marco Polo*), or present Asian nations as outmoded resisters to the voice of American modernity (*The Barbarian and the Geisha* [1958]). Like other films made in the 1950s that sang the contemporary song of cultural pluralism, *Barbarian* is incredibly patronizing, and the Townshend Harris of John Wayne can outwit the Japanese diplomatically with the same ease he dispatched them as a soldier in a number of fictional World War II films.

The Soviet Union, and its overall absence, while not surprising, cannot easily be explained away by resorting to racist explanations. Here, the barrier to representation is ideological in the narrow sense, with studio heads being even more afraid of Communism than they were of the threats of the Nazis. Thus, "Russia" (represented in eight films) had to mean prerevolutionary Russia. Like so many other representations of history, a particularly narrow swath—the doings of royalty—comes to represent an entire nation.

In film, the model of "Russian" is represented either by the subdued nymphomania of the Empress Catherine (variously played by Talullah Bankhead, Elizabeth Bergner, or Marlene Dietrich) or the plight of Europe's "saddest" royal family, the Romanovs. Russia is represented by its rococo, even decadent past, or its "tragic," romanticized, recent past. Musical biopics (of Tchaikovsky and Rimsky-Korsakov) showcase the "otherness" of Russia, presenting it as neither European nor Asian, but a strange, turbulent hybrid filled with swelling music and sad doings. The incredible cinematic possibilities available in the Russian Revolution are of course, off-limits to the virulently anti-Communist industry. Since the American government did not even recognize the U.S.S.R. until 1933, some sixteen years after their revolution, one would hardly expect to find the film industry more forward in embracing their ideology. Moreover, many of the early movie moguls were immigrants from Russia or Eastern Europe, where as Jews, they were subject to a variety of

17. "Churchill" and "Stalin" of *Mission to Moscow* with the real Joseph Davies, American ambassador to the Soviet Union

forms of discrimination and persecution. The sympathetic Hollywood depiction of tsarist Russia, like its construction of WASP, middle-class America, denied the moguls' own experiences through the adoration of the very groups that practiced social exclusion. Rabidly anti-Communist (led by Harry Warner and L. B. Mayer), the studio heads displayed the love they bore their adopted country in their films and their conservative political affiliation. While there would always be room for anti-Communist films well into the seventies and eighties (Stallone's *Rambo* series), the liberalization of Hollywood in the sixties and the changing of the studio guard gave the world some truly bizarre biopics of Communist leaders, with Omar Sharif as the doomed *Che!* (1969) and Richard Burton in Joseph Losey's Italian/French/British production of *The Assassination*

of Trotsky (1972). At one point, Warners producer Jerry Wald con-
templated a biopic of the newest political headliner, Fidel Castro.
Framed in the first moments of his overthrow of the corrupt Batista
regime as a freedom fighter in the mold of other Hispanic warriors
venerated by North Americans (like Simón Bolivar), Castro's life—
he had even played semi-professional baseball—seemed like a
natural for the screen. Himself a shrewd and copious exploiter of
American media, Castro wanted Marlon Brando (who had earlier
played revolutionary Emilio Zapata) to portray himself, and Frank
Sinatra to play his brother. However, as the frame "Communist" replaced "freedom fighter" as a definition of Castro, his desirability as
a cinematic life, or at least a cinematic heroic life, evaporated.
Hitchcock would cruelly parody him in *Topaz* (1969), and Richard
Lester would do the same in *Cuba* (1979).[8]

There were just too many forces militating against producing any
biopic of a Communist or totalitarian leader. Although ideological
censorship may seem to be the most obvious explanation for these
absences, the reasons for this vacuum are more complex than a
simple Manichaean democratic/nondemocratic schism. A substantial number of biopics explain famous people with reference to their
families, their neighborhood or home roots, their education and
friends. Such humanizing touches might render the lives of these
charismatic but forbidden lives empathetic, perhaps even providing
social explanations for their "evil" behavior that might seem to excuse it. Clearly, such humanizing of figures who were elsewhere
presented as Halloween monsters would be antithetical to the pro-
American line taken by all studios. Being masters at propaganda,
Hollywood realized that the normal biopic treatment simply could
not be used for these figures.

In all likelihood, the Hollywood cinema is probably less narrow
in its biographical jingoism than other national cinemas. The
French, Italian, or German film industries (to name three colonialist
nations with active studio systems) do not cover many non-native
biographies (though Ernst Lubitsch's *Madame Du Barry* and *Anne
Boleyn* and the British 1941 pro-U.S. *Courageous Mr. Penn* are exceptions to this trend). To the extent that each national cinema valorizes its own cast of famous persons, one could say that xenophobia
is a trait of all producing countries, and that the American focus on
a select few foreign notables is, in fact, an attempt to broaden the

demographic base of fame, appeal to ethnic minorities in the mass audience, and satisfy lucrative foreign markets.

But Hollywood films influenced not only the home audiences, but audiences abroad. In this way, their distortion of what constituted legitimate fame had a much farther reach than those of other national cinemas, for Hollywood films, in an early one-way flow of information from the United States to other countries, reached larger audiences of "others" than foreign films reached America.

The xenophobia represented in the structuring of the elements of the biopic discussed thus far masks a critical issue; that such stereotyping, distortion, and nonrepresentation were ongoing civics lessons. By the time of World War II, the Capras, Hustons, and Wylers did not have to retool in preparing pro-American propaganda. For, in the world of biopics, these lessons on why we fight had already been presented in the guise of how they lived. Propaganda was merely a brighter spotlight illuminating what, in many instances, people already knew.

Gender and Biography: The Garb of Clio

Gender is one of the most powerful frames informing the construction of fame. The frame of gender controls many of the activities that fall within its boundaries, so that male and female biographies differ according to professions allocated, family attitude toward fame, and, in particular, the consequences of being a famous man as opposed to a famous woman. Here, I will only discuss the allocation of career by gender. Chapter four, "Reel Life" and chapter five, "Configuring the Person" will discuss the specific constructive process in film whereby one attains fame and suffers its consequences.

There are two ways we can approach the numeric data on fame and gender (Table D.3). First, we can look at the relative weight accorded all careers by gender, ranking them in the order in which the specific career is allocated within male or female domains. Here, we will look at the percentage of women who pursued a particular career, or what careers women were "allowed" to pursue. Second, we can assess the degree to which certain careers, by their distribution as male or female, seem gender-coded as appropriate for male or female. There are a number of careers—for example, that of the athlete—that only men pursue; the two careers allocated solely to women are those of the concubine or paramour, and the educator. While men have numeric superiority in twelve careers, films on women dominate only four areas. After paramour and educator, they are royalty and medical.

The overall frame in which all these data must be placed is one in which the biography of the single famous woman accounts for only one-quarter (25.8%) of all biopics. If we add to this total women who are part of famous couple (*The Story of Vernon and Irene Castle* or *Shine On, Harvest Moon*) or who form a portion of some other social unit (*The Dolly Sisters* or the Brontë biopic, *Devotion*) the total is 31 percent. Conversely, men alone account for 65 percent of all biographies, more than twice the number of biopics than women account for. Even the two animal biographies in the complete sample, *The Great Dan Patch* (1949) and *The Story of Seabiscuit* (1949), are about male stars outside the species Homo sapiens. Fame in almost any field would seem to be largely a male prerogative. Given this bias, those careers in which women are numerically dominant—royalty, paramour, medical, and educator—take on a particular weight, for they are instances in which the male domination of the power structure is disrupted by female eminence.[9]

Females almost hold parity with males in medicine and entertainment, where 46 percent of films are either about women as solo acts or as part of a team. First and foremost, then, of all spheres allocated by gender, women are entertainers (29%); it is the single largest sphere in which women perform. It is also one of the few areas in which women have numeric parity with men. In fact, if the three most popular categories for women are combined, it is apparent that "performer" is a metaphor for the image in which women have been constructed. Thus, the paramour (18%) and royalty (17%), after entertainer, are the ways women in biography have been depicted. The latter is a hereditary and largely ceremonial role, the former is a "career" in which the stereotypical attributes of women—beauty and a desire for romance, and perhaps sexual desire—are measures of success. Additionally, the female career is dogged by the conflict between the fulfillment of heterosexual desire through marriage or romance and professional duty. A large number of films of the female famous contain speeches in which the device of male domination is laid bare beneath the marriage canopy: Sister Kenny acknowledges she gave up marriage for her work with children,

18. Gloss: Greta Garbo and John Gilbert in *Queen Christina*—the woman who loses all for love, in life and on the screen

Marjorie Lawrence of *Interrupted Melody* defers her ascent in her spectacular operatic career so her husband's modest medical practice can flourish, and Mary of Scotland and Christina of Sweden give up their lives and thrones, respectively, for the sake of love. Female entertainers are prone to the "Mrs. Norman Maine" syndrome, as their spouses are either manipulative creatures who see them as profitable meal tickets (*With a Song in My Heart, I'll Cry Tomorrow, Love Me or Leave Me*) or else demand that the female star shorten the shadow she casts over his own mediocre career. In a few cases (*The Girl in White* [1952], medicine and *The Dolly Sisters,* entertainment) the male love interest cannot bear competition from the female, cannot conceive of a world where she, and not he, is the star. It is telling that the male version of the career/love conflict has the male star so wrapped up in his career that he is unable to give love. Here, the woman's problem is different: she cannot help but surrender to love, often at the expense of her talent and her career.

Often the female royal figure must choose between her heart and her "professional" commitment to the state. The mere owning up to sexual desire is often taken, by men, as a sign of weakness, so a female ruler can only show her mettle by forgoing things typically "female." *Mary of Scotland* is interesting in this regard, for the formidable Katharine Hepburn, as Mary, voices an almost reactionary creed when she accuses the unmarried, childless Elizabeth of not being a woman, her barrenness and unmarried state a contrast to the thrice-married Mary. Elizabeth's reply, that she is a queen, and that being a woman has not got the imprisoned Mary into a very good predicament, evokes the scornful trump card from Mary: "I've loved as a woman loves, lost as a woman loses. But still, I win. You have no heir. My son will inherit your throne, my son will rule England. Still, still I win." In Maxwell Anderson's version of the Mary/Elizabeth confrontation (which never actually occurred) the fireworks that go off when the two queens confront one another are equal to those depicted vocally by Donizetti in his opera *Maria Stuarda.* Mary's proclivity to love the "wrong man," as so many great women cinematic women are wont, and her biological ability to bear children, define her, in the end, principally as a woman rather than a queen.

This characterization of a woman as chained to the biology of gender is, of course, not limited to biography. One thinks of Bette Davis's speech to Celeste Holm in *All About Eve* (1950), in which the great actress Margo Channing hears, as we say today, her biological clock ticking. Her profession is second to her biological destiny as a woman, though the schmaltzy version of a "Liebestraume" we hear on the radio subverts her speech on this topic, suggesting perhaps that even now, when she is alone, off the stage, she is acting a part, complete with mood music. But the movie Margo Channing is no different than other movie heroines—Mary of Scotland or Ruth

Etting or Lillian Roth—where a male famous figure is ruled by the destiny of his talent, a woman is dominated by the alleged biological demands of her gender. In the end, the female famous person is compelled by biology to do what she must do; males answer to another, different authority. The difference between male and female careers, then, is striking: men are defined by their gift, women by their gender, or their gendered use of their gift.

The woman with a career, be it on the stage or as a paramour, must violate the cinematic convention that would place her in the home. It is by now a cliché to suggest that such depictions of women allocate a public/private locus for them, with males pursuing a life in the public sphere, while women "rule" at home. But the filmic famous, by the very fact of their being publicly well known, rupture this dichotomy, enacting a struggle to accommodate a world that wishes to gaze at women in public, but keep her otherwise located in the backstage area of the home.

One might also add that all three categories—entertainer, royalty, paramour—make the female the object of a male gaze, though of three different sorts. Entertainers are people whose vocation calls upon them to present themselves publicly as an object to be appraised, while royalty, in their ceremonial roles, are also playing parts in public spectacle. It is telling that the dominant female career, entertainer, is one that, as Braudy notes, has always been viewed as morally ambivalent by audiences and the public at large. By performing on a stage, these figures draw attention to the necessity for women to invent themselves, to expand upon the roles allocated to them by society; their public triumphs, constructed of illusion rather than eternal truths, are a constant reminder that society represses women, limits them to a paltry offstage repertoire. Each time a performer flamboyantly breaches the behavioral code, on or off stage, she is breaching the private social code as well. In this way, even though women are held up as objects of male scrutiny, performance, with its reminder that women are forced to fabricate in order to succeed, might be linked to liberation. However, such limited liberation is tamed by publicity that suggested female stars, whatever their screen image, had a domestic side as well. Thus, the historical violation of norms for women depicted in entertainer biopics is balanced by a publicity discourse that assures us, in most cases, that the stars who portrayed these brave women are, themselves, models of domestic virtue.

Courtesans, on the other hand, are more problematic to portray than women with public careers. Courtesans are very much objects to be seen in the private mode; their placement, or misplacement, in the public sphere is often the cause of cinematic moral outrage (*That Hamilton Woman* [1941], *The Gorgeous Hussy* [1936] or *The President's Lady, The Girl in the Red Velvet Swing*).

When women are depicted in scientific spheres, it is typically as a nurse where compassion, rather than brilliance, is a badge of identity. *Madame Curie,* the 1943 story of the great French scientist, was one of two female scientific biopics made during World War II that could be seen as patriotically saluting America's allies. *Sister Kenny* was particularly useful in the hands-across-the-seas campaign, for her greatest triumph occurs not in her native Australia, but in the United States. Her struggle to convince the medical establishment to treat polio in her "radical" way is, as typical of the scientific biopic, not merely an internecine struggle to reveal a scientific truth to a small community. Rather her fight is one of class and gender—a female nurse from the backwater challenging the urban British and Australian medical establishment—and it is fitting that this woman, who is shown counting on the support of "the people" rather than the establishment, should triumph, finally, in America, with its populist tradition of supporting the underdog. *Sister Kenny* (at $660,000, a big money-loser for RKO) salutes our allies, pats women on the head, and embraces progress as a thing almost uniquely American. Thus, even when praising and picturing foreign lives, America often manages to make its presence felt within the frame.

Receiving Difference

I want to avoid generalizing about audience reception that Lacanian film criticism influenced by his writings might see in this or similar material. My readings of the narrative content of these films are one possible set of responses, not as the inevitable, or even the natural way to interact with these films. Scholarship inspired by the male French psychoanalyst Lacan purports to articulate the reactions of those (largely female) viewers who have long been disenfranchised by male-dominated psychoanalytic theories of the identity-formation process we allegedly follow when processing symbolic material like films. However, Lacan's followers act as if all viewers process films in the same way, as if interpretation of meaning were moot issues, processes which long ago were uncovered in film studies, and are now not worthy of further discussion. More dangerously, this highly mechanical view of communications, derived from the model of the individual writer who uses him or herself as a sole informant, suggests all viewers responding to film follow the same interpretive process, albeit down different gendered paths leading to heterosexual desire.

The fact of male placement of female object into professions where it is legitimate to stare at her is, however, a fact difficult to overlook. But the effects upon viewers of this obvious imbalance between the male and female constructions of fame in film are not necessarily easily explainable by the oracular smokescreen of an impenetrable critical language. Even if we grant that Lacan's argument—articulated by Laura Mulvey and others—suggests that the assessment of symbolic material precedes its specific interpretation, such a view of culture reduces members of the audience, and members of society, to ciphers who, biologically made all alike in their difference, are not shaped at all by the crucible of culture. Nick Browne, writing similarly of perceived weaknesses in Althusserian models of the audience member as subject, clearly articulated this position—the never-never-land of the "idealized" audience member:

> This formulation provided only a general abstract conception of the figure of the audience as "subject," one common to all social institutions and specific to none, one that sustained a theory of totalizing ideological discourse. Nowhere did Althusser provide a place for the audience's differential positions and readings according to different levels or instances of social position or practice—for example, according to gender, class, ethnicity, et cetera. (Browne, in Newcomb, 1987:586)

One awaits a theory of reception, perhaps along the grounds laid out by Janice Radway (1984) or Ian Eng (1985), that is grounded less in the eye of the individual author and more in the work of diverse lay readers and viewers. Studies by Dyer (1986), and Bobo and Seiter (1991) with viewers marginalized by culture suggests that despite the surface monolithic quality of mainstream culture, people create readings that are alternative to heterosexual male-dominated views of the world. The reading of "fame" that is "obviously" suggested (to the analyst) by a film need not be the reading that most people could make of a film, given a variety of communication contexts and the diverse contexts in which film might figure.

When xenophobia is dressed in the clothing of history rather than other costumes, it becomes a troubling garb for Clio to wear. Originally Clio, from the Greek, meant to make famous, or to celebrate and, at least linguistically, the term referred to men and women alike. The ultimate irony about the cinematic construction of fame in human, demographic terms is that Clio, a goddess of history, is in film male, white, and American.

CHAPTER

3

■ ■ ■

Night and Day

"Let's agree on one thing at the start, boys. I don't think anybody cares about the facts of my life, about dates and places. I'll give you a mess of them, you juggle them any way you like."
—LARRY PARKS AS AL JOLSON, TALKING TO A GROUP OF
SCREENWRITERS IN *JOLSON SINGS AGAIN*

"As long as we are going to make the Joe Howard story more realistic in its foundation, although we intend to tell it in terms of humor, we should therefore adhere to some of the facts. . . . Now I don't mean to say we should follow his life, or anything like it, but whenever we can use a similar locale without destroying our own story we have created, we should do so."
—DARRYL ZANUCK TO GEORGE JESSEL, OCTOBER 11, 1945,
REGARDING *HELLO MY BABY*

What was the role played by the studio research departments in constructing a life? Every studio had access to historical material, but to view facts as the sole basis of a biographical script is to ignore the many different factors that shaped what could constitute a cinematic life. Historical accuracy was one possible frame to place about a movie. Other issues were powerful determinants of what the final shape of the life might be.

Involved in the making of any biopic were problems of censorship, problems of casting and star image, and a host of legal issues surrounding the depiction of a real person. Most importantly, a powerful influence on the final shape of a biopic was the producer's own strong vision of what a proper film of a life might be. In the end, because of the interaction of specific instances of these four general factors—censorship, casting, legal issues, and the producer's conception of what a life should be—and further, because the film industry as a producer of culture was in each generation reinventing itself in response to extracinematic factors—a life on film tended to reference not historical texts but the almost hermetic systems of reference established in previous films.

Thus, the references used to construct *The Story of Alexander Graham Bell* were not contemporary accounts of Bell's life, or interpretations of what the new invention meant for the nation. Instead, *Bell* was based upon previous Fox hits, only some of which were biopics, like *Drums Along the Mohawk* (1939), *Suez* (1938), and *In Old Chicago* (1938). Bell, like other characters in biopic fiction, is made like Mary Shelley's creature, of bits of previous incarnations of already-lived lives. Because of this ritualistic use of intertextuality, a similar shape to fame, something like an ideological taxonomy of fame, became the norm for making the cinematic life of a great man or woman. Thus Leo Braudy's observation that fame did not consist of a great or noble action, but rather the reports of such action, is nowhere more true than for biopics, where a hit life was constructed out of resurrected hit movies.

The Research Departments and Their Bibles

Since the 1920s, and in some instances even earlier, film production companies' research efforts in narrative, costume, decor, and manners and mores had been organized as separate but integrated departments within the motion picture corporation.[1] The idea of research was present very soon after the movies established themselves as corporations with intensive divisions of labor. All the major studios maintained fully staffed research departments as part of their operating machinery. Many films had reason to make use of these research facilities. For example, fictive films like *Meet Me in St. Louis* (1944) might make use of information on interior decoration, architecture, fashion, or music of the period in creating sets, costumes, and script. Because the historical component of biopics was a commodity used to differentiate it from other studio fare, however, the research involvement in these films was always significant. This was the case even after the script had been approved for production, and, sometimes, even after a film had been shot and was ready for release. Because the research for a typical film was so extensive, often filling several volumes, the organized materials were often used in publicity campaigns to help sell a film. At times, the very fact of extensive research was itself a selling point, as historicity via extravagant research efforts became, along with the presence of a well-known star or a famous director, a quality to exploit.

Once a story had been given the go-ahead and moved from the development phase into actual production, the job of the research department really started. Set and costume designers would want visual information on period details, actors would want information on the biographee to assist them in makeup and characterization, casting would need pictorial information on all the historical figures in the script, the director and producer would want both general and specific information on the settings in which the life would unfold, and the legal department would need a list of all characters in the film, preferably accompanied by signed release forms from living persons insuring their permission to be depicted in a movie version of a life.

To assist filmmakers in these undertakings, the researcher first turned to the studio's own libraries. The Warners library alone contained almost ten thousand books, as well as vast amounts of pictorial material assembled for previous films. Additional volumes could be borrowed, as needed, from area public libraries, special collections at libraries outside Los Angeles, from private universities, or, in rare cases, could be rented from private collections. Generally, one person from research would be assigned to a picture for its duration. However, on prestige productions, or productions in which difficulties arose or in which specialized knowledge was required, more than one person might be assigned to a film. For example, Warners prestige production *All This and Heaven Too* had three researchers (Hetta George, Jean Beck, and Augusta Adler) assigned to it, all overseen by department head Herman Lissauer, Ph.D. They worked a total of eleven weeks. And, although principal photography for the film was completed on April 20, 1940, research personnel nevertheless continued to work for another week on problem areas of this project.

The research for the Bette Davis vehicle was done simultaneously with research on other films. In preparation at the same time as *All This* was another biopic, *The Lady with Red Hair* (1940), a vehicle for Davis's sometime nemesis and co-star, Miriam Hopkins. To meet the research demands of these two projects, the department would weave in and out of historical periods, now concerned with French legal procedure of the 1840s, now interested in acting conventions of the nineteenth-century New York stage.

Although these research teams were occasionally augmented with information gleaned from outside experts or consultants in specialized fields, or were, from time to time, forced to defer to the studio legal department, the range of questions the department was expected to answer on their own was truly astonishing. By the 1920s the procedures necessary to insure a smooth-running operation had been institutionalized, and these departments had become supremely adept at fielding questions. And, because of the cultural weight accorded film as a pretelevision source of public history, studio research departments were perceived as quasi-public repositories of knowledge to which viewers wrote for advice on noncinematic matters, such as etiquette or interior design.

The overall job of the department was to answer specific questions from writers, directors, art directors, producers, and other personnel concerning any and all aspects of production. The reason behind the existence of such an extensive research machine is far from clear, however. As part of the complex division of labor that characterized the producer-unit mode of production Bordwell, Staiger, and Thompson (1985) suggest was the norm in Hollywood during this period, the labor of research had what might be called an instrumental function. But a description of the department's goals in these terms alone—research departments were part of the chain of production—avoids larger issues, namely why studios should be concerned with facticity at all, and how this concept was operationalized by studio research personnel. The ideology motivating the large range of research requests was rather more complex than this research-as-work approach would suggest.

There were competing and contradictory expectations from different personnel as to the purpose of the work that went into the massive research guidebooks (the "bibles") assembled for each film. These bibles were of the utmost importance to a film, for they represented, during all phases of production, the shared basis upon which decisions pertaining to historical accuracy were made.[2] Carl Milliken, Jr., eventual head of Warners research in the 1950s, described the significance of these bibles for an in-house publication, the *Warner Club News:*

> Because the information must be chiefly pictorial, there is prepared on each picture, a compilation of pictures usually referred to as the 'bible.' The department copy of this material is bound in a large volume as a permanent record of the work done on the picture. Copies of the pictures applying directly to their phase of the work are sent to the various people that are directing work on the picture—the producer, director, art director, property casting, makeup, wardrobe, etc. The complete compilation is usually so impressive that the publicity department sends a copy to New York for use in exploiting the picture. (1940:3)

The heads of research themselves, with their staff of in-house experts assembling these bibles, seemed to be after a linear, factual account of a famous life: getting the chronology straight, getting the characterizations accurate or at least recognizable, getting accurate pictures of the costumes and reliable accounts of the mores of the period as described by various reliable primary and secondary sources. They fully expected that their research findings, housed in these bibles, would be used by all film personnel in their various capacities in making a biopic. This use of the bible was standard operating procedure at all the studios, as the directive on the cover for Fox's bible for *Cardinal Richelieu* suggested: "These notes should be read in advance of production as they are designed to give ideas for set dressing, props, modes and manners, business. . . ."

Like other contributors to the filmmaking process at a well-organized studio, the researcher had specific tasks to do, and standard operating procedures with which to accomplish his or her assignments. However, years of working in a fact-dominated environment must have left a mark on those in the research department, and, as in other professions, researchers internalized a set of work values that were specific to their corner of the lot. A "researcher's culture" arose, complete with its own values and hierarchies, and part of this culture undoubtedly was a particular slant on how directors and producers could best use their skills in making a biopic. When researchers' advice was ignored, or some imaginary line demarcating fact from fancy was crossed, given the power structure at studios, the responses of the personnel in research could be quite harsh. In an April 23, 1940, memo, Herman Lissauer, head of Warner's research, upbraids Don Siegel (later a director, but then a member of the insert department) for an inaccurate piece of business in *All This and Heaven Too*. The property department sent a key document to be used for an insert shot in the film, the unjustly accused Henriette's "Certificate of Discharge and Release," to Lissauer for his approval. This verification of accuracy was standard procedure. However, in this instance Lissauer refused to grant his approval, noting:

> This document should bear the title 'Release for Lack of Evidence' or 'Ordonnance de Non-Lieu' instead of 'Certificate of Discharge and Release.'
>
> Some of the errors on this form could have been avoided by use of the information supplied in my memo of February 20th to Mr. Litvak and the Property Department. . . . In all cases of this kind, I would suggest that before any form is made up it should be brought to this department to be checked for errors.

It was important to research that individual artifacts, like Henriette's certificate, particularly if reconstructed for a film, be as close as possible to the original materials unearthed through the department's diligent work. The researchers' devotion to their data, their belief that historical accuracy should be the template for the narrative, was the likely outcome of their particular place in the production chain.[3]

I do not wish to give the impression that the members of the research staff were, like the dictionary compilers of Howard Hawks's *Ball of Fire* (1941), intellectuals from central casting, superannuated creatures holed up in a dark room in pursuit of a truth detached from the realities of the world of movie making. Researchers, as part of the community of commercial filmmakers, were tolerant of the conventions of poetic license used in constructing narratives for biopics. If they had been around a studio lot long enough, they also should have been well-versed in the analysis of the structure of Hollywood power, and on their own, limited role in influencing what appeared on the screen. In most cases, the director and/or producer or the studio's head of production set the tone for how much energy would be expended for research on a given picture. Because their relationship to the labor of making a cinematic life was different from that of producers, however, they held different values. At times their tolerance was stretched too far by the depiction of history in a script. And, although it was not the research department's job to advise the producer on what standards of realism should apply in a biopic but merely to present him with the requested facts, pride in their work and a sense of the contribution they could make forced them at times to violate the standard operating procedures of supplying answers, and instead to confront a particularly flagrant violator of the standards of fact in the biopic.

This was the case in Warners' *The Court-Martial of Billy Mitchell*. In a lengthy series of memos over a period of three weeks, the head of research, Carl Milliken, Jr., who had some twenty years' experience in the movie business, voiced his fears on the dangers of not adhering to the facts as unearthed by research to the film's producer, Milton Sperling. Milliken was addressing a man, Sperling, peculiarly suited to produce *Mitchell*. A former secretary to both Hal Wallis and Zanuck (who had replaced Wallis as Warners chief production executive before founding his own corporation, Twentieth Century Pictures, in 1933), Sperling became a screenwriter in 1936 and a producer five years later. A marine captain in World War II, his interest in Billy Mitchell was more than just that of producer and project (he received joint story and scenario credit). Schooled in the military service and at the feet of Zanuck, Sperling had absorbed definite ideas on how to create a narrative of the life of the controversial Mitchell.

Milliken, a veteran from the Lissauer regime, delivers a kind of researcher's credo on why research departments exist, and what role they should play in a film. In a memo of May 27, 1955, he notes that, from a research point of view, the Mitchell film will be a difficult script to produce, "because you are dealing with factual events and actual people, and also because you have changed those events somewhat and fictionalized the characters to some extent." Then in a memo of June 16, Milliken advises Sperling, "my deep feeling [is]

19. The troubled company of *The Court-Martial of Billy Mitchell:* Gary Cooper, director Otto Preminger, and producer Milton Sperling

that a story such as the life story of Billy Mitchell is best told when the closest possible adherence to facts is maintained." After all, Milliken points out, "The actual events of Mitchell's life were *so* dramatic, that it would be difficult indeed to improve on the drama through fictionalization."

Sperling, in his roles as producer and writer, still demurred.

Finally, in the lengthiest correspondence yet on the project, Milliken specifically spells out his grievances.

> I am sure that you will understand that this department is firmly convinced that the words 'dramatic license' are overworked in this town. This is especially true . . . when our stories have to deal with real people and real events. . . . My reason for this brash statement is that I think that although the overall story holds pretty true to the events and meaning of Mitchell's life—the individual elements have been changed so much that the cash customers will recognize this fact and be disappointed. . . . In *East of Eden,* for instance, Kazan will be the first to tell you that a considerable factor in the picture's success was the care that went into the authentic Salinas background. I *went* to Salinas, dug up a mass of photographic evidence of the way people lived in 1917, *and the result is apparent on the screen.*
>
> This picture, too, should have the benefit of this sort of careful preparation. As it is . . . we are left with a whole mass of research minutiae which we are simply unable to provide and which will necessarily be faked by the various production departments. I can only think that this will have its effect on the finished production. (Emphasis mine)

This overt clash was not a typical way studio personnel articulated or even resolved their different conceptions of research for biopics, but it does illustrate the researcher's credo as contrasted to that of the producer. The researcher evinced a devotion to a rather straightforward telling of the facts. Most significantly, Milliken was certain that his work made a difference to the ultimate quality of the product. Only when standards of research were grossly violated did a researcher change from an observer to an advocate.

The Producer's Culture

With their energies divided among the forces of censorship at Production Code Administrator Breen's office, the legal department's fear of litigation based on either invasion of privacy or libel, and the campaigns to be mounted for publicity and ticket sales, producers, often balancing the demands of competing priorities, were far more pragmatic than researchers were. Experience in the past had told them that getting the facts straight was merely one consideration to be weighed against many other variables in determining what aspects of a person's history would become part of a celluloid life.

A clear picture of the different values producers and research personnel held on the facts in a biopic can be illustrated with the Warners biography of Cole Porter, *Night and Day*. Porter himself was as successful a businessman as he was a composer. He had, through protracted negotiations with Jack Warner, raised the asking price for the Warners' rights to use thirty-eight of his songs in a film based on his life to $300,000. Well aware of the conventions of show business biographies, and experienced in financial negotiations concerning artistic properties, Porter, in order to make a more commercial film, was willing to sign away certain of his biographical rights. To this end, he and his family, including his wife and mother, signed release forms so Cary Grant and Alexis Smith could impersonate them in a film that bore only the most superficial resemblance to their actual lives. Porter's contract stipulated that

> it is understood that Producer in the development of the
> story . . . upon which the photoplay shall be based shall
> be free to dramatize, fictionalize, or emphasize any or all
> incidents in the life of Seller, or interpolate such incidents
> as Producers may deem necessary in order to obtain a
> treatment or continuity of commercial value. (USC,
> Warners Collection, *Night and Day* file contract, p. 6)

Porter realized that the events of his life were not necessarily the same as a story of his life. The direct remuneration and untold free publicity such a film of his life would generate were worth the distortions of the strange concoction that was eventually made.

The Entertainer as Cultural Hero

Making biographical films about entertainers was a fairly new trend in Hollywood. Although *The Great Ziegfeld* had been an enormous triumph for MGM, most biopics made before World War II were about conventional elites, royalty, or current headliners. America's fascination with the entertainer stretched as far back as the days of Barnum and the manufactured veneration of the deeply religious Jenny Lind (portrayed by Grace Moore to Wallace Beery's Barnum in MGM's aptly titled 1930 film, *A Lady's Morals*). However, the arrival of entertainers as great figures in film biographies marked a transition in American cultural values. The rise of entertainers signalled the dominance of performing media, like film and, later, television and recording stars, over other texts of culture as instruments of instruction mediating between a specific lived life and the public's knowledge of it. In 1946, the Porter film was located squarely in the middle of this entertainment-as-culture trend. Its picturing of a life is, in a sense, representative of how Hollywood made the lives of living, popular entertainers into entertainment and instruction.

The apparent rise of the entertainer as the representative biographical figure is also linked to noncinematic trends. The 1940s witnessed several cultural tremors: in addition to the advent of television, the rise of suburbia, changing cultural patterns wrought by World War II, and changing ownership patterns in the studio system, this era also saw the rise of the film star as independent producer. Tax laws enacted in the 1940s had made it more beneficial for a star to defer earnings on a film, incorporating him or herself as a legal entity rather than drawing a straight salary.

> At a time when individuals were liable to pay 90 percent rates if they fell within the top income bracket, the operator of a production company could reduce his or her tax to 60 percent. Moreover, by forgoing a salary, listing profits as capital gains, and selling one's interest in a film as a capital asset, the individual was liable only for capital gains at 25 percent. (Izod, 1988:126)

Additionally, drops in profits in the years after 1946 forced many of the studios to release employees, largely members of craft unions. With a large pool of labor from which to choose, with no fixed overhead and no costs for administrative offices, independent production often lowered the cost of a film by as much as 50 percent. From the mid-1940s on, the age of the studio became the age of the star and the star as producer. Gary Cooper, Bob Hope, Jimmy Stewart, and directors George Stevens and Frank Capra are only some of the names of the major figures who opted for the road to independence. Many studios, bowing to this inevitable trend, granted more concessions to stars like Bette Davis, or producers like Hal Wallis, keeping them under contract but allowing them profit-sharing and other independent incentives.

It is thus no coincidence that the shape of the subject validated by the biopic would shift along with these considerations, as entertainers, newly powerful, became the royal figures where once hereditary royals had ruled. A star-centered economy could produce a star-centered body of biographical texts. Free—or less constrained—to select their own subject matter for a life on film, many stars selected (unsurprisingly) tales of stars in the entertainment media. While ushering in the new era of entertainment, they also bade a fond adieu to the forms that had sustained a definition of entertainment for over fifty years, vaudeville.

Normalizing Genius

Every life presented scenarists and producers with different kinds of problems in narratization. These problems could concern condensation of events, censorship, legal entanglements with surviving relatives, and, absorbing all of these considerations, Hollywood's shifting conventions on what constituted a life worth depicting. In the Porter case, there were more than the usual number of obstacles to overcome. Warners' solutions to these problems illustrate the machinery of studio production at its most characteristic.[4]

Porter himself seemed as adept as any Warners writer at constructing the narrative of his own life. Although he and Linda Lee Porter, his elegant wife, were publicly associated with the glamorous world of opening nights, Porter was also part of a less public, often covert world. Porter was gay in an era when public acknowledgment of homosexuality was, in most instances, not possible. While every member of a minority group has his or her life mediated through the perceptions of mainstream culture, sexual minorities present different problems of representation, both in movies and in their own presentation of self in everyday life. Unlike many ethnic, national, or other minorities who can't "pass" because of certain physical characteristics, the gay man or lesbian can, if he or she so desires, adopt the various public postures associated with heterosexuality. Thus

Porter carried on a very active gay life in private, while his public life as a married cosmopolite was much chronicled in gossip columns. His wife, Linda, was, according to Lawrence Bergreen (1990), a lesbian. Although aware of his gay life, Linda had reached a mutual accommodation with her husband vis-à-vis his (and presumably her) sex life. Simply stated, Porter could act on his gay desires as long as he publicly played straight. Charles Schwartz, a biographer of Porter, notes that Linda Porter's main concern about Cole's gay life was "that if word got out to the media of how he was carrying on, it would be terribly damaging to his reputation and career" (1977:176). Having constructed a front of heterosexuality in his real life, for Porter aiding Warners in perpetuating this artifice was, from his established perspective, in his best interest. Porter bought into the values of the culture that repressed him and other gays and lesbians by energetically putting up the front of heterosexuality and marriage, the values of the world of the Breen Office. Films like *Night and Day,* and men like Cole Porter, merely reinforce a kind of sexual hegemony through their willful banishing of gay elements from their respective scripts. Thus, a history the movies won't make (that of the Cole Porter whose witty songs of "Love for Sale" could have referred to his taste for male hustlers) becomes a nonhistory that is relegated to a kind of symbolic netherworld of alternative, nonmainstream sources. For Hollywood as a sustainer of the social status quo, the first problem of picturing a life, then, might be to eliminate those areas that the culture tells us should not exist.[5]

The second problem of a life is dealing "properly" with the elements that *are* deemed worthy of existence. Porter's marriage to the older, wealthy Linda Lee was hardly the stuff of other Warners biopics of this period. Full of periods of estrangement due to his extramarital affairs, his marriage would be unfilmable were the facts ever brought to the attention of the Breen Office. Of course, since homosexuality (Section II, subsection 4 of the 1934 Production Code) was so far beyond the pale of discussable topics in the 1940s, the nature of the marriage never surfaced as a debatable issue. Nevertheless, while his marriage was a fact, its cinematic depiction—deemed a necessary part of the great life package—was pure Hollywood.

Additionally, Porter in his social attitudes was not the lofty, benevolent individual a great man, in the mold of Arliss, was supposed to be. As Charles Schwartz has suggested in his biography of Porter,

Porter was more than a bit of a snob, and at times even quite bigoted. Although born in Peru, Indiana, he did not identify with middle America, but with the New York-Paris-Beverly Hills axis. He was not Will Rogers. On the surface, Porter's life was hardly the stuff of inspiration for movie audiences.

The Porter life, or rather a story based on a life, had much that could be inspiring. In addition to the wealth of words and music that were strong selling points with various sheet music and record tie-ins, there was Porter's very real courage in overcoming a crippling riding accident that, in 1937, left him, at age forty-five, nearly paralyzed and in excruciating pain. Here, then, in Porter's fight to resume his life and career in the aftermath of his accident, was a Zanuck rooting interest. And, if this particular angle was not enough of a lure for audiences, Warners could—and did—invent other attractions.

A memo of July 7, 1943, to production head Hal Wallis outlined a strategy:

> The life of Cole Porter can be a 'wholesome' story. It is the triumph of the hick. It will be doubly amusing because he triumphs as a sophisticate. . . . Mr. Porter's life, though rich in incident, follows a simple, straight story line.
>
> My talk with Mr. Porter convinces me he will show a very cooperative attitude. He recognizes the plot needs of movie entertainment and agrees to interpretations that will assist the picture's box office.

The memo further suggests guidelines that would help the film's box office. Certain facts of Porter's life would have to be rewritten. Porter had inherited a sizable fortune from his grandfather, and prior to his success as a composer he had, supported by his grandfather's and wife's money, led a somewhat frivolous life. The average viewer, it was reasoned, would hardly find these circumstances—inherited wealth and the seeming absence of a work ethic—congruent with American values. By foregrounding Porter's struggles and physical tragedy, rather than his rather freewheeling lifestyle, and by redefining his relationship with his wife to conform to existing norms of glamorous heterosexual romance, the film could be inspirational. *Night and Day* became the wholesome story Wallis foresaw, the tale of a fellow who, given the gift of music (which he generously shared on the Warners soundtrack) nevertheless created (with the aid of his adoring, loving wife) his greatest work in his triumph over pain. Charm and surface had been transformed into character and depth, and marginalized sexual behavior, first eliminated, was then re-clothed in the appropriate costumes.

Researchers assigned to *Night and Day* were less interested in the value of Porter's life and more concerned with getting its facts in the proper order. Only if the order were so shuffled as to be virtually entropic would this disturb the values of the researcher. The head of research, Herman Lissauer, focused his skills not on the amorous numbers in Porter's love life, but on the chronology of the hit Porter songs that were to appear in the film. In a memo of April 20, 1944, he noted, "A great many songs are out of their proper dates, and I am sure that this is unavoidable as our script is written. However, some of the songs are ascribed to periods so far away from their correct dates it is inevitable that both audience and critics should see the discrepancy right away."[6] In *Night and Day,* the title song appears some fifteen years ahead of its actual composition. But this chronological gaffe was an intentional strategic gamble; Warners traded off the few people who might spot this slip for the role the song played in motivating Porter's love for his wife. In the film, then, he is shown composing the song at the front during World War I, musing about his absent love. His heterosexual romantic desire motivates the specific composition, nicely normalizing the composer, enabling audiences to view the song as a valentine to marriage and love.

In addition to chronology, since many of the participants in the Porter story were living, a number of the research questions were integrally tied in with legal considerations. To assist producers in understanding possible legal problems, Lissauer, as was common practice on biopics, supplied the legal department with a list of all characters in the script, identifying them by their status as fictive or real, and if real, living or dead.

For example, in *Night and Day* the character of Carol Hall, even though given a false name in the script, is identifiable as Ethel Merman. Since American law forbids the unauthorized depiction of persons without their consent, regardless of how flattering the portrayal, the appearance of Carol Hall, easily recoded as Merman, was, noted Lissauer, a problem. Further, she is shown making unreciprocated

20. *Night and Day:* the Hollywood code of biography recasts marginalized sexual behavior in the proper garb—Cary Grant and Alexis Smith as Cole and Linda Porter

(and invented) advances at Porter, a complication different from the mere unauthorized use of a person's image.

Similar issues adhered to *The Lady with Red Hair,* the story of the divorced Mrs. Leslie Carter (Miriam Hopkins) who, having lost custody of her only child in a scandalous divorce (in 1889), takes to the stage as a means of obtaining the money to win back custody of her son. Arriving in New York chaperoned by her naive aunt (Laura Hope Crews in a repeat of her Aunt Pittypat role) unknown, untrained, and unaware of the ways of the theater, she succeeds in gaining the backing of the theatrical genius of the day, David Belasco (Claude Rains). After monumental battles of ego, and under the tutelage of the acerbic Belasco, Mrs. Carter triumphs as an actress.

Here, the potential legal problems were twofold. First, David Belasco's heirs, having read the script for the film, did not like the depiction of their famous relative as a rather charming, but shallow, applause milker who hitched his wagon to the star of Mrs. Carter. Unable to disprove the Belasco family allegations, and fearing a lawsuit, Warners was forced to make some minor changes to please the impresario's surviving family.

Major changes, however, had to be made to accommodate surviving relatives of Mrs. Carter's first (divorced) husband, Leslie Carter. They objected to the unsympathetic depiction of their relative as the cause of the divorce, and Judge Frank Loesch, the Carter family spokesman, wrote Warners attorney Morris Ebenstein that the script libeled his clients Leslie Carter (d. 1908) and Leslie's sister (d. 1933) and that the truth of the Carter divorce, contra the *Lady with Red Hair* script, was that Mrs. Carter's romantic attachments, and not the behavior of Mr. Carter, were the grounds for the granting of the divorce. Although the original script had the wronged Mrs. Carter driven from her own home by an indifferent husband and the machinations of a jealous sister-in-law (it was, after all, allegedly based on Caroline Carter's diaries), creating audience sympathy for the divorced Caroline, the Warners had to bow to the truth of the divorce trial record—and the fear of a lawsuit—and eliminated Mr. Carter as a character from the script. The film thus was reframed as a valiant divorced woman's battle to regain her self-respect and the love of her estranged son after a humiliating and highly public divorce trial. In the modified script, Caroline Carter takes to the stage to defend her honor and make money to win back her son. And, in a scene in which we witness the fusion of jury and audience metaphors, Caroline, on the opening night in her old home town, wins back her estranged friends in her original community through her acting, followed by a scorching speech from the stage apron. Breaking the barriers established by the proscenium—and those established by class and characterization—Caroline Carter directly addresses her former social contacts, now members of the audience

21. Trial as metaphor: Miriam Hopkins as Caroline Carter at her divorce trial in *The Lady with Red Hair*

who have come to judge her. Arguing for the virtues of motherhood and American fair play, she scores a personal triumph as well as a professional one when a member of the audience seated in the cheap seats turns the tide against the snobbish wealthy audience members who have come to scorn her. As in so many other films that suggest entertainment is truly democratic because it is judged by "the people" (e.g., *The Great Caruso, Yankee Doodle Dandy, Oh, You Beautiful Doll*), the applause of the audience, first started by average and not wealthy audience members, signals their surrender.

After years of experience at biopic research, Lissauer had become adept at anticipating such legal complications, and had worked this angle into the normal research procedure for a biopic by notifying the producer of potential trouble with the facts of a life as depicted in a script. In this way, approaches to editing a life became institutionalized procedures at the studio.

Of equal weight to these legal issues were the typical research minutiae on which these depàrtments thrived. Thus, for *Night and Day,* there was a twenty-six-page research inventory of requests, ranging from the correct placement of the Yale insignia on a megaphone, to a May 31, 1945, request as to the year electric Christmas ornaments were first used. A good deal of research attention was given to material that would be used by other departments to create a factual mise-en-scène. These facts—like the historically accurate Christmas decorations—would be mixed with the other rearranged facts that constituted the film's narrative. It could be argued that research supplied the raw materials that would be then rearranged by a host of architects for legal, moral, economic, and aesthetic reasons. The resulting structure, at times, bore only a faint resemblance to the initial blueprint. It was not uncommon, then, to have invented characters moving implausibly, without a trace of irony, through historically accurate sets. The research for any given film was both ubiquitous and submerged, carefully attended to and willfully ignored.

For the producers of biopics, historical accuracy was not the foremost concern. While well aware of the role history might play in these films (Zanuck, for example, could be most articulate on poetic license in Fox biopics), for the most part producers were more concerned with crafting a film narrative that would win audience sympathy, thereby selling tickets. For producers, historicity and accuracy were attractive as long as they remained selling points.

Research data were also used as selling points in exploiting a film's unique qualities. The research effort on a film, such as that extolled in Paramount's road show book for C. B. DeMille's *The Buccaneer,* indicated the prestige accorded the project. Such exploitation of the research effort was a clever public relations gesture, for it appeared to be a flattering and favorable estimation, on the producer's part, of the audiences' intelligence and worthiness; only an audience with the requisite taste and education would be inclined to notice historical anachronisms in a film.[7]

Institutionalizing Difference

While the research work on *Night and Day* may have been motivated by the typically different goals and powers of the studio personnel, normal constraints and conventions of what constituted a biopic kept any disagreement under control. This was not the case with Fox's *The Story of Alexander Graham Bell,* where the producer's perspective of history clashed with a research-oriented one. The making of *Bell,* which made a star out of a Zanuck protégé, Don Ameche, involved a disparate cast of characters and institutions, and is by itself almost as interesting as the struggle depicted in the film. Negotiations to create an acceptable script centered around interactions of research personnel, two large corporations (Bell Telephone and Western Union), and surviving members of the Bell family. At the studio itself, there appeared to be two Bell camps, featuring on one side the Harvard-educated Kenneth MacGowan (the film's associate producer) and Roy Harris (the author of a heavily researched first version of a script) with their research-oriented approach, and on the other side the strong opinions of production head and producer Darryl Zanuck, and his tendency to fictionalize the film in line with previously formulated notions of what kind of life would sell tickets. The problems raised and their resolution illustrate the interaction of the research process and the other components of film production, and show the shifting, negotiated definition of accuracy in biopics as a function of institutional power allocation.

The development of a picture based on the life of a great American was, for Zanuck, the continuation of projects he had undertaken at Warners and at his own company, Twentieth Century Films. After the enormous success of the Warners Pasteur and Zola biopics, Zanuck, ever watchful of story trends in Hollywood, searched about for a suitable great *American* life to enshrine. Though his early experiences with the genre had been successful (*Cardinal Richelieu* and *House of Rothschild* with the Warners' expatriate Arliss as well as *Suez* and *Jesse James* with his own creation, Tyrone Power), none had garnered the prestige of his former studio's releases.

In his early years at Warners, Zanuck had given a good deal of thought to how to develop a cinematic life. He came to the conclusion that there were actually two distinctly different kinds of biography, and each type should be developed according to different rules. One kind of film—the headliner—arose from current news headlines, and was linked with short-lived, exploitable trends. These headliners could either be clearly fictional or could be based upon recognizable heroic or infamous exploits that captured the fancy of readers. In contrast to these headliners, the other kind of biopic immortalized people already famous. The former films created a kind of Warholian fame for their subjects, and in subject matter were similar to made-for-TV movies popular since the early 1970s. The latter films were similar to previously existing forms of veneration in other media (oil portraits, public sculpture, literary and scholarly versions of history) that enshrined a handful of deceased worthies. Unlike figures of the traditional elite, the headliners sometimes dealt with the morally objectionable figure, like the gangster, or else focused on the merely eccentric ("Wrong Way" Corrigan), the unusual (the Dionnes), or the unsung hero (Louise Randall Pierson, an early women's rights advocate). And, just as the headliners displayed the quickness of pace and lightness of tone associated with this type of film during Zanuck's tenure at Warners, the latter films were inevitably serious, and uplifting, carriers of great messages and serious themes.[8] In Bell's life, Zanuck saw the perfect opportunity to create a film comparable to Warners earlier products that would compete with contemporary biopics (like MGM's Edison sagas) or else could hold their own with minor fare, like RKO's headliner on the exploits of aviator "Wrong Way" Corrigan, *The Flying Irishman.*

All of Zanuck's great man films involved substantial research. This was due, in part, to the esteem in which the public held the already famous figure, and Zanuck's belief that the full star treatment, in the form of extensive research, should be given to these luminaries from the nonmovie world. This research occurred on different fronts and could involve background research on the era in which the figure lived, re-creations of the physical environment in which the famous person's great deeds occurred, releases from any surviving relatives, and, overriding all these considerations, a script that would be approved by the Breen Office.

In addition to an extraordinary amount of research, the making of *The Story of Alexander Graham Bell* also involved a great deal of diplomacy. The producer had to navigate between opposing currents: first, MacGowan, in supervising the writing of an acceptable script, had to uphold the images of two of America's most powerful corporations (Western Union and Bell Telephone), whose motives surrounding control of the telephone invention were hardly altruistic.[9] How to tell the tale of the telephone while denuding it of business rapacity was no easy task. Second, the image of the secular saint,

Alexander Graham Bell, had to be presented so as to preserve him as a kind of public-minded benefactor of all humanity, a selfless man who, motivated by love for his deaf wife, created his future empire in a garret. This, too, was a creative job, for the Bell Zanuck envisioned was, in part, a contradiction of the story of a strange, obsessed inventor who suffered bouts of depression and nervous collapse, and who was as eager to profit from his invention as any other nineteenth-century capitalist. Third, the tale would have to please the surviving (and politically powerful) Bell relations, who were sensitive about a number of (sometimes unanticipated) issues, and whose cooperation was essential to the project. Hostile reaction from the family could create litigation that would stall production or enjoin the showing of a completed film. Last, all these elements would have to be arranged according to a schema that Zanuck, the ex-writer and already the producer of several praised biopics, would find congruent with his notions of what constituted a good story.

In MacGowan, Zanuck had an ideal diplomat. Since coming to the studio from RKO, he had already been involved with historical films (*Lloyds of London, In Old Chicago*) often cited by Zanuck, in interoffice memoranda, as exemplars of their genre. His experience as a producer with the Provincetown Playhouse had prepared him to deal with prestigious and controversial products, and he would later leave the film industry to head the Theater Arts Department at UCLA.[10] He was assisted in his negotiations on *Bell* by two refugees from the Breen Office, Lamar Trotti and Col. Jason Joy. Trotti was a former newspaper reporter who would, in the years after *Bell*, become one of Hollywood's most reliable writers—*Hudson's Bay* (1940), *The Ox-Bow Incident* (1943), and *Wilson*—and, still later, a writer and producer of such hits as *Mother Wore Tights* (1947), and such biopics as *With a Song in My Heart, Cheaper by the Dozen* (1950), and *Stars and Stripes Forever* (1952). Colonel Joy, described by one writer as a protégé of Trotti's at the MPPDA, joined Fox in September 1932 as a story consultant.[11] Joy's and Trotti's negotiating skills, in tandem and singly, had been honed during their tenure at the Breen Office, and the demands made by the *Bell* assignment— negotiating which elements of a narrative could remain part of a film—were ones with which they were quite familiar.

The initial script, entitled "American Miracle," was assigned to Roy Harris. Zanuck, known as one of the fastest readers of all the moguls, found the script flat, dull, and unacceptable. His comments in pencil on a Harris draft of March 4, 1938, note "awe-inspiring, needs dramatization and development of human story, but here is an EPIC—it is now submerged by TOO MUCH RESEARCH AND DATA but if we can develop a real romance and human emotional story it is better than [The life of Emile] Zola or [The Story of Louis] Pasteur."

As was his pattern, Zanuck was searching for the rooting interest in the Bell story, the hook on which he, as a surrogate ticket buyer, needed to hang his fancy. He knew from his production of countless scripts that a realistic depiction of the scientific process, or an historically accurate re-creation of Bell's path, would not be such an angle. He believed that historical re-creations could "choke the story to death," and that "an audience will neither understand nor appreciate these things" (Memo dated 3/14/38, UCLA, Fox Collection, Box FX-PRS-1146). What was needed was an angle that would humanize a figure covered with the accumulated dust of respectability and greatness. He stressed this very forcefully in a memo to Julian Johnson, on March 14, 1938. Zanuck felt the romance "seems to be made subordinate to Bell's mechanical and scientific dreams. Even though this may have been the actual truth, I think we ought to throw the romance into higher relief than it gets now," making it "something which shuts out all other considerations." At all costs, Zanuck wanted to avoid any hint that Bell, in his social life, was in any way abnormal. As he bluntly noted in his own copy of a screenplay draft of May 12, 1938, "A man who devotes all time to deaf and dumb can be a freak if we don't make him so real, so human, so down to earth and such a regular guy. A scientific person can be a strange bird." Since there was little room for *rara avis* in Zanuck's vision of Bell, he sought, by normalizing genius, to make Bell, in his own words, "a super salesman with unbounded confidence in himself," one who "almost hypnotizes people, in an amusing way, into giving him money." Bell, the elocution teacher, had become the kind of personality who, had he lived into the mid-twentieth century, might have done very well as a movie producer. To an extent, Zanuck, in his formula for Bell-as-great-man, was re-creating his own success story, selling his own personality through the Bell narrative.[12]

MacGowan, meanwhile, implicitly sided with Harris's historical research-oriented treatment over Zanuck's fabricated one (Zanuck suggested increasing—or creating—dramatic situations around

22. "A scientific person can be a strange bird."—Darryl Zanuck. Don Ameche as the inventor of the telephone in *The Story of Alexander Graham Bell*

Bell's wedding or the birth of his first child). Rather than stating outright that he found Harris's treatment preferable to Zanuck's, he diplomatically couched the issue as a political intrigue, with the Bell family and Bell Telephone at the center.[13] In a March 10, 1938, memo to Zanuck, MacGowan made his pitch for the Harris research-oriented approach: "We are dealing with a family which still has some pretty powerful members alive, and a great corporation which can be either enormously helpful in promotion or enormously hostile. With Harris' knowledge of the facts at our disposal, we can avoid trouble and achieve our ends in the easiest way" (UCLA, MacGowan Collection, Box 887, folder 1).

Zanuck, however, was not swayed. He, after all, knew better than Harris, a mere writer, what constituted a great life. Part of his own success, from his earliest days as a writer for the Rin Tin Tin series, was, he probably reasoned, his ability to get to the heart of a story. The trouble with Harris's script was not only that it contained too much data; rather, Harris had misidentified what made Bell a great man, and what would, consequently, make a great picture.

Harris tried to remedy the deficiencies pointed out by Zanuck, but his script of May 12, 1938, elicited an even more forceful rejection; this time, one that was explicitly based on his overreliance on research materials and data. Again, Zanuck's handwritten comments note, "Dull, flat, undramatic. Lost all punch because it is so swamped with boring scientific babble—some of it good—but this is so loaded it creeks [sic]. Get to the human story and comedy" (USC, Doheny Library, Fox Collection, *Story of Alexander Graham Bell* file). Finally, in a May 21, 1938, letter to Harris, who had pleaded his case through two script revisions and a lengthy letter, Zanuck replied,

> The drama of the story does not lie in the invention of the telephone any more than the drama of Zola's life was his writing. Our main drama lies in Bell's fight against the world to convince them he had something great, and then to protect his ownership.
>
> You have had your opportunity of presenting the story in your way and it has proven obviously incorrect. Now let us proceed my way and stop theorizing. (UCLA, MacGowan Collection)

This is Zanuck at his most characteristic, at turns impressive in his certainty of what will work, but nevertheless chilling in his meglomania when confronted with opinions that differ from his. Harris's original script was quite explicit about Bell's motivation for the invention; he viewed it as a continuation of his, and his family's, long interest in the teaching of elocution. Along these lines, Harris's script opened with a scene, set in Scotland, at which the entire Bell family, including little Alex, play a kind of charades with the "visible speech" alphabet Bell's father had invented to teach the deaf to speak, and with which the real-life Bell set up shop in Boston before becoming, at a young age, a faculty member at Boston University. The prologue attempted to link Bell's invention of the phone with his family's tradition of work with the deaf and his own continuation of this in his work as a teacher of elocution. In this, Harris was historically correct.

Zanuck, however, would have none of this. It was not just that history would not interest the audience, provide them with a figure to root for (and just as significantly, one to root against). Zanuck had other considerations to weigh. Always interested in developing stars of his own at Fox to compete with the rosters at other studios, Zanuck placed great emphasis on the image of the star who would eventually play Bell. The image of the actor cast as Bell would affect both the narrative constructed with this star in mind and, once the part had left its imprint upon him, the role would affect the star's subsequent image away from the screen. At this point of the *Bell* project Tyrone Power was the leading candidate for the part eventually played by Ameche. Zanuck did not like what he saw when he envisioned Power, whose career he had guided with a kind of genius, as Bell the elocution teacher: "Despite the fact that elocution was the rage at the time, casting a leading man of today as an out-and-out elocution enthusiast is like asking Tyrone Power to wear lace on his under-drawers" (UCLA, McGowan Collection).

Harris was removed from the film. With this removal also went his carefully researched vision of Bell. He was replaced by the reliable Trotti, a seasoned pro whose long career as a writer and wide experience as a journalist and Breen Office worker attest to his pragmatic gift of survival.

The film was far from a sure project at this point. Even if foregrounding a love interest in place of historical accuracy, Zanuck still had to deal with the essential narrative of the phone's invention, the attempt by Western Union to steal the patent from Bell, and the establishment of Bell as an icon of American history. The assignment of Trotti, the author of the script for *Alexander's Ragtime Band* (1938), one of Zanuck's pet films, was a first step in insuring that a Zanuck vision of Bell would be the one seen by viewers.

As it turned out, Trotti shared Zanuck's ideas on story construction in biography. Later in the year, at the urging of MacGowan, he was put on an even more famous project, *Young Mr. Lincoln*. There, using incidents that had occurred in his own life—as a young reporter he had attended a murder trial like the one shown in the film— Trotti would embroider Lincoln's life to an even greater extent than he had Bell's. Trotti seemed more likely to produce an acceptable Bell script than Harris. On August 22, 1938, several months after Harris had been removed from the project, Trotti wrote a letter to Zanuck that Zanuck might have dictated himself, so alike were its ideas on biopics to his own. In it, Trotti hit upon key Zanuck themes in biopics: motivation, rooting interest, and a bending of the facts to fit salable contours. "In my opinion," Trotti said, "the basic need of this story is a major theme, or purpose. In every great character story on the screen—Rothschilds, Zola, Pasteur—the principle character, or characters, *have battled against something great for something great*. . . . In this script, this essential theme is lacking, or almost so." And, just as Zanuck had earlier lectured Harris on what the focus of a life should be, Trotti is able to pinpoint what the true thrust of a Bell biopic should not be. "It seems to me that Bell is working for a commercial advantage more than for anything else—for patents, control money, etc. Even the fact that he wants money so he can marry the woman he loves is not sufficient to make him great dramatic material." His solution, the Zanuck solution, is to link the love story—Bell's courtship of the wealthy Mabel Hubbard, daughter of one of his backers—with the invention, thus intertwining romance and commerce. And, as he was to do later with *Young Mr. Lincoln*, Trotti proposed tying together all the loose ends of the narrative by uniting all conflicting parties at a climactic public trial. Bell's primacy of claim would be narratively proven when the devoted Mabel is able to produce key evidence written on the back of a love letter, and the judgment will have the force of law, as well as being a morality play enacted before an entire community.

> . . . the discovery and presentation of the facts about the telephone on the back of a love letter, are wonderful if properly dramatized. There might even be a great scene in court when this can be produced dramatically, with a stirring scene between Mabel and Bell, in which Bell can tell the world the value of the little scientist, struggling in his attic, going hungry, working night and day for something that will benefit all humankind, etc. (UCLA, MacGowan Collection, Box 887, folder 1)

Zanuck approved of the fictitious trial, for it was a much-used but often successful device by which the specifics of a tale could be rendered more universal. Trials and other scenes of public judgment have the commanding function of laying bare the narrative device, of telling the audience what the film is really about (e.g., honor in *Bell*, simplicity and mother love in *Young Mr. Lincoln*, or sexism and ethnocentrism in *Sister Kenny*). And, as Zanuck felt that the

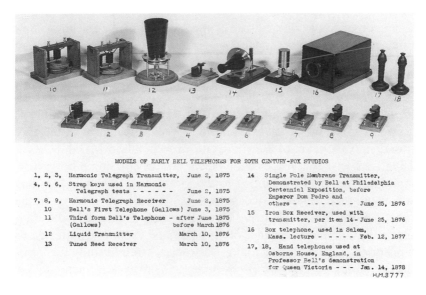

MODELS OF EARLY BELL TELEPHONES FOR 20TH CENTURY-FOX STUDIOS

1, 2, 3,	Harmonic Telegraph Transmitter,	June 2, 1875
4, 5, 6,	Strap keys used in Harmonic Telegraph tests - - - - - -	June 2, 1875
7, 8, 9,	Harmonic Telegraph Receiver	June 2, 1875
10	Bell's First Telephone (Gallows)	June 3, 1875
11	Third form Bell's Telephone - after June 1875 (Gallows)	before March 1876
12	Liquid Transmitter	March 10, 1876
13	Tuned Reed Receiver	March 10, 1876
14	Single Pole Membrane Transmitter, Demonstrated by Bell at Philadelphia Centennial Exposition, before Emperor Dom Pedro and others - - - - - - - -	June 25, 1876
15	Iron Box Receiver, used with transmitter, per item 14 -	June 25, 1876
16	Box telephone, used in Salem, Mass. lecture - - - - -	Feb. 12, 1877
17, 18,	Hand telephones used at Osborne House, England, in Professor Bell's demonstration for Queen Victoria - - -	Jan. 14, 1878

HM3777

23. Valorizing research: Twentieth Century-Fox models of Bell telephones, reconstructed for *The Story of Alexander Graham Bell*

public went to movies to root for a character, a trial was a perfect device to throw this rooting interest into high relief. Thus, both *Bell* and *Young Mr. Lincoln* resolve their hero's fate with a trial in which faith and strong public support—emotional currencies—play larger parts than the more cerebral, but less involving, displays of legal skill.[14]

Although MacGowan would argue with Trotti, in a letter of November 3, 1938, against the use of this type of fabrication, Zanuck liked what he heard from Trotti and this version of the invention prevailed. MacGowan's input vis-à-vis the research aspects of the film would, from this point on, be limited to the depiction of the sundry electrical apparatus shown in the film ("we shall certainly need a man on the set who is familiar with the history of the telephone and the various technical devices such as the original receivers and transmitters of the '70s"), a not insignificant task (UCLA, McGowan Collection, Box 887, folder 1). With Zanuck's point of view on these key points secure, Trotti and Joy were dispatched to

Washington, D.C., in November 1938 as emissaries to the Bell family to help secure their cooperation, paving the way for a completed script.

To convince the Bell family of their integrity in presenting their famous relative's life, Zanuck suggested Joy and Trotti take along films that would show the Hollywood code of biography at its most impressive: morally clean, inspiring, and just accurate enough to bear some relationship to the life being chronicled. His choice of films was a shrewd one, and each film served a different persuasive purpose. Fox's own *Suez* was meant to show the charm of the proposed impersonator of Bell, Tyrone Power, while MGM's recent 1938 release, *Boys Town,* was selected to drive home a key point, "the importance of explaining to the family how essential it is that we would take dramatic license with some of the scenes, as in the case of *Boys Town*" (UCLA, Fox Collection). So strongly did Zanuck believe in the importance of his cinematic version of a life versus a historically accurate one that he instructed Trotti to study the introductory titles of *Boys Town* in order to convey succinctly to the family—and later, to the public—this point of creative biography: "There *was an Alexander Graham Bell, and he did* invent the telephone."

In this belief—dramatic license—Zanuck held firm. Narrative that engaged the audience was a far more important consideration than historical fidelity. On November 10, 1938, in the midst of the delicate Bell family negotiations, when it appeared that the project might stall because of the relatives' disagreements concerning the accuracy of the Bell script, Zanuck wired Joy in Washington, bluntly affirming his stand:

> Appreciate difficulties and am relying upon you and Lamar to settle same without destroying story because rather than destroy present dramatic structure I would be willing to forget name of Bell and other real names and make same plot with fictional character names stop They must realize that from time immemorial there has existed dramatic license which was practiced when I made Disraeli House of Rothschild Lloyds of London Suez and when Warners made Pasteur and Zola stop If you are worrying

about Western Union legal trouble then we can have law
suit against fictional corporation stop

Zanuck's bluster proved to be unnecessary, for the family members were impressed with both the script and the supporting materials. Although each member had some pet criticism, the key
negotiating points centered about a deeply personal concern: that
Mabel Hubbard Bell be shown speaking in a normal voice, and not
the hollow tones associated with the deaf. Joy and Trotti were glad
to comply with this request, and once this was cleared away, full
cooperation was given.

Other obstacles—like Joy's fear of a lawsuit based on the depiction of Western Union as villains—had been settled earlier, when
Zanuck had suggested making an individual, and not the company,
the heavy, thus "softening the Western Union villain angle." Zanuck,
as indicated above, had also been willing to make the well-known
Western Union, the real-life opponent of Bell, into a fictitious
cartoon-figure capitalist rather than risk a lawsuit. As long as there
was someone, either real or invented, to root against, Bell would
appear all the more virtuous, and Zanuck's rooting interest formula
would be satisfied.

Thus *Bell,* with its fanciful narrative and historically accurate sets
and costumes, set the mold for a common procedure in biopics: the
creation of a realistic mise-en-scène painstakingly re-created from
original blueprints and photographs would serve as an historical context for the less-than-creditable narrative.

Censorship and Biography

It was not only attention to audience tastes, however, that dictated
the conservative and ultimately ritualistic content of biopics. The
dual operations of sanitization and moralization of a cinematic life
were also abetted by the forces of censorship at the MPPDA.
Formed in 1922 at the behest of the heads of the major studios, the
MPPDA was at first a kind of public relations organization created
to counter adverse publicity adhering to the movie personnel. With
the promulgation, in 1930, of the Production Code, strictly enforced
from 1934 onwards by Code Administration Director Joseph Breen,

the Breen Office (or the Hays Office, as it was called after its first "czar," Will Hays) and their notion of cinematic appropriateness had a profound and far-reaching effect on American cinema.

Every script had to be submitted to the Breen Office for approval. The sharp eyes—and ears—of the censors took in not only scripts but costumes, song lyrics, and publicity materials and trailers. Virtually no aspect of a film could be passed without the approval of this powerful organization. The Breen Office read every script from all the studios, knew what famous life was in production at what studio. More than any single producer, its readers, with their access to all the studio's versions of fame, had a sense of the shifting content of films, and how the conventions of picturing lives were altering. Although certain producers (notably Hal Wallis) had adversarial relations with the Breen Office, most producers were on friendly, negotiable terms with Breen and his staff, corresponding on a first-name basis, and trading off certain questionable business in a script for other, less essential (and removable) parts.

Wallis ran afoul of the Breen Office early in its tenure. After being warned to eliminate risqué sexual material in *Madame Du Barry,* Wallis, while complying, was, in Breen's words, "sneering and argumentative."[15] In *Dr. Ehrlich's Magic Bullet,* the battle between Wallis, Hays, and Breen (partially documented in Behlmer, 1985) centered about the original title, "Test 606," which, Will Hays felt, drew too much attention to Ehrlich's work with syphilis. Since syphilis and other venereal diseases were taboo subjects under the Code, Hays felt the title desired by Wallis "would be considered as an announcement that the picture is a picture principally about the very thing which all of the effort has been made to make merely one phase of the great accomplishment of the individual" (Telegram from Will Hays to Carl Milliken, 2/13/40, The Library of The Motion Picture Academy of Arts & Sciences, MPPDA Collection, *Dr. Ehrlich's Magic Bullet* file). Breen further warned Wallis that the syphilis patients in *Ehrlich* should not appear to be "too realistically horrifying or shocking," for, in addition to violating the Code's rules for physical explicitness, this might alienate and even frighten the audience. Wallis was enraged at this meddling with what he considered a very important topic, calling the Code (in Breen's words) "outdated, outmoded" and in need of amendment. He threatened to make *Ehrlich* "irrespective of the special provisions of the Code," subdivision II and subdivision (7), which noted that "Sex hygiene and venereal diseases are not proper subjects for theatrical motion pictures." Perhaps fancying himself the heir to the spirit of a previously produced biopic subject, Emile Zola, he decided to release the film without Code approval, presuming that the public would flock to see his version of the truth on the march.

Breen, in an earlier October 28, 1938, letter to Wallis, had bluntly told him of the extent of the Code's power, warning Wallis that any attempt to release the film in violation of the Code (as Louella Parsons had suggested in her column) was doomed, for, "We have no authority to amend, or change, or add to, or subtract from, the Production Code. It is our job merely to interpret that Code, and to see to its Uniform Interpretation." Both sides compromised on *Ehrlich,* with Warners changing the objectionable title from "Test 606," while the Breen Office permitting limited, but specific mention of syphilis.

Historically accurate facts had to be bent to conform to the Code's public notion of how history should be told. As late as 1957, Paramount was warned to alter its story line in *Beau James,* the biopic of New York mayor James J. Walker, to downplay his real-life adulterous relationship with Betty Compton. As Geoffrey Shurlock of the Breen Office noted, "We are very well aware that this is historical fact. However, we stated that the Code endeavors would be along the lines of trying to preserve some regards for the institution of marriage, and of removing any aura of romanticization of these incidents. . . . This is an adulterous relationship. As such, it should be balanced out by a *much stronger* voice for morality."

The MPPDA was an overt agency of censorship, and as such, it conformed to existing public standards of decency published by various religious and civic groups. Because of its connection to other forces of public morals enforcement, its members were almost predictable in their zeal to avoid the subjects of adultery, "pansy action," décollatage, drug use, and other dangerous practices. The producer's themselves, who needed the Breen Office's seal of approval to release their films, were, with their sensitivity to public taste and their need for financial profit, often as conservative as the men at the Breen Office. To engage in a prolonged battle with the Breen Office over a film, or the trailer for a film, would be to endanger the scheduled release and marketing of films. To halt the financial rhythms by which the flow of corporate money was regulated and controlled was a risky venture. Unless the point of argument was crucial to the film, the studios usually acquiesced to the standards of the Breen Office. Particularly at those studios where there was, prior to the Consent Decree, a large chain of theaters to supply with a steady stream of product, producers' hands were tied by the system over which they otherwise were thought to exert so much control. For every Wallis who fought for loosening the bonds of censorship, there was an L. B. Mayer eager to comply with Breen's and the Code's vision of life.[16]

Seeing History as the History of Film

The case studies of the research processes on *The Story of Alexander Graham Bell, Night and Day, The Court Martial of Billy Mitchell, The Lady with Red Hair,* and *All This and Heaven Too* suggest that although the research data accumulated by the in-house departments was a significant component of a film, particularly in shaping the sets and costumes, the vision of a strong producer, like a Hal Wallis or a Zanuck, was the overriding factor. And since these men thought of history in terms of the history of what films had succeeded with the public, a biopic life would have more in common with other models of film biography than it would with sources outside Hollywood's discourse.

Nowhere is this more clear than in Zanuck's case. Zanuck's tendency to remake his hits has been discussed before (notably by Mordden, 1988). His remakes were not the result of a dearth of fresh ideas or plots—few producers were able to come up with plot twists quicker than ex-writer Zanuck. Rather, Zanuck recycled plots, characterizations, and stars because of a firm belief that these biopic star-genre formulations tapped into audience's conceptions of what life should be like. The uncredited partner in shaping the contours of the Hollywood biopic, represented in a plausible proxy by the producer, was the audience.[17] Thus, the producer was always concerned—though not always successfully—with whether a film would play with an audience. Zanuck prided himself on knowing what audiences liked, and his thirty-year reign as head of Fox (1935–1956, 1962–1971) would seem to confirm this.

But shifting production patterns in Hollywood from the early 1940s on altered the once-familiar terrain; tax laws favored independent producers over studio contract talent, studios prepared to divest themselves of their theater chains, the nation prepared to readjust to a postwar culture, and competing patterns of leisure—including the arrival of television—all combined to decimate the once loyal film audience. Particularly in the period following World War II biopics seemed to undergo substantial revisions to keep in touch with perceived audience shifts. Looking over the tortured two-year production history of the biopic of composer Joe Howard, *I Wonder Who's Kissing Her Now* (originally titled *Hello My Baby*), one sees Zanuck and producer Jessel struggling to place the proper frame about Howard's life, well aware that business as usual was not the operative climate, and the rules that, earlier, had made the Zanuck-Jessel *The Dolly Sisters* a hit might not hold for the Howard story.

Allegedly based on "notes in the diary" of the still living Howard, the film was in preparation at the same time as a large number of musical biopics at other studios (Jolson at Columbia, Gershwin at Warners, and Kern at MGM). Noting, in a March 13, 1946, memo that "we are now at the tail end of a cycle of musical pictures of this type" (UCLA, Fox Collection, *I Wonder Who's Kissing Her Now* file), Zanuck urges Jessel to find a narrative frame that will differentiate this product from its competition. For inspiration, he urges him to turn, not to research, but to previous Fox triumphs, notably *My Gal Sal* (1942), *Irish Eyes Are Smiling* (1944), and *Swanee River.*

> *Hello My Baby* has to be about something, as *Tin Pan Alley* . . . was about a young fellow who would rather play around at being a small time music publisher than become heavyweight champion of the world. *My Gal Sal* was the story of a man who turned down his home and family and a career in the ministry because he wanted to play and sing his own songs. *Irish Eyes Are Smiling* was the story of a respected teacher of music who sacrificed his future to go to New York and have his songs published.

Whatever the current climate, a film still had to have an audience hook. Told that *Hello My Baby* had "no rooting interest," it was suggested to ex-vaudevillian Jessel that he might find a solution in telling the Howard tale not in using his own experience as a stage performer from Howard's era, but instead in screening former Zanuck triumphs. Jessel took the suggestions to view earlier movies, but he was unable to come up with a script that pleased Zanuck. In a memo of October 10, 1945, Zanuck told him that he had failed to "scientifically analyze and study the fundamentals in the above pictures" but that "if you study the previous pictures I am certain you will find the necessary elements."

Earlier, Zanuck had put his finger on the uncertainty of postwar production, on why previously successful genres like musical biopics, soon to be reinvigorated by Columbia's enormous triumph with *The Jolson Story,* were now a tenuous thing with the public. "I have a distinct feeling that the public will soon begin to reflect the attitudes of the critics about these pictures, and the critics are beginning to be more and more outspoken about these films which picture the rise to success of songwriters, touching lightly on their actual lives" (UCLA, Fox Collection, *I Wonder Who's Kissing Her Now* file).

Zanuck's remedy was not a Gradgrindian "more facts," but a cry for better character motivation. This was the also the case in nonmusical biopics, like *Buffalo Bill,* where Zanuck suggested a narrative solution to Bill's relationship to his easternized wife by urging his writers to look at how this dilemma was worked out in a nonbiopic example, *Drums Along the Mohawk,* where the genteel character played by Claudette Colbert hides her dismay at husband Fonda's humble rustic abode, as, in *Cardinal Richelieu,* he had pointed the writers toward narrative solutions used in a previous Arliss biopic, *Disraeli.*

This constant use of intertextual references as narrative guides for films, rather than other source material, suggests that the people who created the movies really did so in terms of reference to the world inside the studios and not the historical world outside these boundaries. John E. O'Connor, in his essay on *Drums Along the Mohawk,* notes, similarly, Zanuck's motivations in preparing an historical film text. "They were successful because the producer realized that audiences did not plunk down dollars at the box office to learn a history lesson. They came to be entertained, and Zanuck was particularly conscious of how the story developed in the screenplay would appeal to a mass audience" (1988b:102). This made for a particular insular, conservative (as in non-innovative), and even formulaic world view, as history became reduced to what had worked as a movie of history,

24. Intertextuality: solving Joel McCrae and Maureen O'Hara's marital problems in *Buffalo Bill* by looking back at *Drums Along the Mohawk*

rather than drawing upon other perspectives. As Zanuck himself suggested, the first priority of a film was not to write history, but to make entertainment. The lessons of entertainment were to be found in the studio's intramural history, a history in which the world was very much a stage.

Thus, intertextuality, a reliance on a limited number of film texts as templates for narratives of the lives of the famous, insured that ideas of entertainment and history became so entwined that much of history became a history of entertainment, a strange ontological slant that limited the description of biopic fame to the plots found in a few movies that had found favor with audiences.

A producer was forced to cater to a definition of history that would fill the theater, to create lives that audiences would find watchable, or had in the past found watchable. Zanuck's framing Bell as a "supersalesman" is one example of this approach, that of depicting the famous person as a common man whose cognitive map was just like the viewers', save for one special neighborhood. Alternatively, the famous person could be shown, as was Van Gogh in *Lust for Life* (1956), as so different in every way that the gift that made him special is his only salvation in a world where he is an outcast. This distribution of normal and exceptional traits in a famous life was Hollywood's "Bell Curve," its way of picturing society's boundaries of the acceptable and the deviant, a way of highlighting the distribution of undesirable traits and unusual abilities in a population; the Van Goghs of the world were, after all, the exceptions and not the rules on how to live a life. At all times, fame was constructed with the life of the audience member in mind.

Though there was test marketing, and Irving Thalberg-initiated preview screenings, and an endless round of story conferences in which opinions on the film were articulated and refined, in the end, the definition of public taste often resided in the skill and intuition of men who had been in the business a long time, and whose judgment had proven financially and artistically successful. Because of this closed chain of reference, judgments on what constituted history were very insular, gleaned from past film triumphs. The texts of history were not Pliny, Gibbon, or even Lytton Strachey; rather, the intertextual system of referencing history led a Zanuck to compare Bell to Father Flanagan, and for Wallis to make certain that Zola looked more like Paul Muni than like the character he was playing. Regardless of the era in which a film was set, comparing a situation set in one time to a similar narrative set of circumstances set in a different era insured that all eras would, in the end, have a similar narrative thrust. If history appears unremittingly teleological in Hollywood, it is because producers used relatively few texts as the superstructures that set the narrative conditions under which greatness or villainy could flourish. Such a mode of analysis and criticism became a self-perpetuating machine of judgment; e.g., Zanuck's judgment was good because it had been good in the past. The role of gatekeeper of public taste became one invested deeply with the personal history of the producer's own professional track record, in essence reducing the system of choice to models already known.

In this light, facts and history are the product of institutional pressures that located authority in the hands of one or more powerful figures whose world view was both remarkably narrow, constrained by their own past standards. This is why history in the biopic might be construed as being like the personal histories of the studio heads: a life composed of a series of confrontations culminating in vindication with the public, a tale of struggle to prove oneself and one's judgment to a small contained community. Reading biographies of Goldwyn, or Mayer, or Cohn, or Zanuck, one is struck by the similar narratives constructed about men who were, in many regards, quite different from one another save for their (successful) obsession to master and run a production facility.[18] The "book" on these men foregrounds their ability to fight for what they believed was theirs, and to hold onto it with a fierce grasp and a shrewd eye on industry trends.

The number of films containing such scenes of vindication and triumph—where the lone individual (read, "producer") fights the opinion of experts in his field (read, "the film industry") only to be rescued by the faith of the public who he is trying to serve (read, "the movie audience")—is rather large. Films as different from each other as RKO's *Sister Kenny,* MGM's *Blossoms in the Dust* (1941), and Columbia's *The Jolson Story* all contain scenes of public vindication in which the hero's judgment, doubted by his or her peers, is vindicated by the public in their role as audience/jury. It is not difficult to imagine these scenarios as extrapolations of the producer's own struggles to manifest and articulate greatness in his own histories. A Zanuck viewed the world in terms congruent with those that had brought him to power and nurtured him in his position of eminence; to question the basis of a biopic life would be to question the basis on which he had made his own life.

For all of the reasons suggested above, the resemblance between the actual life of the biographee and the cinematic one was, as the Cole Porter title suggested, the difference between night and day.

CHAPTER

4

■ ■ ■

Reel Life

"Whoever turns biographer commits himself to lies, to concealment, to hypocrisy, to embellishments, and even to dissembling his own lack of understanding, for biographical truth is not to be had, and even if one had it, one could not use it."

—SIGMUND FREUD TO ARNOLD ZWEIG

How do you organize a life on film? Hollywood producers, presented with selection at two levels—both a particular life, and specific episodes in it—needed to develop a strategy that would allow them to shape a biopic life according to conventional filmmaking practices. Yet, the makers of biopics also wanted to provide a unique slant to biopics as a genre, to differentiate them from other dramatic or comic fare, to suggest what was unique about the great individual even while the mode of depiction was strikingly uniform. In short, the producers of biopics articulated the strategy of greatness as a paradox: to find a way to declare that each life—and each film of a life—was unique within the confines of a production system that made certain all products, and lives, resembled one another.

In order to accomplish this difficult task, the biopic developed distinctive narrative strategies, which, with few exceptions, offered particular ideologies of fame based on a limited menu of discourses and situations: romance, the role played by family and friends, and of the idea of fame as a kind of community judgment. Across these discourses, in fact interacting with them, were cinematic narrational strategies like flashbacks and montage that gave the film life a distinctive cast from lives told in other media and provided it with an identifiable profile.

For example, among the most distinctive aspects of the cinematic life was that the biopic almost always started *in medias res,* with the figure past the age where his or her values can be influenced by the family. Because of this structure, explanations of causality other than those involving the family come to dominate the lives of the famous. In place of the family as a model of causality, Hollywood inserted self-invention, that most characteristic American form of personality construction and a dominant mode of the nineteenth century.

Another distinctive aspect of the film biography was self-reflexivity. Entertainers and artists comprise 36 percent of all biopics. With an explanation of life centered on entertainment and self-invention, the biopic created a self-reflexive world in which the lives and values of the men who created movie entertainment became a paradigm for all fame. Although the cinematic lives of the famous take place in locations the world over, and are set in time periods covering over two thousand years, they inevitably reflect the values of the world of the Hollywood studio and their personnel; they are films made by Americans that define the world through the values of a small community comprised largely of American entertainers.

The manufacturers of Hollywood biography oiled their machinery so, with a few basic instructions, it could run (and did run) to turn out a quality-controlled product called "the great life." The workings of this system can be illustrated by a typical configuration of a life, Warners' *The Lady with Red Hair,* the biopic of the American actress Caroline Carter.[1] First, like more than 60 percent of the purposive sample, the film opens *in medias res.* The viewer initially glimpses Caroline Carter at her scandalous divorce trial. Second, there is no mention of the leading figure's family or background. Mrs. Carter thus creates her own identity as an actress, albeit with the strong guidance of David Belasco. Third, heterosexual romance humanizes the character, and Mrs. Carter must choose, like many biopic figures, between love and career. Along this road, she labors to be accepted into the community of her chosen profession; initially ignored, then tolerated, she is ultimately triumphant. Finally, the main focus of this film, like almost half of all biopics, is encapsulated in a dual act of judgment: the society of Chicago judges the divorced Mrs. Carter as a moral being, and the communities (of the audience *in* the film, as well as that watching the film), try her as an actress. As in many other biopics, this judgment is highlighted in a trial scene (at her divorce), and in a dramatic (and triumphant) "trial" stage performance before her hostile hometown. Professions as different as nurse (*Sister Kenny*), artist (*Lust for Life*), inventor (*The Story of Alexander Graham Bell*), and athlete (*The Pride of St. Louis* [1952]) all contain some variation of the four elements above that fit disparate professions into a Hollywood imitation of life.

The Ages of Man

One of the most conventional structures of a life is its division into stages. Whether the stages are those seven enumerated by Jaques in *As You Like It,* or are the three (or four) suggested by Aristotle in his *Rhetoric,* or are part of the conventions of the visual arts in the Renaissance, dividing life into stages orders it into a series of events and provides frames of reference and narratives for each individual's progress.[2]

The model of life articulated by Jaques or suggested by Wordsworth in "Intimations of Immortality . . ." suggests an almost teleological "full cycle," with the father seen, eventually, as the child to man. However, fiction, from the mid-nineteenth century on (with exceptions like the *Bildungsroman*), focused not on a full seven-course life cycle, but instead constructed the life based almost exclusively on the individual as an adult being, one aware of the moral dimensions of his or her actions. In this regard, film resembled print fiction rather than print biography.

While biography often presumes a knowledge of the life from cradle to grave, only three films in the purposive sample chronicled an entire life's history. *Abraham Lincoln* (1930), *The Adventures of Mark Twain* (1944), and *The Great Caruso* are the exceptions in that an entire life is presented. This absence of the full life is puzzling. Less than 20 percent of all the biopic subjects were alive at the time of filming, and it would have been possible to construct a complete life, rather than an attenuated picture of a life, for the other 80 percent.[3]

By opening life *in medias res,* the biopic allows the famous figure to invent his or her own future, just as many a powerful figure in Hollywood had erected a new persona and fabricated an invented life history for him or herself. This angle added weight to the cult of the individual as a sole agent ethically acting in a free environment. As Braudy put it, "America, a whole nation built on the assumption that God helped those who helped themselves, made that attitude an article of national faith, essentially unquestioned until after World War I" (1986:506). The self-made man presented its inventor with

> a new way to justify American progress and character. Thrust forward by the popular press's new resources for focus and celebration, it was a style of social being consonant with the aspirations of the age, and both the self-made man and his publicists were intent on transforming the internal sanctions of the old morality into external structures of behavior and self-display. (1986:510)

Thus picturing the great as largely self-made also created a picture of history as a narrative of powerful individuals, who, by dint of remarkable gifts, are able to override conventional definitions of a social reality held by a restrictive community. That is, the great man can literally write—or rewrite—history. As Neal Gabler noted, for powerful figures in Hollywood, such an explanation of fame justified their own existence, lending credibility to their own fabricated narratives as well as to the narrative films they produced (1988:189). Like Freud's admission, after his falling out with his former confidant Wilhelm Fliess, that he needed strong enemies as much as he needed friends, the early founders of Hollywood needed to populate the narratives of their own lives with strong enemies in the movie community as well as filling their tales with close friends. Indeed, Erving Goffman has suggested that narratives that feature the speaker are always self-aggrandizing, always "so much an abstraction, a self-defensive argument, a careful selection from a multitude of facts, that the best that can be done with this sort of thing is to say that it is a lay dramatist's scenario employing himself as a character and a somewhat supportable reading of the past" (1974:558). Seeing other studio heads and rivals within one's own studio as obstacles within a community enabled the moguls to star themselves in such tales, and to makes films that featured the same plots. The self-made person's achievements—his or her visible success—thus became proof of his or her moral superiority. Like Winston Churchill, the Hollywood producer would make sure that history treated him kindly by producing it himself.[4]

Alternatively, the self-made man, in film and life, can be seen not as a newly devised solution proposed by a new medium, but instead as a continuation of a tendency popular in other arts since (at least) the rise of the novel.[5] Erich Auerbach (1953) noted that, as early as the nineteenth century, the novel and its kin in other media brought about a "democratization" of art by making nonroyal or nondeitic figures the subject matters of artworks. Film can be seen as a continuation of this tendency. In its making self-construction the valorized mode of existence, film suggested that the audience might have the route of self-invention open to it as a path to success. In television biography, we would see a further deconstruction of the idea of fame and its relation to the audience. Here, in film, the biopic reflects the roots of its producers, holding up these narratives as exemplary tales for the possible emulation of the audience.

The Role of the Family

There were however, models of fame other than self-invention. An alternative to the self-made famous are those who inherit fame from their family gene pool. The opening move of a biopic sometimes suggested fame was an inherited commodity, the endpoint of some unspecified buildup in the traits of a group. Universal's *Diamond Jim* opens with the birth of the title character. Holding the future capitalist in her arms, his mother wonders what the future holds for her son, as his heredity contains both the "blood of kings" and the genes of an alcoholic. With these alternatives framing the possible outcome of his life, Brady becomes a kind of king of capital, substituting food for the dangers of drink. "Good" genes win out. Similarly George M. Cohan combines his "Irish" trait of patriotism with his family inheritance of entertainment in a career that opens with his entertainer father placing an American flag into the hands of the newly born child. If one eavesdrops hard enough, one can uncover a key moment—as in *Yankee Doodle Dandy*—in many of the lives of the cinematic famous (at least those whose childhoods are shown) at which at least one person recognizes the extraordinary character of their young charge. The rest of the film, the unfolding of the life, is, in a sense, the journey in which the figure proves this initial judgment to be correct. As Braudy notes, "Biography always dramatizes the past as the direct cause of the present and the folklore of history battens on stories that will end 'and that boy is today' " (1986:109).[6]

Just as the birth of a character gave hints of the individual's nature, an exit—a death—afforded the filmmaker a last opportunity to sum up. The death scene, or the death of the leading character, is present in 29 percent of films in the purposive sample. It afforded one last message to be sent, recapitulating the life in the way that the opening titles had merely suggested. Thus, Parnell and Ehrlich, with pleas for political and ethical tolerance, can address their followers on their deathbeds, Anna and the King of Siam are at last reconciled, Lon Chaney is at peace with his son, Babe Ruth performs one last heroic feat, and Chopin's final wish for a free Poland can be expressed.

The death scene itself could be omitted to spare the viewers a depressing finale, but a monument or commemorative icon, the token of life after death—at least in terms of fame—often concluded the biopic. A monument or monumental depiction is a reminder of the veneration the hero has earned in the living narrative just seen. Thus Lincoln, shown to be "of the people" throughout *Young Mr. Lincoln,* walks out of the frame, and out of mortal life, at the film's end, transformed from the Lincoln of John Ford and Henry Fonda to the Lincoln of St. Gaudens's Memorial statue, a distant figure we revere from afar.[7] Death in the biopic, though rare, is typically uplifting.

What is surprising about the social definitions of fame in the biopic is the relatively small part the family had as a determinant of life and career. Although there are cases in which family is crucial (either as supportive or resistant) to the future career, many famous people existed detached from a family. In the purposive sample, almost half (44 percent) of the famous person's parents are never actually seen, or even mentioned, in the film. The famous are often shown standing alone at the start of their careers even if they gather a company of friends and family along the way. In the purposive

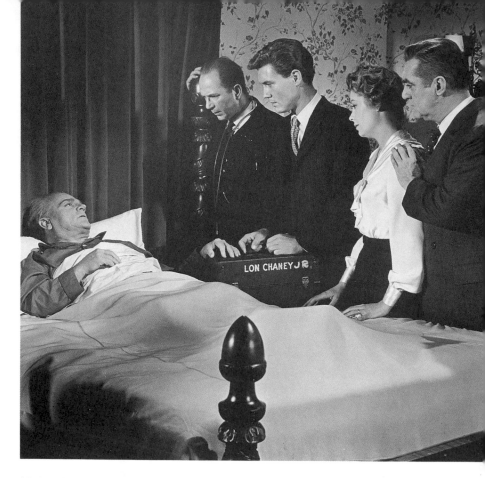

25. Deathbed valediction: In *Man of a Thousand Faces*, Lon Chaney (James Cagney) passes his makeup kit on to his son (Roger Smith). Note the addition of "Jr." to the label.

sample, less than one-quarter (23 percent) of the characters' families held strong opinions about the future directions of a famous person's life.

Significantly, though, many of the families with strong opinions voiced opposition to the career, providing an early—and formidable—example of adversity to be surmounted. More often than not, as the data in Table 4 suggest, in the majority of films (60 percent) life opens at an age—nineteen or above—beyond which the family has prime responsibility for socialization. Self-creation, the free development of talent through the will of an individual who is detached from a family, is the dominant biopic credo.

If the family is often absent from the life of the famous person,

TABLE 4
AGE OF CHARACTER AT START OF BIOPIC

Age	No. of Cases
Infant (0–4)	7
5–10	7
11–18	26
19–25	33
26–35	12
Over 35	15
Totals	100

what is its function? The family is an institution that reigns supreme in television, and, so we are told, holds sway in other film fare. What is the significance of, in many instances, making cinematic fame isolated from family? In Lowenthal's study of biographies in popular magazines, family was a crucible for nurturing the talent that "grew" into the famous person. If the character of the person was not a direct result of chance, he or she is a kind of Pavlovian product of the home environment. In at least half of Lowenthal's famous, the parents or general family background play some part, generally a strong one, in shaping the young child who will become the famous adult. With obvious distaste, Lowenthal referred to such explanations as "primitive Darwinian concept of social facts" that vitiate the individual from playing a large part in the making of his life, instead explaining his gifts as inheritances handed down from ancestors (1944:119). The character of the famous person is explained by his ethnicity (e.g., Clark Gable's stubborn determination stemmed from his Pennsylvania Dutch ancestors). Or, if no racial or national trait can be said to be the "cause" of future behavior, then the general tenor of family life, the quiet examples the parents set for their child, are held up as proof that family and genes determine human nature. In such a way, traditional values, traditional structures of power and knowledge, and ethnic and national stereotypes are maintained through biography.[8]

Of course, the folkways of a particular family can be constructed not as part of the common tradition at all, but instead as radical reconstructions of tradition. In *Cheaper by the Dozen* (1950), the biopic of industrial engineer Frank Gilbreth, unusual power structures and violations of stereotype make up the model of family influence. The eccentric Gilbreths notwithstanding, the family appears to offer the first example of the famous person being estranged from the community. It is the Darwin paradigm in reverse; greatness is maladaptive, and often survives through opposition to the basic social unit of the species, the family. One definition of talent or greatness suggests that the "great" man or woman stands somehow outside of community standards. What marks the famous as different is not merely talent; it is how the talent is received, both at home and later in the larger community outside the home. If one way community is defined is by the notion of cultural continuity, being different—or being perceived as different—threatens the established order, the only order many people know. It is not the fittest that survive; it is the misfits. Following Anthony F. C. Wallace's (1970) dictum that culture is characterized by difference as much as similarity, biopics suggest that resistance to conventional authority breeds a new version of this authority, not its total overthrow. Thus, film's narrative of fame conserves tradition even while seemingly carving it up. To do otherwise would be to subvert its own authority, to question its popular basis.

The Home as a Site of Female Resistance

The resistance to conformity as defined by family structure is particularly strong with women. The spheres in which women are shown to excel are limited mainly to entertainment, love, education, medicine, and royalty. In *The Actress,* young Ruth Gordon's home is an all-powerful institution in which her parents define their child's future. Her father Clinton Brown at first opposes his daughter's desire to go on the stage. Wishing her to follow his own obsession, he wants her to train to be a physical fitness instructor, "so she can earn a living." Despite the fact that Clinton, an enormous eccentric, had rejected his father's preferred career (carpenter) in favor of his own love of the sea, he is oblivious to Ruth's aspirations. He prefers a normal child, with the definition of normal being his domain.

> *Clinton:* As a physical instructor you'd lead a normal life. As an actress, you know, you'll be heading out on a pretty rough voyage.

26. Acting as female strategy: Jean Simmons as the young Ruth Gordon (née Brown) with father Spencer Tracy in George Cukor's *The Actress*

But Ruth is determined, having inherited the trait of stubbornness from her father. She vows to "be someone wonderful, that you read about, and nobody can stop me, not even my own family." In the end, Clinton relents and, pawning the symbol of his own resistance to his father, his beloved spyglass, he stakes Ruth to a career in New York.[9]

An acting career is morally ambiguous in the eyes of the community, but it also glamorous. The woman as performer suggests that she was somehow able to overcome the restrictive limitations of what a woman could do and, courageously, to present a constructed self before an audience in the way a more common career-—nursing, education—did not. Their success as performers attests to the cleverness with which they were able to surmount the obstacles erected in their home; the family, after all, is composed of the very

same people in the audience who applaud the manipulative and de-
fiant facade they have erected. The applause of an audience, then, is
tinged with envy; it is as much for the social daring, I think, as it is
for the talent. As Braudy notes,

> From the mid-nineteenth century on, the performer, par-
> ticularly the female performer, is celebrated in fiction as
> the archetypal self-manipulator who shows her superior-
> ity to social roles by rising to greatness as an actress. Zo-
> la's *Nana* and Dreiser's *Sister Carrie* are only two
> versions of this theme that show business itself sentimen-
> talizes in works like *Sally* or swallows with a dash of *mea
> culpa* in ones like *All About Eve*. In great part the attrac-
> tion of the audience and especially of the fan to the per-
> former thus emerges from the nineteenth century as an
> attraction to the singular, what is outside normal cate-
> gories, an attraction to the ideal as well as to the freak.
> (1986:578)

The female great person, prohibited by cultural prejudice from competing with men in most spheres, must learn to manipulate her self
and others if she is to succeed. The biopics of famous women suggest that a certain dishonesty and wile are associated with the talented woman in a way the male version, with its emphasis on action,
masks. Male talent seems to work more directly, as, exposed to genius, the world caves in. Women seldom have this scenario available
to them, and thus the theater and theatricality become for women,
and other oppressed minorities, both an actual career, cultural
stereotype, and a general strategy.

Without Love

To some extent, the famous cannot exist apart from some construction of theatricality, for fame, in film, is integrally tied in with the
profession of popular entertainer as well as the frame of showcase or
performance used to spotlight all life. But sometimes the spotlight
shines on an empty stage, and that which is expected (the family) is,
as I have said, notably absent. Since the symbolic world abhors a
vacuum as much as the natural one, something must take the place
of the family. Detached thus from family, the biopic figure cannot be
without some sources of human contact. To do so would render him

or her inhuman, and ultimately unlovable. Thus, as substitutes for
the family background the biopic figure loses by starting the life *in
medias res,* Hollywood created omnipresent discourses of friendship
and heterosexual romance. These discourses constructed asymmetrical relationships, so that the famous person is a kind of sun around
which the smaller bodies of the system revolve. The biopic gave
the cinematic life human contact, but it made famous figures remote, takers not givers, sources of illumination but seldom
warmth.

Lowenthal (1944) had noted that the absence of romance and love
was one of the most distinctive characteristics of the magazine biography and was typical of a world that showed the individual detached
from human interaction. But to make a film without romance or romance as a motivation for action was, in Hollywood, almost an im-
possibility, for romance was one of the foundations upon which
almost all films were constructed. As Bordwell, Staiger, and
Thompson noted, romance was one of the two perennial plot lines of
films made during the studio era: "The tight binding of the second
line of action to the love interest is one of the most unusual qualities
of the classical cinema, giving the film a variety of actions and a
sense of comprehensive social 'realism' that earlier drama achieved
through the use of parallel, loosely related subplots" (1985:17).
Even in *Brigham Young—Frontiersman* (1940), a film depicting the
foundation of a new religion (Mormonism), Zanuck wanted to make
sure that the serious subject matter was leavened with romance and
low comedy. In a story conference on October 10, 1939, Zanuck
voiced his concern that the serious tone of the life of one of the
patriarchs of the Church of Latter Day Saints become neither too
formulaic nor overly weighty: "Mr. Zanuck feels that this is a terrific
script but he is concerned about the continual oppression, suffering,
strife, starvation, that runs through the story from the opening
speech to the finish. It is essential that we relieve the heavy drama
by comedy, as was so effectively accomplished in *The Covered
Wagon,* for example" (UCLA, Fox Collection, Box FX-PRS-267).
To alleviate this anxiety, three moves secured the vision of the life of
Brigham Young in conventional biopic terms. First, the original
opening titles that had alluded to a "great wave of religious fervor"
and the proliferation of "countless new sects" was eliminated. Second, a love interest, in the persons of Tyrone Power and Linda Darnell, fulfilled the necessary romantic discourse. Third, actor Eddie

Collins was suggested as a possible addition to the cast for low comic relief, in the way that Francis Ford functioned in many of his brother John's serious films. Thus, the serious—and potentially controversial—subject matter was made commercial by the usual biopic formulation of love, comedy, and just enough history to keep the audiences entertained.[10]

Similarly, associate producer William Cagney and scriptwriter Robert Buckner informed producer Hal Wallis that the life of George M. Cohan, *Yankee Doodle Dandy,* was, on its face, not interesting enough to make a successful film. The problem, they noted, was the absence of love in the life of the cinematic Cohan:

> We needed a romantic personal story, or at least an honest
> and important statement of what Cohan was working for.
> As you know, Cohan has made [it] quite clear that he does
> not want his private domestic life as a major element of
> this picture. He stated that in no uncertain terms to Buck-
> ner, and this is his main reason for reserving the right to
> final approval of the screenplay. (Behlmer, 1985:179)

But Cohan was proving as difficult to deal with on film as he was in real life. Twice married (first to Jewish vaudeville star Ethel Levey), Cohan insisted his "private" love life remain out of the script. Wallis, William Cagney, and Bruckner wrote a personal letter to Cohan, trying to explain to him the necessity of including a love interest in his life story. Their plea is reminiscent of Zanuck's explanation of poetic license delivered to the Bell relatives, and centers on negotiating a degree of acceptable "creative" liberties one must take with a screenplay to fashion a successful film of a life.

> In the life of Knute Rockne, which we believe you ad-
> mired, we could never have produced as fine and well-
> rounded a picture had not his family so graciously
> permitted us to have some freedom in arranging a few
> elements in Rockne's life story. Many scenes in that pic-
> ture never actually occurred as we showed them, but they
> were all true to Rockne's spirit. . . . We did the same
> with Zola and Pasteur. Ziegfeld's life was given the same
> freedom for an excellent picture. . . . It is the only way

in which a biographical picture can be made interesting
and worthy. (Behlmer, 1985:182–183)

After much bickering, Cohan (who died in 1942, before the film
was officially released, but not too late to create enormous headaches
for all concerned) finally permitted the introduction of a "wife" Mary
(Joan Leslie) into the romantic plot line of his life. A stage-struck
girl of eighteen, Mary venerates her husband, a fitting tribute, no
doubt, that Cohan felt he deserved, but wildly at odds with the attitude of either of his real wives.

In so linking historical cause and effect to the presence of heterosexual romance, Wallis and Zanuck were hardly unique. They were
only manifesting principles of screenwriting that had been articulated in films since roughly 1915 (Bordwell, Staiger, and Thompson,
1985:166) and had been inculcated as professional norms through a
variety of institutional discourses, trade journals and "how to" pam-
phlets. If, as Bordwell, Staiger and Thompson, note, "Character-
centered—i.e., personal or psychological—causality is the
armature of the classical story" (1985:13), then biographies of great
individuals can be seen almost as prototypes for all stories. Allegedly based, after all, on real-life behavior, such films will, as both
metanarratives of fame and tales of specific persons, make this formulation even more powerful. Thus, heterosexual romance becomes, in this view, *naturally* linked to biography as a category of
historical explanation via character motivation.[11]

In foregrounding romance as a discourse of explanation, it is important to remember that all biography, not just film, is a constructed
story about a famous person. Hollywood's mediation of the life,
while possibly different from its source material (the short story or
the novel), is not different by dint of mediation alone. It merely gave
new twists—like the necessity of a love interest for the leading figure—to the old rule of recording past events for future telling. Wallis
in the life of Cohan and Zanuck in *Brigham Young* and other films
were pouring a particular set of characters into a well-known, narrative mold.

The Role of Friends

If the family is a site of resistance for the famous person, and romance is both a demand of all films and a stabilizing influence in

most biopics, the role of the friend is more complicated, more problematic. Almost all—88 percent—the famous people in the purposive sample had a close friend. Of the twelve people who had no close friends, seven were entertainers or creative artists, suggesting that the myth of the artist as outsider is strengthened by the biopic.[12] This is in contrast to the magazine biography, where the family is the prime agent of companionship. Of the twelve film "loners," one is the victim of mental illness (Jimmy Piersall), one of alcoholism (Buster Keaton), and one, at least, is an outlaw who lives outside the bounds of friendship (Bonnie Parker). Gender is not a factor in the presence or absence of friends, as this trait is distributed—or not— in proportion to the number of men and women in the sample.

Earlier I suggested that one of the principles of narrative construction for the biopic was what Zanuck called a "rooting interest." This was an angle through which the audience member became an engaged supporter of the leading figure in the film. One of the chief conduits for activating this support was the close friend of the famous person. This could be achieved in a number of ways. First, the close friend could articulate the amazing qualities of the famous person, intoning what makes him or her great.

In *The Pride of the Yankees*, Walter Brennan, as Sam Blake, is a sports reporter whose main career seems to be following Lou Gehrig (Gary Cooper) about, both on the playing field and off.[13] The film's job is to present Gehrig's amazing reliability—he was called the Iron Man—as a virtue in an age when many sports figures, from Walter Hagen or Jack Dempsey to Babe Ruth, were flamboyant entertainers. Here we have talent as pure performance, devoid of the aspect of personality that is the differentiation Hollywood so loves. Sam's debate with a doubting reporter Hank (Dan Duryea in his best obnoxious mode) frames Gehrig's single-minded devotion to baseball as itself a kind of showmanship, which, if not in the Babe Ruth genre, deserves to be appreciated in its own terms.

> SAM: Let me tell you about heroes, Hank. I've covered a lot of 'em, and I tell you Gehrig is the best of 'em. No front-page scandals, no daffy excitement, no hornpiping in the spotlight . . .
>
> HANK: No nothing.

SAM: But a guy who does his job and nothing else. He lives for his job, he gets a lot of fun out of it, and fifty million other people get a lot of fun out of him, watching him do something better than anybody ever did it before.

The film attempts to redefine the very terms of heroism and entertainment in sports, with the friend serving as the historical muse who witnesses and records. Sam Blake represents one of the functions of the friend, that of the chronicler of the great deeds of the hero. Ned Buntline in *Buffalo Bill* and Billy Herndon in *Abe Lincoln in Illinois* both play Boswells to their hero's Johnson. Chronicling need not be written; Clancy, the friend/nurse to Jane Froman in *With a Song in My Heart,* provides the voice-over narration for her charge's life.

A second function of the biopic friend, similar to the chronicler (who is, after all, at times vocationally charged with writing about something), is that of the conscience. These figures are often combined with the official roles they play as manager of the career of the great person, so that managing the professional endeavors is indistinguishable from managing the life. Often older, worldly wise, crusty types, themselves past the prime of eminence in a field, are seen in a number of films: the wise Professor Elsner of Paul Muni to the callow Frédéric Chopin of Cornell Wilde in *A Song to Remember;* Lew Sherwood (James Whitmore), the manager of Eddy Duchin, who must convince him to stop mourning his dead wife and recognize the needs of his abandoned son; Everett Sloane as Cohen, the crusty old pro who manages the career and life of difficult boxer Rocky Graziano in *Somebody Up There Likes Me;* Marjorie Rambeau as Gert, "Queen" of the extras, who, in *Man of a Thousand Faces,* sees in Lon Chaney the stuff needed to lift him out of the corps of faceless performers into the rank of the stars; and Constance Collier as Miss Julia Gibbs, a scenery-chewing grande dame actress who recognizes, in Pearl White, a vitality and honesty wonderfully suited to the movies in *The Perils of Pauline.*

While the friend is rarely responsible for advancing the career of the famous figure, he or she is a kind of moral gyroscope, reminding the great one of the nonprofessional values like modesty, honesty, family, and, above all else, love. It is often the manager figure who points out to the famous person the daily needs—like romance—

they are too myopic to see. These friends see clearly from the perspective of normal life a vista often blocked to the great person by his or her extraordinary talent. Most great people are presented as *idiots savants,* creatures whose cognitive maps are drawn straight to professional success, but lead them astray in other terrains. It is the job of the less gifted to guide the figures through this alien turf. In so doing, their "normal" behavior—often accentuated by plain speech or homely appearance—illuminates the unusual qualities of the hero. Like Lord Rochester's monkey, their very ungainliness and lack of talent make the gift of the leading figure more dazzling; at the same time, their friendship for these extraordinarily ordinary creatures endows the great man or woman with the desired common touch. Their presence is often required to provide comic relief, and, as Darryl Zanuck's notes for *Brigham Young* and *Young Mr. Lincoln* suggest, they are used to lighten otherwise "heavy" material.

While friendship seems to be a prerequisite for most great people, relations between the great and their friends are seldom symmetrical. As Lowenthal suggests, "the hero appears in his human relationships as the one who takes, not as the one who gives" (1944:120). Here, too, the findings are similar to those of Lowenthal, who found that "there is very rarely an episode which shows our heroes as active partners of friendship. In most cases their friends are their helpers." More often then not, the friend is a kind of worshipful member of an entourage whose life appears to be given meaning by association with the great person. William Demerest's Steve Martin, who lives through the greatness of Jolson, epitomizes this figure. While there are occasionally morally superior friends who give the famous person advice—Brother Mathias in *The Babe Ruth Story* and Captain Peoples, the prison warden, whose will reforms Carbine Williams, or Professor Elsner who keeps Chopin away from the clutches of George Sand in *A Song to Remember*—friendship is a kind of mirror used to reflect the bright light of the leading figure's glory.

The friend can be a representative of the larger public that acclaims the great man or woman. Providing the trappings of normal behavior—companionship, interaction, loyalty—like a Greek chorus or knowing stage manager, the companion signals the audience to applaud or occasionally to villify the behavior of the leading figure. The friend articulates common values, and acts as a kind of surrogate for the imaginary audience member. In this way, the presence in a script of these figures is a guide to the audience, getting us to empathize with these great figures, but also to revere them. While purporting to show how normal, underneath it all, the famous person is, the figure of the friend instead convinces us the opposite is true. Despite their presence in these films, the one-sided relationship friends enjoy with the famous suggests, both in print and on the screen, the price of fame is often estrangement from friends and family. Friends of the biopic famous are just as distanced as the audiences watching the tales, and their distance within the film may signal the real audience watching the film that such a pose is appropriate.

Causality in Life

Whether one explains fame as a divine gift (*The Great Caruso*), the result of family inheritance (*Yankee Doodle Dandy, Young Bess*), or the result of hard work and the proper social atmosphere (*The Pride of the Yankees*), all life on film exists within a logical frame that proffers an explanation of why the famous deserve their special niche in society. Whether the explanation is biogenetic or sociogenetic, biopics reduce causality to individual, identifiable factors. In film, it is not so much the case of the universe being perfectly bifurcated, with one cause or another predominating. Rather, Hollywood films, and the biopic, represent a mechanical view of the universe, in which cause and effect can almost always be isolated, attribution comes easily, and stable patterns of success and failure are homeostatic devices regulating world history. The emphasis on clear-cut causality, rather than chance, distinguishes film biography from its magazine counterpart.[14]

All fame is, and therefore must be shown to be, specifically motivated. But there are several levels at which this can be accomplished. The specific motivating, explanatory episode can be a single case or instance that changes a life—as in the mystical intervention that turns the drunken Alvin York from a sinner into a man imbued with religious faith, or the divine intervention that shows Peter Marshall the path to religion in *A Man Called Peter* (1955).

In *Sergeant York* the title character is first shown as a kind of hillbilly cavalier who openly scoffs at the religion of his family and neighbors in rural Tennessee. So craven are York's early actions—

he sometimes blasphemes at the very door of the church he later comes to revere—that our expectations are aroused that either he will receive his just punishment or he will have a dramatic revelation and change his ways. Cheated by a sharp storekeeper out of the valuable land he had worked for in order to impress his fiancée, York vows to kill the perpetrator of the swindle. En route to the murder, his gun is struck by lightning outside the church he had earlier shunned. Not only is the gun struck by lightning, but it is twisted out of shape, "beat into a plowshare," so to speak. His pacifism stems, then, from direct intervention from above. He takes this as a sign of God's intention, and, following the ways of his mother and the advice of (yet again) Walter Brennan as a preacher, mends his ways. The larger message of the 1941 film is one of anti-isolationism. *Sergeant York* suggests that, in the year America entered the war, there is no such thing as neutrality, and the film opens with a hymn "When the roll is called up yonder, I'll be there." York's dilemma is to accommodate his newly found religious pacifism (God) with fighting the Germans in World War I (country). It is important to note that a particular incident and a particular kind of agency change York's path forever.[15]

Roughly 79 percent of the films in the purposive sample explain fame through a specific motivating episode. For example, told by her father that only unattractive women who can't marry seek careers, Sister Kenny is determined to prove his view of her capabilities and of the world incorrect. Throughout the film, she battles this prejudice against women—and also against her outsider status as an Australian—that is first raised, in a key episode, by her father. Similarly, Emma Gladney in *Blossoms in the Dust* is first shown as an upper middle-class debutante with few cares other than which beau to select. Her interest in illegitimate orphans arises when her adopted sister, shamed by the revelation of an illegitimate paternity, commits suicide under her very roof. The later loss of her only child propels her, in conjunction with the memory of her sister's shame, to make all children, especially the illegitimate, her charge. Thus specifically motivated turning points alter the life of a woman of the upper class, one whose breeding and class mores emphasize pedigree, the very issue that would have constrained her from championing the causes of such "socially unacceptable" creatures as the illegitimate.

The specific foregrounding of motivation and causality in the life of the famous person is congruent with Hollywood's general notion that character construction is not necessarily related to believability, but rather is connected to the function a character plays in the narrative. It is also part of the screenwriting creed that it is important to delineate the nature of the character in an economical, direct way.

Sweet Mystery of Life at Last . . .

Specific motivation is often introduced with the very opening titles of the film. Introductory titles directly and economically proclaimed a film to be true. But they also performed other functions just as important as the establishment of veracity; they could suggest certainty. In one variation of the opening of a life, certainty, rather than mystery, framed the assertion of talent. Thus, in addition to the truth of the film, we were given a statement of its outcome, told before the fact what the famous person did to be worthy of a film.

However, another strategy can frame a life so that mystery rather than familiarity shape the narrative. Sometimes introductory titles framed the film not in certainty, but in uncertainty, using the rhetorical strategy of having a character or a narrator voice curiosity as to the outcome of the life. A film, feigning its unawareness of an already written script, was presented as the unfolding answer.

Young Mr. Lincoln is a well-known example of this strategy. Nancy Hanks, Lincoln's mother, returns as a ghost and asks, in the Rosemary Benet poem that opens the film, a series of questions about the future of her son.[16] It is presumed that every viewer knows the answers to the questions of what happened to Lincoln, but the device adds poignancy to the tale, and allows the viewer to see young Lincoln before he attained fame.[17] The poem, added very late in the production history of the film, frames the narrative as the answer to a series of questions. It is an uncommon device, and must have been developed after more conventional formulas did not work.

In *Young Mr. Lincoln,* since we were supposed to see Lincoln as ordinary, rather than famous, some device had to be created to frame this most famous American as an unknown figure. Darryl Zanuck, producer Kenneth MacGowan, and writer Lamar Trotti grappled with this difficulty. In a story conference on January 13, 1939, Zanuck had rejected one solution to the puzzle of framing Lincoln as unknown. In an early draft of the film, there had been a mystical section in which Lincoln, talking with an unseen figure, is told about his future: his marriage to Mary Todd, the Civil War. In this vision, he is even allowed to see his own funeral cortege. The film then dissolved to the Lincoln Memorial (UCLA, Fox Collection, Box FX-PRS-786).[18] Zanuck wanted little to do with mysticism and uncertainty. He preferred terra firma to the Elysian fields, and found the opening poem preferable to the ghoulish specter of Lincoln seeing his own death.

Only five films in the purposive sample use this strategy of opening with uncertainty. The bulk of purposive sample biopics, then, reveal their hands to the audience by asserting their facticity and the trajectory of certainty the viewer will witness. Presumably, the pleasure the viewer obtains is derived, as in other genres, from seeing familiar expectations fulfilled within a tradition of performance or witnessing the reenactment of a particular kind of entertainment.[19]

Talent as Doppelgänger

Talent cannot be segregated and controlled. It often trespasses—jarringly—into the everyday lives of entertainers. Its very presence, even its very nature, that of transmuting the everyday into a strange and different set of codes, is a threat to normal institutions, for it establishes the legitimacy of a double persona for an individual, and makes an essential part of their nature public, rather than private. The borders between performances on stage and performances in life are not simply drawn. Entertainer biopics draw our attention to an aspect most of us would like to ignore in our own lives: the often warring dissonances in the different presentations of self necessitated by the everyday roles we assume. By segregating the performing persona of soprano Marjorie Lawrence from her "woman's" identity, *Interrupted Melody* suggests that fulfillment is found only in a kind of "honest," one-person, one-personality performance. This is a line of thinking wonderfully congruent with Western notions of the integrated "self" and "individual" and with 1950s image of womanhood, both of which suggested static types as ideals, standing outside of history.

I suggest that entertainer biopics displace onto their subjects the problematic conflicts all people share. By isolating such allegedly dishonest behavior to a small portion of the population—the famous, or famous entertainers—these movies allow audience members to walk away feeling intact, and perhaps a bit smug, about their own integrated personalities. What makes talent special, then, is a particular brand of behavior that would be non-adaptive in normal settings. By defining talent's relationship to the individual's self as abnormal, sacred myths of the individual, or at least a definition of what a normal person consists of, are secured from the comparative pathology of the talented.

Talented people are different. Such difference is a matter out of their control. This is not unlike Lowenthals's observations that the famous person in magazines was often the beneficiary of help from others, or had inherited greatness, and was thus a kind of passive recipient of fame. It is as if fame is a substance that can be injected at birth, or somehow obtained through contact with the right supplier. And, although many of the famous protest that they want what "everyone" wants, it is not merely a matter of willing one's life into normality. Try as they might, the famous, like Ernest Hemingway supposedly said of the rich, are different from you and me; they have more talent. Talent is often characterized as a kind of double, convenient when performing, but dreadfully out of place off the stage.

The Social Construction of Fame:
The World of Entertainment

The picturing of the lives of entertainers had been gradually undergoing transformations since sound film made possible a definition of talent that included singing and dancing, rather than movement and spectacle.[20] In the 1930s, entertainer biopics were rare, comprising less than 10 percent of all biopics of that era. By the 1940s, this percentage had nearly doubled, increasing to 17 percent, and in the 1950s, nearly three times (28 percent) the proportion of biographical films were about entertainers. As the form evolved, mere repetition of the same life's progress became no longer desirable. Producers felt audiences were tiring of such predictable formulas. Fearing a loss of audience, producers attempted to alleviate viewer boredom by encouraging novel treatments of the lives of entertainers, and gradations within genres of the entertainer biopic emerged.[21]

This shift in the content of entertainer biopics—from the revue image of life exemplified by MGM's Rogers and Hart biopic *Words and Music* (1948), to the more dramatically motivated tale—was the result not only of personal observation of prescient individual producers. There are a number of possible explanations for the new angle brought to entertainer biopics. First, this increasingly "dramatic" approach to a life (I hesitate to apply the word "realistic" to these films) was abetted by the weakening bonds of the Production Code. Although the Breen Office would hold power into the 1960s, post-*Paramount* decree (1949) Hollywood saw a loosening of the power of the censor. By according film the same First Amendment rights as other forms of speech, the United States Supreme Court in *Paramount* opened up new possibilities of film as a mode of free artistic expression. Although censorship was still a very powerful factor, post-*Paramount* biopic lives benefited from this less sanitized approach to telling stories. Second, the rise of the independent producer and exhibitor loosened the hold of self-censorship under which the Code had flourished. Since post-*Paramount* exhibitors were no longer obliged to rent from the oligopolistic "big eight" companies, the collusion between the Breen Office and these corporations was not as effective, allowing for a potentially freer content. From the early 1950s on—when the power of censorship was directly tested by Roberto Rossellini's *The Miracle* (1950) and other films—"American cinema discovered new material, themes and styles—and a new audience which in the 1950s and 1960s television could not steal" (Izod, 1988:131). Biopics made after *Paramount* featured such stark content as alcoholism (*I'll Cry Tomorrow, The Buster Keaton Story* [1957]), drug addiction (*The Gene Krupa Story* [1959]), and mental illness (*Fear Strikes Out* [1957]), material deemed inappropriate for the revue-oriented biographies of the 1930s and early 1940s.

By the 1950s, the notion of the life of an entertainer had changed dramatically from the 1930s and 1940s strategy of whitewashing. Considering the genre initially was purported to be escapist fare at the time of its genesis (cf. Bergman, 1971), by the 1950s, people might have been going to other genres, like musicals, to escape the anxiety induced by these once cheerful but now increasingly problem-laden biopics of musical performers. The tales of nonmusical performers—like *The Buster Keaton Story*—also exhibited this more "adult" approach to life. Once filled with bravos and cheers, life could also be shown as a difficult struggle to overcome obstacles;

talent was no longer enough to guarantee a happy ending. Thus, though genre considerations were one factor in shaping a life, concepts of a genre changed, sometimes within the course of a single decade.

Darryl Zanuck grappled with these shifts. A Fox film in production in 1949 (though not released until 1953), *The I Don't Care Girl,* the biopic of Eva Tanguay, shows just how many factors had to be considered in shaping the life depicted. Produced by vaudevillian George Jessel (*Variety* had already alluded to a Jessel "stable" of vaudeville films at Fox), the film was made on the cusp of the transformation from the biopic as showcase to the biopic as drama with musical entertainment. Zanuck, keenly aware of this shift, noted the difficulties in shaping this life at the critical juncture of Hollywood's history. At a conference on June 13, 1949, he outlined his thoughts on how to shape the Tanguay life:

> Now Eva Tanguay is not so famous or so great that the public is going to sit around and await the story of her life, even if this happened to be the story of her life, which it isn't. Therefore, since we are devising a story and since we have a potentially good set of characters, we should be sure that we have a good, fresh, entertaining story, and work out the story we have in such a way that there is some excuse for making it other than to just spot some numbers. (UCLA, Fox Collection, Box FX-PRS-1185)[22]

In his desire to have the life narrative integrated with the songs, even to have the songs motivated by the events in the life, Zanuck was not breaking new ground. Director Vincente Minnelli, with producer Arthur Freed, had been able to integrate plot with numbers in *Meet Me in St. Louis,* and on Broadway, the success of Jerome Kern's and Oscar Hammerstein's *Show Boat,* in 1927, and to some extent Kern's earlier "Princess" shows, suggested such an approach was both artistically justifiable and financially appealing. But nominal producer Jessel and writers Michael Abel and Jules Buck (the latter, a future producer, whose London-based firm produced the notable 1964 biopic *Becket*) were unable to come up with a script that pleased Zanuck.

The problem of the Tanguay life, and the picturing of other lives like it, resisted a simple solution. In the past, Zanuck might have urged his writers to screen "older" biopic triumphs—like *The Dolly Sisters*—or quasi-historic films—like his favorites *Alexander's Ragtime Band* and *In Old Chicago*—in order to come up with acceptable solutions which had already proven workable. But things had changed, and the gaudy Technicolor entertainer tales that had previously been Fox fare were not always acceptable templates. Two months after the June conference at which he had articulated his ideas on biopics of lesser known figures, Zanuck continued, from his vacation site in the Antibes, to push for an integrated approach to showcase the Tanguay life. In a memo of August 22, 1949, to Jessel, he noted that other recent entertainer biopics, including Warners biopic of Ziegfeld star Marilyn Miller—*Look for the Silver Lining* (1949)—had dealt with fairly dramatic, even potentially depressing situations. Given his willingness to open up the list of allowable plots for a life, he wondered if his writers, "clever fellows like you two" couldn't take these new possibilities and create a fresh rooting interest for Tanguay that was not transparently in the revue tradition.

There were other problems with the project from the outset. Although part of the pantheon Jessel had, in his mind, erected as his own shrine to vaudeville, Eva Tanguay was hardly a star as well-remembered as Marilyn Miller, or as revered as Jolson, and this lack of recognition presented a problem for picturing the life. Most film biopics were about people who were already extremely well-known before the film was made. Tanguay's marginal status with the public presented a problem: "Eva Tanguay is associated with only a couple of songs and neither of them is very good, so we would have to commence from scratch on this angle." Zanuck suggests the writers start anew, throwing away the conventional musical showcase treatment, and

> try to tell a real story of her life with the blindness angle
> and everything else. They got away with some pretty
> heavy drama in the last part of the Marilyn Miller story;
> therefore, perhaps if we tell a realistic tragedy and tell the
> whole story honestly and legitimately we might come up
> with a sympathetic story. We failed utterly as I felt we
> would fail with Herman Mankiewicz, but you insisted on

hiring him. What Jule and Mike [Jules Buck and Michael Abel, the writers] must look for is a basic theme. *Maybe they will get a cue out of her life; maybe you will have to invent it.*

We note that shifting genre considerations, public perception of the magnitude of a star, and awareness of what—and how—other studios were producing similar films were all factors in bringing a particular kind of narrative to the screen. It was not life being imitated, in biography, but other films of life.

Still, the proposed production dragged on. The film passed through at least six revisions over a period of four years. Finally, the very difficulty experienced in finding the best way to frame the life on film became, in the end, the frame used to film the life.

In an extraordinary autobiographical extrapolation from the production history of *The I Don't Care Girl*, the final version of the film featured a kind of displacement that Freud himself would have applauded. Jessel—stepping outside his role of the recipient of Zanuck's harangues about how to construct a script—played himself as a Zanuck-like figure who harangues a writer (a Jessel surrogate) for his clichéd version of the Tanguay tale. The actual dialogue for the film spoken by Jessel, as Jessel, was derived almost verbatim from material Zanuck dictated to Jessel, under the heading "Story Revision" in a memo of October 26, 1950, some three years before the film was completed. Its subject matter was a favorite Zanuck topic, character and story motivation. Thus "Jessel," through the pen of Zanuck, notes:

> This is great stuff. But it's all worthless . . . it only proves Eva Tanguay was famous. . . . But it doesn't tell me why. Find out what made her madcap, find out why she sang "I Don't Care," . . . I don't want alibis or psychoanalysis—I want Eva Tanguay, the woman. Underneath those sequins and feathers and the mop of wild curls was a woman's heart and a woman's brain—maybe even a woman's soul—that's what I want. (UCLA, Fox Collection, script dated May 23, 1951)

Typically producers of films hid the process of filmmaking so that the problems of production would not be visible on the screen. At

27. Laying bare the device: George Jessel, as himself, articulating Zanuck's biopic credo to two writers of the film within the film in the Eva Tanguay biopic, *The I Don't Care Girl*

most, such problems could be submerged within the text, transformed from a direct representation to an indirect one, as in the highly coded Hollywood treatment of ethnicity and sexuality. But in the script for *The I Don't Care Girl,* we have the rare opportunity to have the biographical device laid bare. The Zanuck amenuensis, Jessel, articulates some of the problems Zanuck had encountered in creating a motivated character for this and other biographies. The processes that shaped this utterance, and the forces that moved this film through its production, sum up what Hollywood meant when it attempted to construct, within the borders of conventional production practices, an individual life from the template of previous textual experience. A life on film meant, really, an imitation of life, one based on previous popular mediations (best-selling books and stories) and previously used film incarnations of fame.

Holding It Together

The self depicted in these films, if one can draw a kind of composite figure based on numerous occupations, is full of contradictions. Famous people have friends, but their relationships are asymmetrical. Famous people are self-made, yet need heterosexual partners as a kind of gyroscope to balance them in the world. Those who lack this gyroscope don't topple over; they are merely framed as lacking some integral part of life. For them, the fame that brought them renown is, at times, a substitute for heterosexual fulfillment. The famous person can inherit the gift that brings fame, but little is seen of the family that nurtured this. Balancing these tensions are the given bulwarks of romance and democracy, discourses that, separately or interactively (anyone can marry anyone else for love in Hollywood film) pervade every famous life. Thus, two key structures the audience could relate to—democracy and romance—are part of the stable constellation that holds in place the shifting contours of biopic fame that might, because of the pull of the contradiction inherent in each life on film, become unstable.

The very basis by which entertainers stay famous—maintaining the favor of the audience—is at the heart of entertainer narratives. At the heart is a homage to democracy that flatters and coerces the current audiences. Thus, to validate entertainment is to valorize democracy and popular judgment. The biopic fuses the gestures of democracy and romance, and in so doing makes them natural indexes of the very idea of popular entertainment upon which all movies are based. The acts of giving an entertainer a fair hearing on a popular stage (democracy), and then, after the courtship of the ups and downs of a career, taking him or her into their collective hearts (romance) are powerful rituals nearly all famous people undergo in the Hollywood biopic. But such a cycle is even more powerfully codified with the audience/performer/stage relationship than with other configurations.

Finally, I do not want to suggest with this talk of democracy that biopics articulated Andy Warhol's idea that everyone would be famous for fifteen minutes. This ultimate leveling is rare in film and typically was limited to biopics of war heroes or individuals, like Douglas "Wrong Way" Corrigan or the five Dionnes, for whom one eccentric event informs a life. A democracy of fame is not the province of the movies. Such a redefinition of fame was years into the future. It would not flourish within the studio walls. But long after the studios were gone, it would emerge as the dominant discourse on fame in the domain of television.

What the biopic suggested is that we can all benefit from the presence of the famous in our communities, a different proposition indeed from a comradeship of fame that television proposes. Being grateful for the Edisons, the Lincolns, and the Gladneys in our midsts validates the idea that out of the large mass of people, somehow leaders emerge at regular intervals to help the ordinary citizen see the correct path in science, music, literature, and aviation. It is, however, the comforting genius of these films to suggest that despite the untouchability of their deeds, despite their unusual gifts, most of the greats are normal, just like you and me.

CHAPTER
5
■ ■ ■

Configuring a Life

Si monumentum requiris, circumspice
[If you seek his memorial, look round you]
— INSCRIPTION ON THE TOMB OF CHRISTOPHER WREN, ST.
PAUL'S CATHEDRAL, LONDON

Some day you will learn that there is no substitute for a story
and that while occasionally Van Johnson and Esther Williams can take a piece of material like *The Thrill of Romance*
and turn it into a hit because of their personalities, this is not
the rule. It is sometimes very good to include vaudeville acts
and ancient routines, but first you must have a story in
which the audience will want to root for the characters. This
is a simple a-b-c kindergarten formula. . . . How you could
have ignored such a fundamental rule is beyond me. It is
like having a circus without a tent.
— DARRYL ZANUCK TO GEORGE JESSEL, SEPTEMBER 29,
1945, REGARDING *HELLO MY BABY*

Does the biopic constitute a particular kind of historical discourse?
Are there factors specific to film that make a film version of a life
differ significantly from its biographical kin in other media? Or, as
Hayden White suggests, is a film biography a mediation like any
other? These and other questions are at the heart of the biopic as a
cultural object, and any attempt to understand the biopic as a genre
or to assess the role these films played in shaping public history will
focus on issues of cinematic mediation: the kinds of source materials

for film biography, the devices peculiar to film or frequently used by filmmakers—for example, montage—that afford a life a uniquely cinematic shape, the role played by the star actor in casting and shaping a life, and the three basic configurations—resistance, the struggle between innovation and tradition, and the importance of the big break—that give shape to the universe in which fame is placed. There is also the significance of trial scenes, the metanarrative device found in almost half of all biopics, that ensure the "lessons" of the film being telegraphed to the viewer, securely linking the ideology of a particular film to the patterns formed by other historical narratives.

Erecting the Tent

The conventions of film storytelling are among the strongest determinants of how historical characters are embedded in specific plot lines developed as film biographies. Every text is composed of conventions from related texts; each particular film narrative can be said to combine and recombine particular textual permutations in novel or familiar combinations, orders, and emphases. But a biography, the story and explanation of a life, is that rare thing, a microcosmic view of the world. In it most of the forces that shape destiny are brought to bear not upon the community, but instead upon a single individual. While this description might easily apply to most narrative fiction since the nineteenth century, the biopic—and to some extent, the print biography—differ from these related narratives to the extent that they emphasize individual causality—detached from most other factors—as an explanatory model of the world. Because biography is both a model of and a model for causality in the world at large, it will appropriate sometimes dissonant discourses—from descriptive science and mass entertainment—to secure a contradiction; a popular, mass-produced narrative of a life whose uniqueness is in opposition to such quality control. The narrative models for film biography contained in these different discourses become critical indexes of the kind of historical vision film attempts to construct.

The source materials for the purposive sample of 100 films (see Table 5) suggest just how strongly intertextual practices shape the events pictured in a life. Rather than being inspired by first-hand accounts of a life, Hollywood biopics are usually based on secondary,

TABLE 5
SOURCE MATERIAL FOR BIOPICS

Source Cited	No. of Cases*
Short story	26
Memoirs/autobiography	13
Play	12
Suggested by life or works	10
Biography	8
Relative's reminiscenses	7
Novel	5
No specific source cited	21

*The number of cases (102) is higher than 100 because more than one source was sometimes cited for a film.

mediated structures. At times this second-hand observation bears the imprint of kinship; the scripts for both *Madame Curie* and *Jack London* were based on books written by the daughter and wife, respectively, of the leading figures. Other times, the film is only loosely connected to any sort of mediation; the Joe Howard biopic, *I Wonder Who's Kissing Her Now,* is based on "incidents in the life of" the composer. These data on source material refer to only those sources officially listed in the films' credits, of course; an enormous number of uncited sources—both verbal and visual—also shaped the narratives. A cinematic life has already been mediated through these source materials. The kinds of source materials upon which most biopics were based underscore the extent to which intertextuality in film and in print was the foundation for building a narrative of a life. Here we have the data, for film, that illuminate Leo Lowenthal's gloomy perceptions for magazine biographies; that the same finite set of plots and structures were used to explain diverse individual lives and careers. Thus, the uniqueness of fame is rendered, ironically, similar by the repeated use of these controlling narrative mechanisms.

By relying on already mediated and abbreviated versions of a life—almost a quarter were based on short stories—the biopic assures that a life will be fully explained, that it is congruent with other narratives in a culture. What E. A. Poe—and, earlier, other writers like Prosper Mérimée—discovered in the mid-nineteenth century about the short story was no less true one hundred years later: namely, that a short story was not merely a shorter version of a novel. It was a story meant to be consumed in a single sitting. The life on film is meant to be taken in one ninety-minute slice. Given these conventions, the condensation and abbreviation demanded by the organic nature of the form had to be codified, and frequently used sources of such codification were previous incarnations of the life in the shortened form of plays, short stories, and previous films.

We see this process of cinematic mediation at work in John Ford's *Young Mr. Lincoln*, released by Twentieth Century-Fox in 1939. The life of Lincoln is a good illustration of how the cinematic great life is mediated. Audiences, exposed to the construct "Lincoln" in school, on postage stamps and currency, and in countless other symbolic forms, approach a film version of the life with a certain degree of prior knowledge. What makes a cinematic mediation of the already famous life at all tenable is the extent to which a particular bricolage of these known facts contains either a new slant on a life or else "classically" organizes what is already known. The strategy of mediation on film thus takes popular conventions extant in a culture and arranges them according to principles that make one particular life congruent with others. In film, this is accomplished by configuring the person within the four moves suggested at the outset of this chapter, and these can be illustrated with the Ford film.

First, the film relies heavily on popular notions of Lincoln encoded in other media. Entire episodes and snatches of dialogue— like the confrontation between Lincoln and Buck in front of the jail—are appropriated verbatim from Carl Sandburg's popular biography of Lincoln, published in 1926.[1] Sources other than the immensely popular Sandburg narrative were also used to link the film to current popular tastes; Zanuck himself urged Lamar Trotti, in a memo February 20, 1939, to read an (unspecified) new book of Lincoln anecdotes.[2] Second, the film makes use of specifically cinematic devices to tell its story. It starts when Lincoln is already a young man, and moves the pace along nicely with such specifically cinematic techniques as montages (the July Fourth festivities at which Scrub White is killed) and dissolves. It was Zanuck who suggested the dissolve that propels the viewer from Lincoln beside the frozen river at the winter graveside of Ann Rutledge, to Lincoln in the spring, getting on with his life (and career) amid the now melting

28. Henry Fonda as Bell's assistant, Watson: the star actor actualizes the historical figure with his specific attributes.

ice. Visual and aural transitions, like the dissolve, also link narrative events in a specifically casual chain, offering explanations for a life that secure fame within interpersonal (often romantic) ties. Third, the star Henry Fonda, seen also that year (1939) in *The Grapes of Wrath* and in the biopics *The Story of Alexander Graham Bell* (as Bell's assistant, Watson) and *Jesse James,* gives the Lincoln character his flat Midwestern accent and homespun star persona, endowing the script with a corporeal reality that mere lines of dialogue or stage directions only suggest. As in all other biopics, the historical figure in *Young Mr. Lincoln* becomes realized and actualized for the viewer through the physical presence of the star persona. Last, the messages of the film are encapsulated at a fictive trial, a device suggested by Zanuck and eventually based loosely on one Trotti, as a young reporter, had covered.[3]

By adhering to these four structures—a limited number of textual sources, a specific narrational logic dictated by film's time frame, the star persona, and the summation of the film's message via a trial—Hollywood configured the life of the famous man or woman within a stable and controlled trajectory that still left room for an individual personality and face.

Tempus Fugit: Montage and Flashback

To state that intertextuality was a prime influence in shaping the biopic tells us, in a general way, how film was related to other films as well as other systems of popular culture. But film had its own signifying practices; in addition to codes derived from other media, cinema developed its own characteristic ways of telling stories that lent a distinctive shape to its products.

All media had to condense the raw data of a life into an abbreviated form. In the eighteenth century, Edward Gibbon could write his seven-volume history of Rome, just as today, Leon Edel might create the life of Henry James on a similar scale.[4] But it is far more common to demarcate the life on a less massive scale than either Gibbon or Edel do, to put it into a consumable length fit for the mass market. Thus, every medium has developed ways of and conventions for representing a life within a manageable (and for commercial popular culture, salable) form. If plays and short stories had developed a repertoire of devices to divide a life, and move it forward, to condense and select, film had its own methods of briskly getting on with it. Film could open the life at the jumping off point of fame, and, more economically, deal with the particular representations of success through montage or flashback.

One out of every five films in the purposive sample used flashbacks to present the tale of success. For example, *Young Bess* opens with the faithful servants of Elizabeth I celebrating her imminent coronation. They reminisce over the rocky road to queendom, and her governess's voice-over narration sets up the tale of Bess's struggles to obtain the throne, and her uneven relationship with a procession of stepmothers, the wives of her father Henry VIII.

Yankee Doodle Dandy uses a flashback narrated by its leading figure, as George M. Cohan explains his life to none other than the president of the United States. He tells Franklin Roosevelt:

It started with a very funny incident about sixty years ago. It was in Providence, Rhode Island, on the Fourth of July. There weren't so many stars then, in the flag or on the stage, but folks knew more were coming. They were optimistic, happy, and expectant, the beginning of the Horatio Alger age. . . . The first thing I had in my fist was a flag.

From its opening narrated flashback, the life of Cohan is linked to the American consciousness, so his brash proclamation—that America expected to expand its territory and add to its entertainment pantheons—links his destiny as a flag-waving patriot to the growth of America as a world power. The film fleshes out his assertions.

One of the functions of the flashback, then, is to retell history from the vantage point of a particular narrator. This privilege allows the narrator to frame the life not just in terms of the order and content of events, but to frame its significance. Cohan and the flag go together just as Elizabeth and England are wed. This use of a framing device is similar to, but not identical with, the device discussed in Chapter one, the use of opening titles that assert the facticity of the tale that will follow. The titles assert not only truth, but truth constructed from past events observed from the vantage point of a particular individual, truth constructed with the slant of personal observation. The prison warden who narrates the life of *Carbine Williams* or the historian who narrates the story of German General Erwin Rommel in *The Desert Fox* (1951) are self-consciously setting out to reframe the life so that it is (finally) properly understood, only because the life has been, prior to this point, so badly misconstrued. A flashback creates its own internal sense of time. The present tense of the narrative is contrasted with the "history" of the flashback, imbuing the film with its own validity as historical data simultaneous with the creation of its history.

The use of such framing devices as flashbacks characterize film biography, but are largely minor elements in biography in other media. Although William Manchester's mammoth popular biography of Winston Churchill, *The Last Lion* (1983), opens, like a biopic, on the eve of World War II, situating the prologue so that the life of the rescuer of the British gradually builds, with all its abrupt shifts and reverses, into a triumphant culmination, this is not a common device. More likely, written biographies of the modern age, like Michael Holroyd's *Lytton Strachey: A Biography* (1971), or Peter Gay's *Sigmund Freud: A Life for Our Time* (1988) open with, or shortly after, the birth of the leading figure.[5] While we discovered in chapter four that the actual depiction of a birth is rare in a biopic, it was, until very recently, the standard opening in print. Thus, although print has imparted to the biopic general principles of narrative construction, film had its own ways of telling stories. Once upon a time, in film, means once upon a carefully selected moment.[6]

If flashbacks economically situate a tale, frame it with a particular set of references, montage moves it forward or back so the essence, the unique angle, of the life on film can be accorded the time it merits. More than 80 percent of films in the sample used montage.[7]

Montage was originally used by the Soviet avant-garde and, later, German directors to impose a director's interpretation of events or to suggest altered states of consciousness, but the avant-garde roots of these devices soon became tamed within the confines of the American cinema. Montage became not a key to the unconscious, but a shorthand of narrative action. Montage thus does not take us into the mind of the great man or woman—this is done largely through set speeches or scenes of public judgment—but instead for a rapid tour through his or her career. Montage is the abbreviated evidence of the success that made the person famous. As such, it is as essential a part of the biopic as other components that differentiate this genre from other films; the opening titles that assure us of the films facticity, the use of flashbacks, the foregrounding of romance, and the resistance heroes encounter in their home environments.

Montages showing the rise to fame of entertainers were almost predictable: rapidly shifting newspaper headlines, theater posters, record labels, or charts that show box-office receipts. One of the more creative montages of the rise-to-fame variety appears in *The Story of Vernon and Irene Castle*. To show both the Castles and their dance style "sweeping the nation," we see the Castles dance across a map of the United States, as once-empty spaces are filled with little dancing couples, all doing the "Castle Walk." In *Madame Curie, Doctor Ehrlich's Magic Bullet,* and other films about scientists, montages consist of repeated failed experiments, indices of frustration, until the eventual, and dramatic, moment of discovery. Oliver Wendell Holmes's contributions to jurisprudence are summed up, in

The Magnificent Yankee, by a montage of his opinions in famous cases, his "greatest hits" as a member of the Supreme Court. In short, montages supply viewers with "facts," but not slowly enough for us to take them in or to really interpret their significance.

Montage can also characterize the development of a figure's life: Emma Gladney's increasingly wealthy—but hollow—lifestyle in *Blossoms in the Dust* is shown by a montage of anniversary gifts that grow, year by year, in splendor. This marks the passage of time, but it also shows a progression in the focus of her life.

Montage moves the plot forward by presenting an abbreviated version of a narrative event that is important, but too long to be shown in its entirety. Thus, we see Daniel Boone's hardships, in *Daniel Boone;* witness the growth of the five Sullivan boys, as they go through baptism and episodes of childhood, in *The Sullivans* (1944); or observe the impact of a cholera epidemic in *The Barbarian and the Geisha,* all in brief montage sequences.[8]

Historical montages do not only chronicle triumphs, they can also show failures. Montage gives us Lillian Roth's decline—her frequenting of a series of ever seedier drinking spots is a chronicle of her alcoholism and the ruin of her career. Montage also shows us the reversals of the showman of *The Great Ziegfeld,* as, one by one, the theater marquees that were filled with his shows darken, their spent illumination emblematic of his fading power.

Typically, though, the montage asserts the qualities of greatness. In *Edison, The Man,* an extraordinary montage shows the now aged Thomas Edison marching (in place), as the capitals of the world are illuminated with his lightbulbs, overlaid with bold letters proclaiming,

1,150 Patents
creating jobs
industries
wealth

Montage is the most powerful marker of the teleology of fame, of its relentlessly forward march to a predetermined goal. Having established the greatness of an individual, the rapidity of the shots, often edited in dynamic combinations of overlapping dissolves, canted frames, altering scales of images, and the like, reinforce a sense of overwhelming certainty, of irresistible fate. Montage is the (nonlinguistic) stylistic equivalent of the linguistic superlative, a device whose very energy sweeps the viewer along; we rush to follow the cascade of images.

Trials: Making Public What Is Private

While montage is a narrative device that can telescope events in the film biopic, the extreme abbreviation of life's events necessary in a film—compared, say, to a book-length study of a life—dictates that a more powerful condensing device is required. One narrational strategy that is extremely important to the biopic is the trial or trial-like setting.[9] Just as the emphasis accorded entertainers is a comment upon the very production procedures of film, so trials lay bare the specific messages of the biopic, encasing one narrative within another on a parallel level of commentary. The presence of trials suggests the purpose of the biopic is to offer up a lesson or judgment in the form of a movie.

Although the great figure can articulate his or her goals in life—and frequently does—it is often the case that a public trial affords a better stage for the drama of fame than personal interaction. Few biopics can carry off the spectacle of a figure orating his credo. For such speechgiving, unless it comes from a Disraeli or a Voltaire (who are accused of stage-managing their lives), is an infrequent occurrence in day-to-day private life. Since a prime feature of Hollywood narrative was the motivation of a character (and not necessarily credible plotting), narrative is better served by linking message-laden credos to dramatic scenes involving not accord, but conflict; they are played out not with a dyad, but before an entire community. The trial is a specific view of causality, one that reduces history to a kind of evening school psychoanalysis: all motivation is overlaid with a few basic human drives, all art is tied to a charming narrative episode. In trial scenes, the imputation of causality itself is the object of everyone's attention.

The public trial provides several benefits in the script of a life that mere small-scale interaction cannot offer: a clear rooting interest in the roles of defendant and prosecutor. A trial often states the issues in balder terms than they could be in another setting; it creates the drama of clearly opposed sides; it allows heroes to address the community with impassioned pleas for whatever it is they hold dear to their hearts. In short, it is a kind of metastructure of fame, with the famous standing outside community standards, his or her cause being resisted, a dramatic turning point (in which love often figures), and an official and public triumph, vindicating the cause with a finality seldom seen in other real-life contexts. A trial also seals the verdict of history. Even though such scenes (as in *Young Mr. Lincoln, Houdini* [1953], and *The Story of Alexander Graham Bell*) are often fabricated, the subtle mixture of fiction within the threads of fact creates an impression of judgment that has the weight of law and community behind it.[10]

Trials or trial-like scenes of formal adjudication figure in thirty-two films in the purposive sample. For example, in *Stanley and Livingstone* the Society of British Geographers sits in session to judge the maps that prove Henry Stanley's reported finding of Scottish missionary David Livingstone. In addition to tribunals or formal panels, scenes of audience/performer triumph, in which a performer is challenged, often by an "old guard" member (as in *Houdini* or *The Great Caruso*), to win over an audience at a particular show, occur in at least eight of the biopics. There are also a number of instances in which the biopic figure addresses a mob or crowd gathered for purposes opposed by our hero or heroine (*Young Mr. Lincoln, Brigham Young*). The biopic figure is able to alter opinion through rhetoric, or by the rhetoric of performance.

While not formal trials, such set-piece scenes use the public as a metaphoric jury, and, as such, are similar to actual trials, affording the great figure the opportunity to show the mob what is really important. Combining these totals, we find that the trial structure occurs in nearly half (47 percent) of the biopics.[11] Just as Jane Feuer (1982:28) suggests that internal audiences in movie musicals function as a bridge between the audience response depicted in the film, and the audience responding to this depiction in a theater (or watching television), biopics with audience and jury metaphors are simulacra of shared judgment; we too, are won over by the virtue of a cause or the genius of an entertainer. Judgments of applause or jury verdicts are a conduit to our own assessments of the life and the aptness of its filmic version.

A trial is an illustration of just how far from conventional behavior the great figure is. A trial tests whether the hero's ideas can be incorporated into the conventional modes of adjudication that signify the force of the community and the judgment of history. In *Blossoms in the Dust*, Emma Gladney (Greer Garson), speaking words written by Anita Loos, emotionally addresses the Texas legislature for her Birth Certificate Bill which would wipe out records of illegitimacy. A legislator argues with her, noting that such a bill, removing the stigma from the child of an unmarried parent, would "be a direct blow at the sanctity of the home." Further, the passage of this bill would "result in anarchy." Unperturbed by such shortsighted accusations, the great figure proceeds with the good fight, because her knowledge of the world, as shown to the viewer, is derived from gripping personal experience. Conversely, the arguments of the opponents of the great man or woman are often framed as shaped by lack of exposure to the world, or else are depicted as a desperate clinging to outmoded "conventional" ways of thinking. As such, opposition is a kind of straw figure, painted in Gramsci-like strokes of false alternatives. Emma Gladney's campaign for the rights of the illegitimate is fought against an opposition composed of heartless grande dames, cynical politicians, and repressed religious fanatics who would deny children loving homes.

> LAWMAKER: Madame, this is evolving into an argument of what shapes human destiny, heredity or environment. That argument has never been answered yet by the scientists.

> EMMA: Then ask the scientists to come to me, I'll tell them. . . . Believe me, gentlemen, there are no illegitimate babies, there are only illegitimate parents.

Against such opposition, Emma Gladney easily carries the day.

The famous person is spurred on by resistance. In one of the large ironies of the biopic, the great person fights organized social power that is hostile, reactionary, and often abusive of power. This is an odd referent for a sitting social establishment. But its hostility is vitiated by the fact that no matter how entrenched or corrupt the system, the great person, representing the will of the people, triumphs. The system is maleable enough to adjust to the extraordinary vision of one person whose crusade it is to see truth carry the day.

29. Gramsci in Hollywood: Greer Garson as Emma Gladney faces opposition to her Illegitimacy Bill in *Blossoms in the Dust*

The depiction of the construct "social change" in the biopic leaves little room for criticism of the status quo. Even when the point of a film is that the world is a place full of corruption, there will always be biopic panaceas to cure all ills, to right all wrongs. This idea— that all ills can be cured—is precisely the biopic's message. It is naive to suggest that one very conservative social institution (the motion picture industry) would criticize the culture that nurtured and sustained it. In fact, the MPPDA made certain such a situation never evolved. Greatness, in biopic terms, meant uncritical (or safely critical) acceptance of the society that served as the crucible for movie and nonmovie figures alike. One only has to read the MPPDA censorship files at the Library of the Academy of Motion Picture Arts and Sciences to appreciate how jealously the Production Code minions guarded this reactionary definition of great men in history, and how eager to comply, in most cases, studio personnel were.

To suggest, however, that the overt censorship of the MPPDA shaped the biopic's vision of social change would be to isolate a single cause in a process that was otherwise both polyvalent and organic. Biopics were conservative because so many of the public institutions endowed with power shared and sustained a similar view of the world. Criticism of the world, then, was displaced to genres where mythical horror (Frankenstein, King Kong, the zombie) masked everyday ills. Biopics were made in an era in which film culture was interlocked with and helped to define public culture. Film biography—which self-consciously glorified America by sustaining various myths of inclusion—dealt with social change in its own convoluted but safe way. Hollywood could not, and did not, turn biography into something of potential danger, a crusade with a broad social base. Instead, these films safely framed social change by personalizing it, making it into a love story or a case of singular honor.

The body of biopics nicely illustrates Antonio Gramsci's notion of hegemony, in which the warring ideas of resistance and instability characterize the domination of culture. By making the biopic hero or heroine triumph by virtue of "common sense," a particular set of circumstances can be rendered universal. The differences among the very people who sit in the audience (often falsely depicted) are disguised beneath this illusion of common consent upon which film greatness is constructed.

By personalizing evil—often as a corrupt or venal establishment figure, like Dr. Wolfert (Sig Ruman) in *Dr. Ehrlich's Magic Bullet*—the triumph of history is rendered individualistic and the outcome, even after struggle, seems both obvious and predetermined. Thus, Elizabeth Kenny, whose treatment for polio was opposed by the medical establishment, is told that she is wrong, but not because her practice has been shown to be inefficacious. Rather the Australian nurse is wrong because she contradicts authority. Like others before her who fell victim to a similar quandary, Kenny holds up personal experience as her shield. When she is accused, in her new treatment of infantile paralysis, of violating medical norms by the reactionary Dr. Brack, she can only reply, like the Maid of Orleans, that she knows what she sees and hears.

30. A different drum: Sister Elizabeth Kenny (Rosalind Russell) confronts the male, British medical establishment, with ally Dr. McDonnell (Alexander Knox)

> DR. BRACK: I think it's a pretty serious thing . . . to encourage a nurse to contradict the greatest orthopedic authorities in the world.
>
> KENNY: I'm not contradicting anybody. But I cannot deny what I saw with my own eyes.

When she is refused a public hearing by the powerful Brack, she resorts to what today we might call guerilla theater. Appearing at one of Dr. Brack's lectures at the medical school, she confronts him in a dazzling piece of drama. As portrayed by Rosalind Russell, Sister Kenny, who sacrifices marriage and family for her larger goal of tending to the children of the world, strikes just the right balance of assertiveness and humility. Standing atop the lecture amphitheater, framed dramatically so she opposes Brack visually, Kenny, accused by the medical establishment of preaching gibberish, articulates the biopic credo of the person who has personal visions where others merely wear blinders.

KENNY: Dr. Brack, I don't like this any more than you do . . .

BRACK: These are not scientific terms. They're gibberish. You invented them.

KENNY: Yes, for a new concept. New ideas need new words. The words I use describe the things I see.

BRACK: Well, how is it we don't see them?

KENNY: Because you've got a book in front of your eyes. Whole libraries, words. If you're interested in what I mean, you wouldn't quibble about the words I use.

BRACK: Without the strict and careful use of words, there could be no science.

This scene, or a close variation of it, appears in a large number of films, particularly films that venerate novelty in science, art, or even business. Whether the name is Pasteur, Van Gogh, Reuter, Jolson, Gilbreth, or Bell, the impact of such scenes is the same. At stake is not a particular fact, but the honor of the field, the paradigm that gives meaning to the scrambling for public recognition of its participants. The public, after carefully sitting on the sidelines while giants in the field take shots at one another, finally judge the hero as the carrier of the truth.

Vindication, though taking place in a public forum, often begins with a domestic, private indication of faith in the hero. Thus, both Alexander Graham Bell and Paul Ehrlich are saved by wifely interventions, not the forces of law or logic.[12] Sister Kenny's and Emma Gladney's triumphs are popular before they are official. In short, these individuals are shown representing the will of the people married to the sanctity of domestic relations. These "trials" validate the powerful alliance of democracy (the jury system) and romance (marriage) within the notion of community suggested by the system of public entertainment represented by the movies.[13]

Men (and Women) Who Knew Too Much . . . and Men and Women about Whom Too Much Is Known

The triumph of the biopic hero through public trial foregrounds what is ordinarily an unpopular trait: knowing too much. This knowledge and other undesirable aspects of personality can be tempered by the star image of the actor impersonating the great figure. In this way, social outcasts deemed unappealing in real life can be transformed and transcended by their screen representations. The creation of the historically famous is done partly through the pen of the writer, and partly through the impersonation of the actor.

Because star actors are valuable commodities, they must be placed in a setting that sympathetically showcases their "appeal," that is, the qualities that make them popular. In this way, the relationship between the characteristics constructed for, say, George M. Cohan, are an interaction of how Cohan was perceived elsewhere, outside of film, and how James Cagney's own qualities shape this construction. Such a mutual construction is compounded by the question of how much control the star—or any other individual involved in making a biopic—has over his or her own image. In the case of Cagney impersonating Cohan, both the real Cohan and Cagney had a good deal of say about the script. The picturing of Cohan in *Yankee Doodle Dandy* was thus a negotiation between different constructors of star image and text.[14]

George M. Cohan, by many accounts an unbearable tyrant off and on the stage, is rendered merely "cocky," part of the charm of actor Cagney's established screen persona.[15] Similarly, Elizabeth I of England or Mary of Scotland take on the auras of their respective impersonators, Bette Davis and Katharine Hepburn. Both actors were frequently showcased in films that showed them as existing outside the normal bounds of heterosexual desire, to the extent that marriage was not an option in their scripts. Both stars cultivated this image offscreen, though Davis, with her quartet of marriages, was also pictured in conventional domestic settings. Elizabeth and Mary do not end up happily ever after, but instead invite audience identification with sublime suffering that was often associated with their portrayer's roles in film. It is presumed that a "Bette Davis" film or a "Katharine Hepburn" vehicle could have an ending in which the heroine is denied happiness. In fact, one could go further and suggest that it

31. Gender and fame: Henriette Desportes (Bette Davis), in *All This and Heaven Too,* left to her schoolchildren after love has failed

might be expected that any figure portrayed by these actors, historical or not, would likely have such an ending. All of Davis's biopic figures—the two Elizabeths, Empress Carlotta in *Juarez,* and Henriette Desportes in *All This and Heaven Too*—end up bereft of happiness, though Elizabeth has her nation, and Henriette has her class of adoring schoolchildren.[16]

A fuller answer to the questions of how the star persona shapes the life portrayed in the biopic is beyond the scope of this book. Richard Dyer's two books—*Stars* and *Heavenly Bodies*—have superbly laid the groundwork for the study of stars as social phenomena. Here, I will suggest ways that the concept of the star shapes the portrayal of a historic figure. It is useful to recall that Dyer in *Stars* suggested four different categories into which stars, as social types, were presented in media texts. The four categories are useful for segmenting an otherwise difficult array of material surrounding the star as a social entity. Dyer suggests that the "star image is made of media texts that can be grouped together as promotion, publicity, films, and commentaries/criticism" (1979:68). Here, I will focus on promotion, films, and the studio's own perceptions of what a star image was good for.

Availability

In the studio era, often the sheer fact of a star's being under contract shaped the qualities of the life depicted or whether a life could be depicted at all. While it was possible for a particular property to be purchased for and tailored to a star, in the studio era, more often than not, properties were developed with some combination of star/genre formulation in mind. That is, the star, though a key part of the package, was a replaceable commodity. The list of major films (for example, *Madame Curie*) created for one star (originally Greta Garbo), but portrayed unforgettably by another (Greer Garson), is a long one, testifying alike to the powers of both post hoc analyses and the genius of casting. As Thomas Schatz (1988:6) suggests, the machinery of the studio system was created to run smoothly, with or without individual participants.

Stars under contract represented a material investment, a kind of overhead that in order to be deemed valuable had to be consistently used. Assignment to a biopic could be the most routine of casting, almost as if one were making a Monogram Western, but it could also mean a dramatic reach for a performer, as when Clark Gable portrayed Parnell or Doris Day, Ruth Etting. The fact of a star's availability was one consideration used in casting a film or casting about to see what kind of film to develop. The cases of Muni and Arliss, as figures identified with the biopic, have already been discussed. But such considerations were also operative with less exalted personnel.

Biopics of performing artists—and the use of the stars showcased in them—may be the most determined of all cinematic professions. Entertainers represent a kind of ur-life on film. Building their lives on film comprises the moves that make up the plots of almost all biopics: resistance by family, public triumph, and the eventual construction of a new form of popular entertainment. While the opening

32. Revue as history: Mary Martin, playing herself, reprises her star turn "My Heart Belongs to Daddy," increasing the marquee value of *Night and Day*

titles of nonperformer biopics must present the viewer with an angle, a theme that will define, from the outset, the nonperforming life as entertainment, entertainer biopics, *sui generis,* wear the familiar and expected masks of Thalia (comedy) or Melpomene (tragedy) shaped into song or dance. One does not watch ninety minutes of Marie Curie's routines of "performing science" in the same way one does the biopic of Jerome Kern, with the expectation it will be loaded with production numbers. The entertainer biopic frames history as a revue, biopics of those outside the Hollywood orbit as the review of the life.

Zanuck saw *Golden Girl,* for example, the biopic of vaudevillian Lotte Crabtree, as a buildup for his new discovery, Mitzi Gaynor. Made in 1951 (the studio's lowest profit-earning year since 1940 and the start of a generally declining period in box office receipts), at a point in the studio history when reliable genre pictures were no longer bringing in the same returns, *Golden Girl* shows Zanuck constructing the life of Lotte Crabtree through the prism of economic scarcity. The strategy of using contract personnel (as well as previously built sets and musical numbers in the public domain) was particularly important at such a juncture.

In a memo of May 23, 1950, to producer George Jessel, Zanuck suggests how the availability of a certain actor could shape the project:

> If she registers in *My Blue Heaven* . . . we might easily find ourselves with a new star and a fresh face. This is especially useful in a story where an actress is called upon to play an historical character. If an established personality plays such a role, she is never accepted as readily as is a talented newcomer. (USC, Fox Collection, *Golden Girl* file)

Thus, unless one had—or developed—an actor whose association with the biopic was natural, or became naturalized (an Arliss or Muni), the actor could be inserted into the role, with the role undergoing specific modifications. Too powerful a screen persona would limit the roles a figure could play, though some of the most interesting cases of casting against type have occurred when a star's part ruptures the seams of the image previously established. As Zanuck's memo suggests, this limitation or strength of the star persona in historical casting could present producers with a problem, unless, of course, one were willing to argue that the historical persona and the Hollywood star were perfectly congruent constructions, a kind of transmigration of souls over the centuries. This notion of the "perfect fit" between established star and historical personality was a studio publicist's dream.

In his autobiography, *The Ragman's Son* (1988), Kirk Douglas tells how John Wayne (who considered him a fellow action star) warned Douglas against playing such a "weakling" as Van Gogh in *Lust for Life;* this posture was not appropriate for a star with a clearly defined persona, one of the few "male" images left in Hollywood. But, notes Douglas, he was more than a star; he was an actor. He ignored Wayne's advice. Tied to Van Gogh by a startling physiognomical resemblance (and, later, by his ownership of an impressive

33. The Ragman's Son as alienated genius: Kirk Douglas as Vincent Van Gogh in *Lust for Life*

collection of Impressionist and Post-Impressionist art), Douglas reported a curious bond between the Lutheran pastor's son and the ragman's offspring. Coming across the strolling Kirk/Vincent roaming the streets where Van Gogh painted, surviving villagers who knew the real Van Gogh allegedly crossed themselves when the physical apparition of Douglas as Van Gogh passed by. "Il est retourné," muttered the townspeople, so perfect was the match of actor and role. Here a previous star persona, cultivated in a series of "tough guy" roles, was subverted by a natural affinity between two artists, a connection made despite separation by a continent, religious and ethnic heritage, several eras, and a number of tax brackets.

The reverse of this "genetic link" could also be used to confirm the correctness of star casting.[17] Actors with strong personas that were physically remote from the historical figure could "tone down" their star image (that is, they could act), and critics would remark favorably upon this muted star energy as inspired casting. Thus, Frank Sinatra, known for his stylish phrasing of songs, and offscreen for his "Rat Pack" drinking and womanizing, successfully muted the former attributes and brings out the latter in his impersonation of Joe E. Lewis in *The Joker Is Wild*. This was appreciated by the critic of *The Motion Picture Daily* in an August 28, 1957, review of the performance:

> Only the most ardent devotees of Lewis will be able to tell how close Sinatra comes to imitating the special delivery the comedian employs. . . . Anyone in the audience should be able to perceive, however, that Sinatra is giving it a good try—especially in subduing his own unique mannerisms in early scenes in which he sings several songs.[18]

Just as intertextual forces delimited the shape of a life, so too did star considerations reconfigure the historical person. Unlike the model suggested by Kirk Douglas (as Vincent Van Gogh) or Raymond Massey (as Abraham Lincoln), if the actor was not born for the part, the part could be altered to suit the gifts the actor was born with. The Dolly Sisters, brunettes in real life, became Technicolor blondes because June Haver and Betty Grable, their screen impersonators and luminaries in the Fox heaven, were showcased for the very blondness that contradicted the Dollys darker real-life hue. Similarly, diminutive (five foot, six inch), balding Cole Porter was portrayed (as was his wish) by Cary Grant, who at six feet, two inches and forty-two years of age makes an intriguing contrast to the diminutive Yale undergraduate from the Midwest. In such cases of star casting skewing the biographical portrait, we have modification of history through the power of the actor as a commodity.

34. Star casting: Garbo as Queen Christina, and . . .

This modification of star casting is seen in the casting of the romantic lead in *Golden Girl,* in the part of the Confederate agent Mark. Originally written as a kind of serious political character, the part was reconsidered when Zanuck looked around and saw contract player Dan Dailey, a breezy song and dance man, in the part. "Mr. Zanuck would like to use Dan Dailey in this role and therefore it will be readily seen that a complete change must be made in this role,

CHRISTINA GVSTAVI MAGNI FILIA,
SVEDORVM ETC REGINA

35. A contemporary portrait of the Swedish monarch

character-wise" (USC, Doheney Library, *Golden Girl* file, memo, 8/1/50, p. 5). As it happened, Dailey was not cast in the role that went to Dale Robertson; but the casting of either Robertson, a young, nonmusical talent, or Dailey, an established musical performer, would shape the script, the life, and the characterization.[19]

This shaping the life to suit the talent is seen even more clearly in another Fox musical biopic, *Oh, You Beautiful Doll.* The film—the life of composer Fred Fisher—presented Zanuck with a problem. For, unless one had an elderly star, like an Arliss, to carry a film, Zanuck did not believe people went to the movies to see the stories of old people. They went to be entertained by youth and beauty. This he believed to be particularly true in movie musical biopics, where one could showcase young singers involved in romance.

> The real value of this version lies in the fact that it gives us an opportunity to cast a good girl as the daughter and a good leading man as the boy. My whole worry about this story has always been that if the emphasis is on the old man [Fisher] it cannot be a success. People are simply not interested in watching the antics of an old man in a musical when they expect to see youth and beauty. . . . In this version the boy and girl emerge as real leading characters, and thus we can cast them with good people—Mark Stevens and June Haver. (UCLA, Fox Collection, Folder FX-PRS-1146, story conference of September 29, 1948)

The story of one of America's most popular composers ("Chicago," "Oh, You Beautiful Doll") becomes, because of the logic of star casting, the story of his romance-besotted daughter. The father's compositions, the ostensible "hook" for the viewer, become an excuse for the daughter to shine; the father was old, the daughter, June Haver.

Star Value

The ultimate goal of star/genre formulations was the creation of a successful performer, or better yet, a successful pairing of performers, so that one "naturally" associated a Betty Hutton or June Haver with a certain type of film, and one ineluctably joined Jimmy Stewart to June Allyson, Katharine Hepburn to Spencer Tracy, Myrna Loy to William Powell, or Greer Garson to Walter Pidgeon as properly coupled names on a marquee. The pairing of two actors as a team was also a consideration in creating a biopic. The successful chemistry between two MGM contract players, Greer Garson and Walter Pidgeon, apparent in *Blossoms in the Dust,* led to their pairing in *Madame Curie* and four other nonbiopic films. Other attempts at star

36. Star couples: Walter Pidgeon and Greer Garson as the Gladneys in *Blossoms in the Dust*, one of six films they made together

pairing—Mark Stevens and June Haver in two Fox musical bio-pics—proved less durable. By successfully pairing two leading actors, a studio developed an angle for promotion that added the aura of heterosexual love and marriage to a life. Advertisements for *Madame Curie* emphasize many angles, one of them the pairing of a successful acting duo. Thus Marie and Pierre Curie are advertised in

Mr. and Mrs. Miniver . . . . together again!

GREER GARSON

WALTER PIDGEON

give their best performance in their best picture

MADAME CURIE

Directed by MERVYN LeROY Produced by SIDNEY FRANKLIN

Presented by M.G.M.

With a brilliant supporting cast, Henry Travers, Robert Walker, Dame May Whitty, Elsa Basserman, Van Johnson, Albert Basserman, C. Aubrey Smith, Victor Francen, Reginald Owen, Margaret O'Brien · Screen Play by Paul Osborn and Paul H. Rameau. Based on the book, "Madame Curie" by Eve Curie. A METRO-GOLDWYN-MAYER PICTURE

37. Ad for *Madame Curie* with a focus on the star couple Garson and Pidgeon

one poster as, "Mr. and Mrs. Miniver . . . together again! Greer Garson and Walter Pidgeon give their best performance in their best picture."[20]

The determinism of the star/genre formulations, star availability, star offscreen image, star promotion, real and imagined star/historical figure connections, and the negotiations used to create the texts themselves are mutually interactive considerations in bringing a biopic life to the screen.

The fact that the permutations of the star persona have been brought to bear on historical figures has repercussions far larger than the affects of stars on nonbiopic narratives. Since I argue that the shape given to history in these films cultivates the notion of the "great man" who shapes history, these specific images (the great man or woman as star) are carried away from screenings and become part of popular constructions of a real, historically constituted human being. The glamour accorded stars spills over into the specifically determined historical impersonation in a single film—Errol Flynn as George Armstrong Custer—and into the larger arena of real life, where, in the age of infotainment, we expect our leaders to be as worthy of fan worship while carrying the mantle of statehood as Spencer Tracy, Bette Davis, and George Arliss, and to deal with crises as neatly as their film counterparts. As Ronald Reagan shrewdly noted, at first he worried that because he was "only an actor" that he was not prepared for politics. Later, he came to wonder "how you could be President and not be an actor."[21] Were they to run for public office today, patrician, bald John Quincy Adams or three-hundred-pound William Taft—neither figure very telegenic—could never compare, in the public's eye, with a candidate reminiscent of the Lincoln of Raymond Massey, or with any other candidate (e.g., Dan Quayle as Robert Redford) whose construction of self has been nurtured by the cosmetic imagery of the biopic specifically and Hollywood in general.

Family Resemblances

Chapters three and four suggested that many of the biopics are intertextual reconstructions. Within this interlocking network of borrowed plots and derived characterizations, biographies of entertainers occupy a special niche, ur-texts of how Hollywood constructed fame and the life. First, entertainer biopics comprise the largest category of profession represented in the studio era. All told, entertainers and creative artists account for 36 percent of all biopics made between 1927 and 1960. In the last decade of the studio age, 1951 and 1960, entertainers and artists account for 42 percent of all biopics. Additionally, I have earlier advanced the argument that entertainer biopics can be seen as extensions of the lives and the values of their producers, in the sense that they canonize the judgment and the triumph of an individual within a closed community, and valorize a kind of entertainment that was fast fading away under the lights of new electronic media that catered, in many respects, to different conceptions of the mass audience. One of the reasons these films were dear to the hearts of men as disparate as Harry Cohn, Darryl Zanuck, Jack Warner, Hal Wallis, Louis B. Mayer, and co., is that they sell success as the ultimate assimilation—to be worshipped is to be accepted. The triumph of the popular arts, increasingly the sphere of the biopic's focus, is first the triumph of the men that made the movies, and last the vindication of the movies themselves. Although this last fact cannot be "proven," since it is unlikely that such sentiments would be formally put in writing, nevertheless the films themselves display a remarkable quality of similarity in three main points, points that also illustrate the role of the movie industry worker/Hollywood producer in American culture.

Every one of the 104 entertainer biopics contains some variation of three moves: the big break, resistance, and the struggle between innovation and tradition. These three moves explain a key part of the equation of the biopic; together, they give a shape to the universe in which the biographical subject excels. Although each move is not indexically linked to a single issue, it can be said that the big break offers a model of causality, resistance deals with community, and the last move, innovation/tradition, looks at the role of convention in a profession, as well as the social basis of entertainment.

The Big Break

Leo Lowenthal suggested that in making luck, like a big break, the predominant explanation for fame, magazine biographies "seem to demonstrate that there is no longer a social pattern for the way up. Success has become an accidental and irrational event" (1944:127).

Earlier, when non-entertainer biographies dominated magazines, "To a very great extent they are to be looked upon as examples of success which can be imitated. The life stories are really intended to be educational models. They are written—at least ideologically—for someone who the next day may try to emulate the man whom he has just envied" (1944:113).

Of twenty-four entertainer or artist biopics in the purposive sample, over 90 percent feature the biographee demonstrating his or her talent in a big breakthrough scene, or as being the beneficiary of a stroke of fortune. These scenes demonstrate just how unique or talented the heroes are, or else establish the hero's talent or point of view as the dominant point of view. They also show that a single "break" can establish a career. In a similar construction, non-entertainers are shown having their lives inexorably changed, made famous, in a single dramatic episode that illustrates why they have been honored with a film. This occurs in 79 percent of the cases in the purposive sample. Thus, the trope of sudden or dramatic success, found in 82 percent of all films in the purposive sample, presents fame and its recognition as a kind of dramatic performance, one in which the theatricality of sudden revelation is as important as the talent unveiled. Whether one is a performing artist or not, the "star turn" and the notion of "overnight star" became an established part of the biopic repertoire for all professions, a legacy of the entertainment superstructure as an explanation of fame.

In *Jack London,* the hero establishes his reputation as a journalist by scoring a tremendous, unprecedented scoop while covering Japan's invasion of China. The dramatic breakthrough, seemingly an impulse, makes him a "headliner" as a journalist. Sudden recognition comes to preacher Peter Marshall, in *A Man Called Peter,* when, preaching to an unruly crowd, he is able to fill a group of cynical lapsed Christians with revivalist fervor. In *The Five Pennies,* Red Nichols, of Ogden, Utah, persuades a doubtful Louis Armstrong (playing himself) that he really can play jazz with the best of them. Mounting a stage in a Harlem nightclub, his rendition of "The Battle Hymn of the Republic" (played before a largely black audience without a hint of irony) persuades the crowd (and his date) that he is fit to share the stage with Armstrong. In *The Pride of St. Louis,* Dizzy Dean, the "rube" minor leaguer, defeats the Chicago Cubs in an exhibition game, giving a compelling single "performance" from the pitcher's mound, complete with predictions of how the game will go. And Marjorie Lawrence, forced by the sudden death of her father to give up voice lessons, makes, with her teacher's assistance, an unexpected and spectacular debut as Musetta in *La Bohème* at the Monte Carlo Opera. All of these single episodes transform the lives of the biopic heroes, catapulting them from one community to another, revealing them to an audience or an influential group as worthy of attention.

Fate, we see, is an unpredictable author. Previous models of biography encouraged hard work as the way to elect status. In such a world, success and fame had distinct moral dimensions; biographees were examples that could be emulated. With luck as a mentor, rather than family or hard work, emulation is more difficult; the best one can do, since there are apparently no preconditions to fame, is either invent oneself or imitate the style of the famous. Appropriation of the image, then, becomes a substitute for the internalization of the principles that had previously brought fame to those who worked for it. And, as Walter Benjamin noted, there is one thing to be said about style: it can be mass-produced, so that a kind of false egalitarianism, the democratization noted by Erich Auerbach in literature, can be worn by those who are less than equal to those they imitate. The biopic made the style of fame as important as success itself, transforming an emulation of character into a desire for consumable goods.

Innovation and Resistance

By one kind of definition, all entertainers have demonstrated the ability to win over an audience. They have to be able to engineer the big break that is supposed to come by chance. Often, they must vanquish not an actual individual, but instead contend with a different performing style. Tradition in performance is their enemy. Through their skill—and often with a good deal of brazen nerve—they must convince the audience that the second entertainer biopic move, innovation, deserves to become part of a new tradition. Thus, the cycle of innovation controlled by the mechanism of popular acceptance becomes the model in biopics, a model strikingly similar to a box office-dominated industry like the moving picture community. Such a model also congratulates the very audience watching the film on their own prescient good taste. Having judged a historically established great entertainer as worthy of their applause, audiences in film double for the acts of real audience members watching the film.

In chapter four, I remarked that the family is often an early site of resistance for the very career itself. Here, the community of fellow carcerists makes entry difficult, suggesting that entertainment has to be renewed every generation or so to rid the profession of these vengeful dinosaurs who hang on to their turf long after their time has passed. Both Jolson and Cohan must surreptitiously sneak in a number on a vaudeville bill to get a hearing for their new styles of performance; Houdini must interrupt a magician's convention to show his new kind of magic; and, in one of the more unusual roads to fame, Franz Liszt, championing Robert Schumann (but unable to conquer Clara Schumann) convinces an ex-lover of his, a princess, no less, to seduce a conductor into playing his friend Robert's opera. Lon Chaney, after being told he is not leading man material, shows up at a casting call in a preposterous disguise, and, undetected, proves his point about variety in casting by being selected for a part by the very person who had told him he had no future. Once heard, the famous entertainer, the herald of the new, inevitably triumphs. But this first hurdle is the most dramatic; it is talent on demand. When Buster Keaton gets his first job, it is because, despite his atypical appearance, he is able to make a tough casting director laugh on the spot.[22]

It must be added that seldom do films articulate precisely what is new about an entertainer. Caruso is said to represent a more democratic approach to opera, but precisely how this is manifested in his stage performances is left to our imagination. Spurned by the philistines of the Metropolitan Opera because he is "a peasant," he is told by his future wife, Dorothy, to "Sing for [the gallery], Mr. Caruso, and you'll like America." In similarly vague terms, Johannes Brahms, also, like Liszt, madly in love with the Clara Schumann of Katharine Hepburn, can only say of Robert Schumann's music that, "It's different, it's strange, it's a new kind of music," hardly a professional assessment from one composer about the music of another. It is enough to be told that an entertainer is radically different without having to explain—or to demonstrate—why this is so. Having to secure claims of radicalism in a conventional format is a difficult task. The irony of the limitation of the narrative form on claims of radicalism is apparent, though seldom investigated. The best Hollywood can do to convince us of (past) radicalism and innovation is to surround it with hyperbole and verbal avowal.

Non-entertainers, on the other hand, can be framed as radical because they deal not in art, but in the knowledge business. Thus, opposition to them is opposition to progress, and scores of biopic films tell us science is nothing else if it is not progress. Following principles of script construction, this opposition is personalized, so that the opponents of these great men and women are virtual ogres, creatures of Wagnerian darkness who, if they are representative of the establishment of a given profession, represent fields utterly different than those traversed by our heroes and heroines. The science of those who oppose progress is utterly bankrupt and resistant to change, obviously ripe for redefinition. It is as if Gramsci himself wrote some of these scripts, rather than his famous notebooks from prison, so fatuously is the picture of the "opposition" presented. Resistance to such creatures appears to be merely a matter of common sense. And, this being the case, it is often the common people, rather than the experts, who are the first to recognize and appreciate our heroes. The community of experts battled by the biopic heroes are really stalking horses for a kind of aristocracy, complete with "high class" accents and stuffy dress; the hero is the democrat doing what comes naturally. Thus, we are told that "the people" can judge in *Sister Kenny, Yankee Doodle Dandy, The Adventures of Mark Twain,* and a score of other films. Resistance to innovation is framed as resistance to the will of the people, securing a specific vision of a single individual within the matrix of populism.

Often resistance to these men and a few women comes in instrumental, life-and-death ways, increasing the stakes, and upping the ante of the rooting interest. In *A Dispatch from Reuters,* Julius Reuter, whose innovations in message transmission revolutionized the dissemination of information, first proves his pigeon couriers useful in saving the life of a girl who had inadvertently been sent poison medicine via the coach mail. Reuter sends a message via pigeon post that beats the land-based means of transport, saving the life of the patient, and ridding himself of the insulting nickname "the pigeon fool," given to him by envious men of lesser vision. Later, director Dieterle has an Eisensteinian inspiration when Reuter's pigeons are literally killed by colliding with the new medium of information transport, the telegraph wire. Eulogizing his beloved pigeons, Reuter comes up with this viable biopic definition of progress in art and science.

WIFE: Julius, progress can't destroy us, can it?

JULIUS: Of course not. It killed my pigeon post, but at the same time it moves another step toward making the world a little smaller. I believe in progress, just as I believe in a smaller world where men may come closer to each other, get to know each other. That's the ultimate objective of all progress—knowledge and, through knowledge, the truth.

These great people are shown to be radical in their discoveries and their temperament, as if their field of endeavor virtually defines their personality. Thus, Reuter is scolded, as a child, for being too curious; Marjorie Lawrence is told by a strong-willed stage director that her ideas on operatic acting are unconventional; Pasteur is told by a rival physician that "Too many things occur to you, that's your trouble!"; and Ehrlich is told, by the head of his hospital, what many a biopic hero has heard: "Men like you usually have a very difficult time in this world because they do not know how to conform. You must learn, Ehrlich. It's conform or suffer."

Anatole France's eulogy for Emile Zola—that he was "a moment in the conscience of man"—holds true for almost all biopic figures. The biopic famous live for the common people, resist so we can have the one world of Ehrlich, the world without pain of Sister Kenny, Lou Gehrig's brand of baseball, and Pasteur's science in the service of humankind. The biopic great are often so ornery because it is indeed frustrating to try to be so good for so many, and to be constantly rebuffed by individual greed, entrenched power, and pure selfishness. Whatever radical programs they may have held, by the films' end they are contained as revered members of the establishment they tried to overthrow. In this way, the radical calls of these figures are muted by the co-optation into an establishment elastic enough to accommodate their abrasive talent. Ultimately, much of fame is transmuted into accommodation. And, all their avowals in their ghost-written memoirs put aside, accommodation is one thing that the men who made the movies knew about.

Idols of Production

Film biographies represent, in many ways, a kind of last gasp of a pre-electronic world in which a lone figure ran the world, those individuals who, like Max Weber's Protestant elect, stood before God as masters of their fates. In an age where critics heaped jeremiad upon jeremiad upon the "mass society" media helped create, the movies gave a ghostly shape to fierce individuals who forced a community to take them on their own standards, reshaping history so that the mass-manufactured suburbs became, instead, the inspired cities upon the hills. Biopics became pacifiers that assured us that we had not lost our communities, and that the redefinition of the self from producer to consumer still left room for a greatness that had individual contours. In an age when such tales were viewed in the splendor of movie theaters, unsegmented by the banality (and originality) of commercials, such a dream seemed possible. But this view of the great man did not outlive the studio system that created and sustained it.

The shift Lowenthal detected in magazine biographies, from idols of production to idols of consumption, was cemented finally by the rise of a truly consumer-based medium, television. The small screen (and to a lesser extent, the radio networks out of which television grew) gerrymandered entertainment from the hands of the movies.[23] Although movie and radio stars first fared well in the new medium of television, eventually television developed quite a different relationship to its audience than film, and developed stars who were different from their film equivalents. No longer was it necessary to convince moviegoers that the self was constructed in relation to great figures fit to lead us in times of peril. Rather, with a good deal of the country uprooted after World War II, with regional cultures everywhere either in ferment or in decline, with patterns of leisure shifting, and with the very outlets for the movies divested from their parent companies, moviegoing became not a mass pastime, but a fragmented one.

Television was a new form of mass narrative, which sold products along with programs. With this different relationship between the teller, tale, and audience, came a different kind of narrative of fame. The fact that diverse television viewers were at home, receiving programming at different hours, made producers rethink the very nature of the content of the tales wedged between commercials. If a mass audience in the age of the studios had given rise to the conceit of democracy, television gave rise to the reality of demographics. And, as the new medium was tied to corporate sponsorship in ways the movies only dreamed of, the notion of the famous soon shifted from producers to consumers. Lowenthal had been right about this shift; only he had not seen far enough into the future. He had not watched television.

6

■ ■ ■

The Frame Shrinks

"Revenge is the dark side of adulation."
—LEO BRAUDY, QUOTED IN *THE NEW YORK TIMES*,
JUNE 1990

In the 1950s as the Hollywood studio system disintegrated, the biopic passed through a final set of permutations before entering a post-studio era of virtual extinction.[1] As the studio mode of film production drew to a close, television began to penetrate the lives of Americans, seizing the cultural terrain once occupied by film. The kind of narrative of fame constructed by cinema and the studio system that spawned it would soon give way to the new and different symbolic world created by television. From the 1950s onward film would no longer be synonymous with the concept of public culture. Rather television (and a combination of televisionesque print journals) performed the ritual of shaping public history that film had once so powerfully accomplished.

Television rose to its new challenge of defining culture by employing a well-known strategy: as Marshall McLuhan had predicted in *Understanding Media* (1964), the content of the new medium borrowed liberally from the repertoire of the one it had supplanted (film). Early live television biographies—like *Christopher Columbus* (1949)—were still the great man, civics text lessons that had dominated the first decades of the Hollywood studio era. In contrast to these early TV biographies, made-for-TV biopics—first broadcast in 1971—shifted attention away from the elite famous and focused instead on the lives of everyday people to whom unusual things happened.[2]

The world of the television biopic valorized the ordinary. The unique Puritan-inspired city on the hill, projected quite literally as the final vision of much previous cinematic greatness, became, in TV-land, a very different site. The community in which the TV famous dwelled was filled with ordinary people living in undistinguishable suburbs. These towns were illuminated by the glow of the new television sets people purchased in increasing numbers throughout the 1950s.[3] The owners of these new sets defined a novel sort of community, one linked by the common culture of the cathode tube rather than the shared myths that had been enshrined in print media, plays, and films.

The different contexts of reception surrounding television and film altered the rituals by which one received these new video biographical narratives. By changing the ritual surrounding the reception of fame, television changed the public's perception of what constituted history as well. Clio, once remote and formal in her cinematic guise, became, with the intimacy of television, both close and casual. The drawing rooms of the great became the rec rooms of suburbia.

In suggesting that the TV biopic performed a cultural role once the province of print journalism and film—that of publicly defining fame—I am arguing for the continuation of a pattern of culture rather than its disruption. Television is merely the most recent holder of a territory once occupied by film, magazines, and other mass media. But, not content with merely replicating previous media definitions of fame, TV has seen fit to alter them.

Framing Change

The changing TV definitions of fame through biography cannot be accounted for by a single dramatic factor, nor (*pace* McLuhan) are they the result of "inherent" differences between the media of film and television. Rather, the different profiles of fame found in the movies and television are the consequences of a host of factors, and different combinations of factors: the different industry structures of film and TV, the changing face of TV itself as an industry in the 1980s with the advent of cable networks, and the shifting cultural values located in the nonstatic societies that TV or film mediate as worthy of narrating.

Cutting across these factors was the new image of fame created by unpredictable permutations of interactions among the different media, print and electronic. In a process in which culture resembles a moebius strip of reciprocity, popular magazines like *People* and *Us* (that in their graphic look have been so influenced by the visual and narrative conventions of television) have come to shape the very biographical subject matter of the medium that first spawned them. As Douglas Gomery (1987:207) notes of the made-for-TV movie in general, the subject matter of these films "emerged straight from the pages of the daily newspaper, the *National Enquirer, People,* and/or various features in broadcast journalism." Biography on television resembles these tabloids to a similar extent that the films of the studio era were inspired by great plays, portraits, or print biographies of their era. The redefined contours of fame suggested by television reflect an interrelatedness of different aspects of media culture; TV as a signifying system cannot be assessed isolated from other media.

Tabloid Famous

The general trend in TV is away from remote powerful figures and toward the immediately recognizable "common" person to whom something unusual has occurred. Biography thus becomes not the civics text it used to be, but a better-selling commodity, the tabloid or the tabloidlike talk show.[4] Notoriety has, in a sense, replaced noteworthiness as the proper frame for biography; short-lived, soft news has replaced the harder stuff, history. In place of Warners presenting the life of Zola or Pasteur—ennobling, uplifting, serious—tabloid fame comes to figures of a different type. For example, perhaps inspired by the "sex change" operation of Renée Richards depicted in *Second Serve* (1986) in the summer of 1990 on her talk show Joan Rivers presented Erica, an allegedly pregnant transsexual, comforting the distraught mother-to-be ("I'll be there in the delivery room") when an on-air gynecological exam failed to detect a fetal heartbeat that could prove her extraordinary claim.[5] Unlike film, the source material for biography on television is no longer exclusively the past, or even written narratives based on events in the past. The source material is now, to a great extent, the "news" of today, narratives increasingly influenced by the entertainment context of the news and the lurking presence of the tabloid press, which, despite all condemnation by "serious" people, continues to outsell prestige newspapers.[6]

In a situation worthy of Plato's famous cave, the biographical images we see on television have been foreshadowed in the tabloid press, so that seeking to find which mediated reality—print or video—we use to shape our public perception of fame becomes the pursuit not of corporeal beings, but the watching of a shadow play, a ritual in which fame demands that a new set of faces be placed weekly beneath a spotlight. The perennially famous have been supplanted by the momentarily observed. None of the recent TV biopic figures from headlines—Ryan White, Sidney Biddle Barrows (the "Mayflower Madame"), or Jessica McClure—were famous before a single episode reported in the press "catapulted" them to renown. Short-lived fame thus takes the place of previously identified "historical" figures from the past that formed the bulk (more than 90 percent) of the biographical film canon.[7]

The Seasons of Television

If the tabloids provide the subject matter and the tone for TV biography, the year-long ritual of TV watching provides the frame to which many people secure these narratives.[8] The TV schedule segments the year for our culture. Much has been made of the role sporting events play in creating a new sense of "the season"; football in the fall, baseball in the spring and summer, the bowl games nestled about the turn of New Year. But the very concept of season in the United States now refers more to the new fall lineup of TV shows than to a progression of the agricultural life of a community. Biographies play a significant part in this ritual of the sacred and profane, for the appearance of a particular life at a particular time of year acts as a kind of seasonal benchmark. Thus, spring, once signalled by the horological clock, is now marked by *The Pride of the Yankees, The Babe Ruth Story, The Winning Team,* and other biographical and nonbiographical baseball fare; St. Patrick's Day valorizes Irish Americans of achievement in *Yankee Doodle Dandy, My Wild Irish Rose,* or the *The Sullivans.* Previously existing social orders are reaffirmed while new ones (Martin Luther King Day) are created and cemented through media scheduling in the form of biography and other "special" material tailored to commemorate a special day or to inaugurate a time of year.

Nick Browne's notion of one of the cultural functions performed by television—its general structuring of its texts to the prevailing social order—is similar to my notion about biopics. Browne suggests that TV naturalizes the existing social order by correlating TV programming and TV commercials with the actions of key demographic groups. If one accepts this assumption, one arrives at a view of the audience confirmed by a programming strategy that presumes all men "naturally" watch football, and purchase the cars, beer, and redolent aftershave lotion pedaled during televised football games, and that women are home during the day tending to the house and watching soap operas.[9] As Browne notes, "The most relevant context for the analysis of the form and meaning of the 'television text' consists of its relation to the schedule, that is, to the world of television, and second, of the relation of the schedule to the structure and economics of the workweek of the general population" (1984:589).

The idea presented here is a bit narrower in its focus than Browne's formulation. After Browne, I suggest that the pattern formed by a specific genre—the television biopic—affirms old concepts of the social order, and supports—and occasionally reshapes—the contours of the seasons of fame.

The TV season is divided into key ratings periods, called sweeps, that occur in November, February, May, and July. Programs are planned and produced with these key time periods in mind, for the ratings earned during the sweeps periods help set the rates networks charge advertisers for air time. In addition to large temporal markers like the sweeps, two other variables shape television programming decisions: first, programming is created, bought, and sold with regard to the competition of its neighboring texts, the other programs that surround a particular show in a time slot (e.g. lead-ins).[10] Second, like other social texts, the made-for-TV biopic is shaped by the historical events, existing outside of the network's control, that surround all of the world, including television.

Both film and television hope to reach large target audiences in order to generate a profit. But TV's typically short production schedule creates the potential for producers of TV programs to grab an audience with a short-lived topic of the day in a way that filmmakers only rarely can.[11] In several instances, different networks rushed on the air with biopics or docudramas on the same current topic.[12] The presumption on the part of TV producers is that viewers exposed to the same daily headlines will want to see the "true" story of the recently famous only within relatively close proximity to the events that placed them before the public. Thus, late in 1988, a short time after his death from AIDS (in February 1987), viewers could witness within a period of one week in October dueling Liberaces on CBS (*Liberace: Behind the Music*) and ABC (*Liberace*). They could also watch competing versions of the courtship of Prince Charles and Lady Diana Spencer: ABC's *Charles and Diana: A Royal Love Story* aired on September 17, 1982, while CBS came in with *The Royal Romance of Charles and Diana* three days later.[13] In a similar scramble to connect viewer awareness of the news with its TV narratization, Princess Grace's body had barely been laid in the Monacan soil in September 1982 when ABC capitalized on public interest in her fatal automobile accident by broadcasting her biopic, *Grace Kelly*, some six months later on February 21, 1983.

Why this apparent rush to write history with a camera? One possible explanation may lie with people's expectations about television and its role as a mediator of fame. A number of writers (Braudy, 1986; Schickel, 1985; Kubey and Csikszentmihalyi, 1990) have suggested that TV has become a kind of celebrity agenda setter. If one is not mentioned on TV, one is deemed, circularly, simply to be not worthy of mention at all. A story of putative high interest in the news justifies a biographical narratization of it, securing, with this narrative, the official worthiness of a life. TV produces only lives that have already been marked as worthy by their appearance in other media. Like other "reality maintaining" devices of culture, TV, in the words of Kubey and Csikszentmihalyi (1990:100), produces psychic entropy because it depicts that which is familiar. In this sense, television is not the first, but often the last link in a media chain. The TV biopic does not serve the purposes of novelty or information—for surely these are done better by newsprint and weekly magazines. Instead, TV is the preserver of already-told tales, the official muse of a culture which has long since ceased to inscribe permanently its doings through writing. Television is the ultimate version of twentieth-century myth making. The tales it tells are suited to the reading habits of its audience, where reading means looking at an imbalanced ratio of pictures to text that newspapers such as *USA Today* and magazines like *Us* have made the norm.

Celebrities and the Balkanization of the Audience

Several writers—Mark Crispin Miller and Leo Braudy, among them—have suggested that the celebrity is the new figure in our media-dominated society, the pseudo-person to go along with Daniel Boorstin's pseudo-events. Interest in celebrities goes as all the way back to the times of Alexander the Great. But television's obsessive quest for the slightest trivia about public figures—indeed, the very terms it uses to define who constitutes a public figure—makes novelty and recency (both for the already famous and in the recently famous) tactical advantages in the wars for viewer attention. Viewers expect TV to present them with a dramatically engrossing explanation of a life recently in the news. The life need not be meritorious or instructive, as in the film biopic; it only has to be known.

News and its narratization has become one possible choice of "what's on TV." There may always be a parade of Kennedy biopics, but few remember Jonestown, Jim Jones, or Congressman Leo Ryan except as the "stars" of *Guyanan Tragedy: The Story of Jim Jones* (CBS, April 15, 1980), occasionally rerun on a local affiliate or independent station. But, while reducing all events to equal importance—"what's on TV"—television may serve Clio better than critics suggest. Ironically, it may be that through TV narratives—and not through disposable newspapers, magazines, or education—that news, the smaller subset of history, often forgotten and replaced, lives on in the minds of its consumers.[14]

Further biases—other than timeliness and rootedness in the tabloid press—differentiate contemporary television biopics from their film counterparts. Today it is the new structures created by the audiences for cable TV that shape TV content as much as the old formula of "lowest common denominator" that was allegedly the structure of all pre-cable programming. John J. O'Connor, in "The Small Screen Has Its Shining Moments" (1990:H-27), notes that "the new structural configurations of the television industry, especially with the growth of cable, have significantly broadened the medium's content possibilities." Factors of TV production that differed from those of film—lower production values, shorter conventionalized time frames—were once considered drawbacks in attracting viewers. Today, with the balkanization of the audience, these limitations are seen as creative possibilities.[15]

Television's typically smaller budgets enable it to tackle dramas of more intimate scale than film. In TV, the production values do not differentiate one product from another as much as they do in film. Further, TV, once seen as a prisoner of its rigid one-half-, one-, or two-hour programming formats and schedules, now appears to have greater flexibility than film. With the mini-series (currently, I am told, in low repute at the networks) TV has an expanded time frame (as long as twelve hours) in which to extend the range of classical narrative possibilities that were so highly conventionalized by the shorter duration of Hollywood feature films. Freed from the conventional ninety-minute or two-hour narrative time frame that shapes all but "blockbuster" Hollywood films, television can tell the tale of an entire "dynasty," as ABC's 1989 series, *The Kennedys of Massachusetts,* showed. And while these long nights of television seldom are compared to Wagner's *Ring Cycle,* another work revolutionary in its time scale, they nevertheless make possible on a mass scale new forms of storytelling. The 1989 Kennedy family saga, a familiar retelling of stories of the Massachusetts political family, was already the grist for several made-for-TV films, and even more paperback books. Despite the familiarity of the tale and even with its extreme length, it outdrew the first network broadcasts of two blockbuster films, *Indiana Jones and the Temple of Doom* (1984) and *Robocop* (1987). Unlike film (which rarely releases a feature over three hours for a mass audience), television seems, with the proliferation of mini-series, willing to take this chance that epic time slots will lead to equally epic ratings.[16]

A Vernacular of Fame

Perhaps the key distinctive feature separating TV fame from movie fame is the vernacular perspective used to present a famous life. Television's recent emphasis on the lives of typical people—though hardly with ordinary things happening to them—throws the difference between fame on TV and fame in the movies into sharp relief. The nature of the person illuminated by fame differs in the two media. The well-known or already famous comprise 93 percent of all film biopics. In film, to be famous meant to be, prior to the movie, already a figure of veneration who had succeeded in a specific field of endeavor. The famous cinematic figure had already been written about, had his/her portrait painted, has had a postage stamp issued in his or honor. Conversely, TV fame articulates the lives of the ordinary, the everyday famous. These people are figures who, prior to the TV biopic or recent news story, were not public figures. More than 40 percent percent of all made-for-TV biopics are about the lives of people who, prior to a single event, led lives presumed to be ordinary.[17]

This shrinking of the dimensions of fame in biography on TV is echoed by the diminution of the distance between the film viewer and the once distant object of their desire, the famous. As Mark Crispin Miller notes, "The rise of television has created the excessive importance of celebrity today while simultaneously breaking down the connection between them and us. . . . The movie theatre was a cathedral where stars could be worshipped, but the TV in the living room brings them down to size and dispels the attitude that we should be polite to them" (*New York Times,* June 1990).

The very context of experiencing fame in the theater seemed to call for a distance between the subject of biography and the life of the viewer. Along these lines, Leo Braudy noted that, unlike the TV performer who is seen in commercials and on talk shows, the movie actor of the studio era rarely addressed the spectator directly, either by look or verbal interaction in film, though stars made frequent appearances on radio or in print advertisements. This cinematic distance created a kind of "special status" for the performer, and the fan's response "is a compound of envy for the actor's special status and relief to be free of those public pressures, fascinated by the freak and yet reassured of one's seeming normality" (1986:578). The distance between fan and star, very much a part of film, is much less the case in television. In film, such distance framed achievement of figures from the past in the mode of nineteenth-century oil painting, with the subject looking beyond the gaze of the spectator, embedding this image in a narrative of veneration. While films also made the great man or woman "regular" in key emotional issues (love interests, family, etc.), the very notion of biography as greatness is a hallmark of the movies and not television.

This is not to say that, with its smaller budgets and ineluctable link to timeliness that film rarely demonstrates, TV has totally dispensed with the Emersonian "great man" of history in favor of tabloid-inspired heroes and heroines. Rather, the TV redefinition of—perhaps even the TV attack on—fame has been twofold: first, by replacing the distant "great" with the contemporary "average" as a subject for veneration, TV seemingly—though this might not be the best word—democratizes fame, shrinks its contours. Second, by applying new, harder standards of scrutiny to the once sacred lives of the "good" famous (e.g., extramarital lovers for Presidents Eisenhower, Kennedy, and Roosevelt, once taboo revelations about Rock Hudson and Rosemary Clooney), celebrities once constructed as "wholesome" are reconfigured in line with a tabloid point of view. Television redefines the character of the famous, reshapes the mythical moves it takes to get to the top, or get noticed, reformulates, in fact, our very idea of a kind of moral superstructure that should support fame. Feet of clay, more often than not, have replaced marble as the material of choice in the construction of memorials.

Unflattering, or (once) inappropriate coverage of a life is the new price of fame; star images, once controlled by a studio in the same way that star roles were shaped, are now under attack as part of the new celebrityhood. In the hands of certain TV and print journalists, gossip becomes an electronic form of voodoo, lessening the power of its object and increasing the leverage of those who wield it. As Leo Braudy asserted of such "attacks" on the characters of the once sacred famous, "Revenge is the dark side of adulation," and in recent made-for-TV biopics, we are frequently seeing the dark side of celebrityhood.

The Already Famous versus the Everyday Famous

Jessica McClure—the child from Texas whose fall down a well made her a national celebrity—is the TV famous person par excellence; a person whose everyday existence is so ordinary, "like you and me," that her daily ritual is not worthy of a chronicle until one event of an extraordinary nature happens. In TV, the everyday famous occupy specific positions in the constellation of fame; they either are the victims of a particularly heinous, bizarre fate (McClure), or they do one thing that violates the rules for the type of person they are thought to represent.

Television biopics are filled with physically handicapped people who overcome vast odds to excel at sports (*The Terry Fox Story*, HBO, 1981) or to pursue careers normally closed off to them (*To Race the Wind*, CBS, March 12, 1980, on blind Harvard law student Harold Kreuts), or to violate in some other way expectations for the category "handicapped" and thus become interesting.[18] What we are witnessing in the biographies of the everyday famous is a society's definition of what constitutes normal behavior, and how a community deals with its violation. As Erving Goffman suggested generally in *Frame Analysis* (1974), cultural categories such as those found in TV biopics ("retarded," "normal") illuminate the boundaries of ability we are not supposed to cross; conversely, these films can signal the official change of once immutable cultural markers, just as the shift in cinematic fame from the 1940s onward signalled a new valorization of idols of consumption rather than the earlier idols of production. The lives of the everyday famous on TV reshape the agenda of fame to include the once absent subjects who used to sit in the audience.[19]

What is particularly intriguing about the TV conception of "ordinary" fame is that it equates fame with being a victim; subjects of made-for-TV biopics are more likely to be the victim of an illness, accident, drug problem, or crime than to control fate through excellence in some sphere. The data on the distribution of fame by status of the biographee (everyday famous/already famous) and by the whether fame is equated with being a victim suggest that more than twice as many ordinary people (36%) as contrasted with the already famous (16%) have been the victim of fate in a painful form; their battle against—often their overcoming of—this fate is their reason for fame. The already famous battle tragedy much less frequently, suggesting a greater control of their lives. Moreover, while tragedy can "strike" the already famous, it is not the sole defining parameter of their lives. Both Jane Froman (*With a Song in My Heart*) and Lon Chaney (*Man of a Thousand Faces*) were renowned for their talent before illness disrupted their lives. The TV victim, on the other hand, has attained no public recognition prior to the intervention of fate in the form of mental or physical calamity.

Thus, television is unlike film in two very important aspects of its taxonomy of fame. First, it creates a populism of fame: to be famous can also mean to be ordinary. Second, this oxymoron—fame after all has almost always meant to be extraordinary—is played out by a

TABLE 6

BIOPICS BY GENDER AND NETWORK

Subject	Network				Totals
	ABC	NBC	CBS	IND*	
Male	20	24	31	2	77 (52%)
Female	11	17	15	2	45 (31%)
Male/female	4	3	2	0	9 (6%)
Male/male	0	3	2	0	5 (3%)
Female/female	0	0	0	0	0 (0%)
Family/group	4	3	3	1	11 (7%)
Totals	39	50	53	5	147

*IND = non-network programs (syndicated, affiliates, cable, etc.)

neat dialectical homeostasis: the price paid by an ordinary person is that he or she is a victim of a fate outside his or her control far more often than the already famous conventional elite. TV famous, by and large, are the victims of tragedy far more frequently than their film counterparts. In the purposive sample of film biopics, while the famous battle illness, financial reversal, and misfortune in love, not a single figure is defined solely through his or her suffering.[20] TV not only "democratizes" fame; it also makes ordinary people relatively powerless as they don the guise of the famous—they can only attain public recognition through tragedy over which they exert little control.[21]

TV and Gender

At first glance (see Table 6) the distribution of the fame by gender, as depicted in television biopics, suggests that television is a more egalitarian mode of representation than film. In film, 26 percent of all biopics were about women, while 65 percent focused on famous men. Moreover, film biopics about women limited the spheres in which women might excel mainly to arenas or stages in which, as entertainers, royalty, or paramours, they were "legitimately" the object of both male and female public gaze.

While women constitute a slightly higher percentage of the TV biopic population than their film counterparts, there are two codas one must add from these data before concluding that TV is more egalitarian in regard to gender. First, women in TV biopics—famous or everyday—are victims far more often (nearly twice as often) as their male counterparts. Twenty percent of all ordinary men are victims, while 38 percent of all ordinary females are victims. Second, TV's most common denominator places an emphasis on the family or familylike group as narrative a unit (7.5%) in a way that the film biography rarely did. Inevitably, focus on a family is a focus on an ordinary group of people in extraordinary circumstances, fighting for basic rights that are presumed to be the norm for Americans. In film, family biopics are rare (2 Dionnes, the Foys, the Gilbreths, the Sullivans, the Dorseys, the Brontës). Moreover, cinematic families have extraordinary things happen to them: all the sons are killed in war (*The Sullivans*) or all the children are amazingly gifted (*Devotion,* biopic of the Brontës, *The Fabulous Dorseys,* or *The Seven Little Foys*), or the very makeup of the family is biologically so extraordinary that daily living becomes the stuff of wide interest, as in the two Dionne biopics, *Five of a Kind* (1938) and *Reunion* (1936).

Television biopics, on the other hand, enshrine normalcy. The bulk of these family or familylike biopics argue that the family is the rock that supports all else in a society; people will—and implicitly should—do anything to preserve this form. While the encroachment upon the institution of the family is typically the traditional "authorities" (e.g., social service agencies, the courts), it is possible to read the villains in these family valorization tales as stalking horses for threats "too awful" to narrate; thus, gays and lesbians, unmarried female heads of household, and other threats to mainstream definitions of family, though present on TV talk shows and even on religious cable networks, are rarely the threat spelled out. Reaching back to the nineteenth century, TV families are melodramatic units threatened by orphanages and closeminded members of society who, like figures in some ghostly replaying of a Shirley Temple film, can't see past their own definitions of what should constitute this unit. CBS's *The Ordeal of Bill Carney* (December 23, 1981) chronicles the court battle of a quadriplegic for the custody of his children, combining the frames of family and society's definition of physical limitation into one drama. Tellingly, these films are often shown at holidaytime, during what was once called "the family hour," reflexively cementing the togetherness of families watching TV as they look at families on TV staying together.[22]

These family excursions into Bradyland occupy the same moral ground as comparable sitcoms of this period, where the sanctity of the family is preserved through various forms, the most interesting being unconventional: merger in the form of marriage (*The Brady Bunch* and *Eight Is Enough*); single parent homes with bizarre surrogate parents, both male (*My Three Sons, Bachelor Father*) and female (*My Mother the Car*); and unusual adoption situations (*Family Affair, Diff'rent Strokes*). The endless stream of intact nuclear family sitcoms (*Leave It to Beaver, The Donna Reed Show, The Cosby Show*) also proliferated, valorizing some form of the family as an ideal type of social unit.

The apparently higher number of women in TV biopics does not therefore translate into a pro-feminist message. It merely reinforces an image of women as less powerful than men while valorizing a living arrangement—the nuclear family—that more often than not places women in the role of homemaker, monarch of the domestic scene but victim of the world outside this sphere. One could even argue that TV's female famous have taken over the function traditionally assigned to certain films of the studio era designated as "women's pictures," in which suffering was suggested to ennoble its victims.

These TV female victim films—twice as prevelant as male victimization tales—take a variety of guises. Early in the history of TV biopics, ABC broadcast *The Longest Night* (September 12, 1972), the grotesque tale of Karen Chambers, a young woman kidnapped and buried alive in a small box. One could witness the spectacle of woman as victim in NBC's *Death of a Centerfold*, the story of Dorothy Stratton, a Playboy magazine model who was murdered by her husband/manager when she attempted to break free and control her own life and image. It is telling that almost all of the TV biopics dodge the question of sexism, making individuals culpable of murder—as in the twice-told Stratton tale—but refusing to indict the society that nurtures violence toward women, particularly in publications like *Playboy* and modes like TV fiction. While only a few made-for-TV movies featured the actual murder of a female victim, the motif of women ennobled by suffering is a continuation of male dominance fantasies from the studio era. For, in these films, if the woman's body is ravaged by illness, she is typically under the ministrations and dominance of a male physician. The spirit these brave individuals display—both famous like Patricia Neal (*The Patricia*

Neal Story, CBS, December 8, 1981), Babe Zaharias (*Babe,* CBS, October 23, 1975), or Maureen Connolly (*Little Mo,* NBC, September 5, 1978) or unknown (*Walking Through Fire,* CBS, May 15, 1979), the tale of a pregnant woman battling Hodgkin's disease—like many of the female victim biopics, all appear to promote acceptance of one's fate.[23] Although putative victims sometimes emerge triumphant from their dramatic crucibles of pain, the solutions most often affirm the system, and are always mainstream, unquestioning ways of dealing with victimhood. As George Gerbner (1958) noted of confession magazines, in which ordinary women were the victims of the most amazing fates, made-for-TV biopics similarly tie individual motive to the victim, but rarely link the possible causes of misery to a structural problem in society.

These female victim tales are similar to "male weepies" (like *Brian's Song*) for, in the words of Douglas Gomery, they "reaffirm basic values and beliefs" (1987:206) while simultaneously controlling "hot" topical issues—like women's rights—within individual suffering. If these films suggest that the true heroes of life are those who "do their best in the face of adversity" (1987:209), as the Kiplingesque lesson of male suffering in the cinematic form of *The Pride of the Yankees* or *A Man Called Peter* suggested, then triumph is merely a metaphor, and the real issues of the role of women in society (and on TV) can often then go undiscussed.[24]

Professions and Television Fame

The greatest shift from film to TV biography in the professional sphere (as suggested by Table 7) is the virtual elimination of a conventional career, or arena of excellence, for many of the TV films; the subject matter is suffering or victimization, a view of life that reduces a career to cries of pain and not gestures of work. Such a construction of career or life suggests that the travails of the ordinary folk seen on TV provide comfort to those watching at home, witnesses and not participants in tragedy.[25] New subgenres—plane crash survivors, tales of false imprisonments in mental institutions, tales of drug addiction culled from "actual" diaries—attest to the enshrinement of the ordinary subject as victim. As I have said earlier, while less than 8 percent of film lives were "ordinary," almost half of TV biographees are. Given the enormous place—temporally,

TABLE 7

BIOPIC PROFESSIONS BY NETWORK

Profession	Network				
	ABC	NBC	CBS	IND	Total
Entertainer	7	4	6	2	19
Artist	1	1	3	0	5
Government/politics	5	8	5	0	18
Business	0	0	1	0	1
Religious figure	3	5	4	0	12
Military figure	1	4	0	1	6
Athlete	4	4	4	0	12
Outlaw	5	5	5	1	16
Law enforcement	2	0	0	0	2
Medical/scientific	0	1	2	0	3
Royalty	0	0	0	0	0
Explorer/adventurer	1	2	0	0	3
Paramour	0	1	0	0	1
Inventor	0	1	0	0	1
Education	0	2	2	0	4
					103
Misfortune					
Illness/handicap	3	6	15	0	24
Crime	2	3	1	0	6
Accident	1	0	1	0	2
Drugs	1	0	0	0	1
War/politics	0	1	1	1	3
Other	3	2	4	0	9
					45
Total	39	50	54	5	148

culturally, as a form of leisure, as a form of companionship—occupied by TV, it might be more reassuring to have video neighbors who are more like you than the fabled celebrities of the cinema past.

Like the world pictured in film, TV biography is dominated by a self-referential stage where the most common sphere in which a person obtains fame is that of entertainment (13%). Unlike film, where artists account for almost 18 percent of all professions, in TV artists are rare creatures, accounting for less than 4 percent of all figures.

In addition to the absences of the artist (largely male) and the paramour (exclusively female) as spheres of fame found in film, there are two main categories of profession in which the world of TV differs from the world of film.[26]

Film and TV are both populated by gangsters (11% each)—film, particularly in the 1950s. Both film and TV focus on military figures (6.5%), and government or political elite (8.5%). These conventional leaders—or villains—have been augmented, on TV, by religious figures and athletes (8%), who we largely learn about from television. Unlike the cinematic famous, well known for their historic contributions to society, the TV famous are the products of very contemporary intertextual validation through multiple appearances in a variety of tabloid forums.

Patricia Neal (film actress), Rosemary Clooney (singer, actress, and talk show guest), or athletes Ron Le Flore (baseball player) and John Capaletti (football star), are all figures the viewer encounters through the world of TV before they are encountered through the world of TV biography. Mediated already as electronic figures in baseball, football, or on a talk show, these lives are given a more specific frame than "baseball player" or "actress" through the narratization of their story in a TV biopic. The biopic fleshes out the video image of the figure whose performance has been observed by TV, differentiating one small figure in a jersey from another by telling, in the case of Capaletti, the tale of his relationship with his younger brother's illness (*Something for Joey*) rather than chronicling, as in the film biopic, his feats on the gridiron. While football may first place John Capaletti in the arena of fame of TV, it is his unique "human" tale that establishes a narrative context worthy of a biopic. Made-for-TV biopics clothe the body, seen previously in the variety show format, heard on records, or cheered on the playing field, in a variety of costumes rather than just one, connecting the dots between previously encoded performance events with "new" information often gleaned from previous soft-print features.

TV equalizes these entertainers by bringing us up close to their tragedies. While this was occasionally done in film, particularly with courtesans or female entertainers, TV seems to have started a new chapter, a kind of autopsy of the still-living famous that delves deeper into previously private or restricted material. Thus, several years after portraying film star Mae West in ABC's *Mae West* (May

2, 1982), Ann Gillian plays herself in the narrative of her battle with breast cancer. Wholesome singer Rosemary Clooney's tale of alcoholism, first revealed in her written autobiography, is brought to the TV screen with Sondra Locke playing the singer in CBS's *Rosie*. What we have here, in the biopics in which the figures play themselves (as Ann Gillian, Marie Osmond, Sophia Loren, and Theresa Saldanas did), or else are alive at the time of the films' broadcast, are fascinating simulacra of audience proximity to distant stars. By revealing "all," or by permitting all to be revealed, the famous figure benefits several times over from such exposure while still retaining a high degree of control over his or her biographical image. Talk show appearances, both before and after broadcast, complete the simulation of intimacy that these biopics create; inspired by the tale—or at least reminded of the sphere in which the biographee is famous—you buy the album, video, book, or exercise tape. For, unlike their film counterparts, the living subjects of made-for-TV biopics often benefit in a real, financial way from media attention.

Time and Place

Television is even more insular than film in regard to nationality and historic era depicted. Only 6 percent of TV biopics are located outside the United States, while almost one-third of film biopics were. TV, a creature of the twentieth century, narrates the time of its invention: 89 percent of TV biopics are set in the twentieth century, with the majority of them set after World War II; this compares to 60 percent of films set in times other than the recent present. When TV does travel outside the United States, or ventures into a century other than its own, biblical settings account for a significant number of locations (67%) and time frames (37.5%). Thus, the past is rendered male, Christian, and white, an echo of the construction of the present that belies other realities, ignores different interests.[27]

Stretched out comfortably on your couch, tired from a day of work, it is easier to digest the doings of American Elizabeth Montgomery in a suburban kitchen, coping with amnesia, than to deal with Bette Davis ranting about her unfaithful younger lover as she paces about the Tower of London. Television normalizes fame, tames the text, as it were, so that it is safe to invite it into your home. It is unlikely that TV, in the manner of a Dieterle biopic, will lecture

you about some pressing topic. The values represented by the Dieterle cycle are "big public issues" that, Santayana-like, we are urged
to attend to lest we pay the dreadful price almost paid by the figures
in the movie. These values, notes critic David Denby (1990), are out
of synch with the TV population.[28]

In answer to the critics who denounced its impoverished content,
film once selectively strove to be a religious and educational pulpit,
a reformed Chautauqua in an era where mediated discourse had
overshadowed the voice echoing in the covered tent. Today, notes
Denby, "school values have lost their authority, especially among the
young, and have been replaced by media values. Nothing is taken
seriously. Everything is hip; everyone is in the know. We don't even
believe in greatness anymore; it embarrasses us. . . .We are all, in
our minds, guests on a late-night talk show" (1990:35).

Part of the media values Denby rails against in his fond recalling
of the crepescular form, the movie biopic, are found in TV's redefinition of fame as the province of ordinary people. Just as the viewing
context of most television is more mundane than the sacred environment once conjured up by movie houses, the morals of TV biography are on a similar, smaller scale—more comfortable, though
hardly more "hip," than those of the studio era.

Where Adorno once suggested that the authoritarian bent of much
popular culture prepared people to "take their medicine" in real life,
television seems to suggest the opposite. The gentle green glow of
the screen flatteringly bathes the room in a cool light as, turned on,
it is present even when no one is watching, a kind of white noise for
the postwar world. Medicine is taken in discrete doses; television is
not. Part of our nightly interpersonal ritual of engagement of disen-
gagement from interaction, its figures recognized almost as members of our inner circle of friends and near-friends, the parade of
people on TV lives in miniature in our homes, in spaces public and
private. Tragedy happens to others, and the famous don't have it
nearly as good as we thought. It is comforting to be safely at home,
watching these horrible things happen to my neighbors, and not to
me . . . on TV.

APPENDIXES

■ ■ ■

Appendix A
Methodology and Coding Sheet

The Samples

There were 291 biopics produced by the major studios and independent production companies in the period 1927–1960. I gathered the titles by first going through lists of films of the major studios contained in the series published by Crown, *The MGM Story, The Warner Brothers Story,* and so on. In addition to volumes in this series, I used other studio histories, such as *Hail Columbia.* These books contain complete film lists and, significantly, narrative descriptions of all films. It is hard to tell from a mere title, for example, *The Lady with Red Hair,* that a film is a biography. Not every film announces its family membership with "The Story of . . ." in its title. Films from the smaller studios, or from independent production companies, were gleaned by reading film lists, where available (like Richard Hurst's *Republic Studios,* or Ted Okuda's *The Monogram Checklist*), or were constructed through several scannings of Leonard Maltin's *TV Movies and Video Guide* (1991). Lists were double-checked against *The 1961 Film Daily Yearbook of Motion Pictures.* It is likely that a very small number of films was missed in the sample by utilizing this method of search.[1]

Data will be drawn from two kinds of sample. One order will be drawn from the total biopic sample, hereinafter referred to as the complete sample, or the **CS.** Data here will include occupation, nationality, gender, and other demographic characteristics of the films that are available without a close viewing of the particular film. A second sample, one that is a purposive sample (**PS**) of 100 available biopics, will be used to draw conclusions about narrative construction, gender depiction, and other values. The purposive sample was constructed to insure that several variables—gender, profession, studio—present in the **CS** were represented proportionately in the **PS**. This use of a smaller sample was necessary because not all biopics have survived or are readily available on film or tape. Every attempt was made, in the purposive sample, to replicate the shape of key variables, such as profession, gender, releasing studio—suggested by the patterns in the complete sample. Again, I do not claim that this smaller, purposive sample is as good a context of description as a saturation sample would be. However, given the lack of availability of some of the (particularly early) films, I felt this method to be the most apt for my research goals.[2]

The Coding Categories

Each film was coded according to the categories constructed for the content analysis. The categories were initially derived from Leo Lowenthal's work. However, Lowenthal divided the occupational domain into three large categories: political life, business and professional, and entertainment. I have constructed sixteen occupational categories. I felt that there should be finer gradations in certain categories (e.g., entertainers), because artist might mean one thing for a male and quite another for a female. (See Appendix D for a list of professions.) Moreover, while Lowenthal's analysis of the narrative construction of biographies continues, forty-eight years after it was first published, to be prescient, it is more impressionistic than it is systematic. That is, his analysis of, say, the childhood environment of the famous person is done only for a few select figures rather than his whole, rather large, sample of over one thousand biographies.

These categories were pretested using *Lust for Life* and *Young Mr. Lincoln*. (See below for the coding instrument.) Every fifth film from the **PS** (N = 20) was coded by a research assistant who, after receiving the content categories, looked at the films on a VCR. Results will first be presented quantitatively, to see the relative distribution and intensity of characteristics over the entire corpus of films. Later, in-depth analyses of individual works would illustrate specific aspects of the patterns discerned from the entire body of all biopics.

The categories represent the major areas of investigation of the content analysis. Though the coding sheet contains twenty-seven categories, for purposes of analysis, I divided these separate items into three content areas. These three content areas focus on different aspects of the films: formal elements (e.g., title cards, music, montage, credits, etc.), character demographics (age, sex, ethnicity, etc.), and the narrative components (role of parents, friends, reception by members of the field) used in constructing a cinematic life. These categories will attempt to objectify Braudy's observations that fame is made up of four elements: a person, an accomplishment, their immediate publicity, and their reception by posterity (1986:15).

Like Goffman's concept of frame, masterfully presented in *Frame Analysis,* categories like biography, or, even more broadly, fame, are examples of society making certain symbolic forms (and not others) available to render the world understandable. For Goffman, a primary frame "is one that is seen as rendering what would otherwise be a meaningless aspect of the scene into something that is meaningful" (1974:21). What was critical to Goffman's perspective is also a tenet here; frames of reference, like film, as part of the ongoing stream of social interaction, are subject to special vulnerabilities and transformations. To assume a static view of fame or even biography over time and across variables would be to see social processes themselves as static and unchanging. Since such a view is hardly tenable, my content categories are useful to the extent that they form a set of configurations that are reconstructed in a host of arenas, analyzable or cross-tabulated from a variety of perspectives. Data in the purposive sample will be analyzed using the methods of content analysis and through textual analysis of individual works. In the cases of early films that are unrentable as videos or films (such as the 1929 *Disraeli* with George Arliss) screenings were arranged at different archives and museums that contained prints or tapes of the films. TNT network was also an invaluable source of films, screening many early, rarely seen Warners and MGM films.

Coding Sheet

TITLE: YEAR:

STUDIO:

DIRECTOR: PRODUCER:

SCRIPT:

SOURCE MATERIAL:

Running time: _____   at _____(speed)

---

1. Subject:
2. Sex: M _____   F _____   Couple: M/F _____   M/M _____
   F/F _____   Other _____
3. Age at start of film:
   infant _____   5–10 _____   11–18 _____   19–25 _____
   26–34 _____   Other _____
4. Period of time covered in film:
   + birth shown   y/n
   + death shown   y/n
   entire life _____   childhood _____   adult (18 +) _____

middle age ____ (35 +) ____ old age ____ (55 +)

5. Occupation or sphere of fame:

entertainer	military	royalty
artist	athlete	explorer/adv.
govt./pol.	outlaw	courtesan
business	law enforcement	inventor
biblical/rel.	medical/sci.	education
other (specify)		

6. Country of birth:
7. Era depicted:
8. Schooling:

some school ____ college ____ other ____ not shown ____

9. Family:

+ mentioned y/n

+ shown   y/n

both parents living ____ siblings ____ other family ____

10. Attitude of family:

supportive (who) ____ opposed (who) ____ n.a. ____

11. Change in attitude of family:
12. Friends:
13. Rupture in friendships caused by career?

How resolved?

14. Older figure in professions:

y/n

advice given by older figure:

15. Reception by members of field:

supportive ____ hostile ____

16. Change in reception by members of field:
17. Critical incident in which opinion is changed:
18. What is unique about this person's fame?

innovation:

classicism:

19. Tragedy:

physical ____ psychological ____ monetary ____ other ____

20. Marriage:

y/n

divorced ____

widowed/widower ____

21. Does person have children?

    y/n

    relationship to children:

22. Do titles or voice-overs introduce film?

    titles _____   voice-over _____

23. Is there a credit for research?

24. Is the subject, if living, involved in any way?

25. Does music introduce film?

    y/n

26. Social class:

    upper (servants, etc.) _____   middle _____

    lower (poor housing, mentions of poverty, etc.) _____

27. Ethnicity

    specified _____

    alluded to _____

    indeterminate _____

■ ■ ■

Appendix B
Purposive Sample (PS) of Biopics (N = 100)

Abe Lincoln in Illinois (RKO 1940)

Abraham Lincoln (UA 1930)

Actress, The (MGM 1953)

Adventures of Marco Polo, The (UA 1938)

Adventures of Mark Twain, The (Warners 1944)

Alexander Hamilton (Warners 1931)

All This and Heaven Too (Warners 1940)

Anna and the King of Siam (TCF 1946)

Annie Oakley (RKO 1935)

Babe Ruth Story, The (Allied Artist 1948)

Barbarian and the Geisha, The (TCF 1958)

Beau Brummel (MGM 1954)

Beau James (Par 1957)

Belle Starr (TCF 1941)

Bob Mathias Story, The (Allied Artists 1954)

Bonnie Parker Story, The (American International 1958)

Boys Town (MGM 1938)

Buccaneer, The (Par 1938)

Buffalo Bill (TCF 1944)

Buster Keaton Story, The (Par 1957)

Carbine Williams (MGM 1952)

Cheaper by the Dozen (TCF 1950)

Daniel Boone (RKO 1936)

Desert Fox, The (TCF 1951)

Devotion (Warners 1946)

Diamond Jim (Universal 1935)

Dispatch from Reuters, A (Warners 1940)

Disraeli (Warners 1929)

Dr. Ehrlich's Magic Bullet (Warners 1940)

Dolly Sisters, The (TCF 1945)

Eddy Duchin Story, The (Columbia 1956)

Edison, The Man (MGM 1940)

Fabulous Dorseys, The (UA 1947)

Fear Strikes Out (Par 1957)

Five Pennies, The (Par 1959)

Flying Irishman, The (RKO 1939)

Girl in the Red Velvet Swing, The (TCF 1955)

Girl in White, The (MGM 1952)

Great Caruso, The (MGM 1951)

Houdini (Par 1953)

I'll Cry Tomorrow (MGM 1955)

Interrupted Melody (MGM 1955)

I Want to Live! (UA 1958)

I Wonder Who's Kissing Her Now
(TCF 1947)
Jack London (UA 1943)
Jesse James (TCF 1939)
Joker Is Wild, The (Par 1957)
Jolson Sings Again (Columbia 1949)
Juarez (Warners 1939)
Lady With Red Hair, The (Warners
1940)
Left-Handed Gun, The (Warners 1958)
Life of Emile Zola, The (Warners
1937)
Love Me or Leave Me (MGM 1955)
Lust for Life (MGM 1956)
Madame Curie (MGM 1943)
Madame Du Barry (Warners 1934)
Magnificent Yankee, The (MGM 1950)
Man Called Peter, A (TCF 1955)
Man of a Thousand Faces (Par 1957)
Marie Antoinette (MGM 1938)
Mary of Scotland (RKO 1936)
Mighty Barnum, The (TCF 1934)
Million Dollar Mermaid (MGM 1952)
Mission to Moscow (Warners 1943)
My Wild Irish Rose (Warners 1947)
Oh, You Beautiful Doll (TCF 1949)
Parnell (MGM 1937)
Perils of Pauline, The (Par 1947)
Pride of St. Louis, The (TCF 1952)
Pride of the Marines (Warners 1945)
Pride of the Yankees, The (RKO 1942)
Queen Christina (MGM 1933)
Roughly Speaking (Warners 1945)
St. Louis Blues (Par 1958)

Sergeant York (Warners 1941)
Shine On, Harvest Moon (Warners
1944)
Sister Kenny (RKO 1946)
Somebody Up There Likes Me (MGM
1956)
Song of Love (MGM 1947)
Song to Remember, A (Columbia 1945)
Spirit of St. Louis, The (Warners 1957)
Story of Alexander Graham Bell, The
(TCF 1939)
Story of Louis Pasteur, The (Warners,
1936)
Story of Seabiscuit, The (Warners
1949)
Story of Vernon and Irene Castle, The
(RKO 1939)
Stanley and Livingstone (TCF 1939)
Stratton Story, The (MGM 1949)
Till the Clouds Roll By (MGM 1946)
Toast of New York, The (RKO 1937)
To Hell and Back (Universal 1955)
Virgin Queen, The (TCF 1955)
Voltaire (Warners 1933)
Walk the Proud Land (Universal 1956)
Winning Team, The (Warners 1952)
With a Song in My Heart (TCF 1952)
Yankee Doodle Dandy (Warners 1943)
Young Bess (MGM 1952)
Young Mr. Lincoln (TCF 1939)
Young Tom Edison (MGM 1940)

Appendix C
Biopics by Studio (N = 291)

Columbia (14)

The Eddy Duchin Story (1956)
The Gene Krupa Story (1959)
Harmon of Michigan (1941)
Is Everybody Happy? (1943)
Jeanne Eagels (1957)
Jolson Sings Again (1949)
The Jolson Story (1946)
The Law and Billy the Kid (1954)
Masterson of Kansas (1954)
The Return of Daniel Boone (1941)
A Song to Remember (1945)
Song Without End (1960)
The True Story of Lynn Stuart (1958)
Valentino (1951)

MGM (47)

The Actress (1953)
Annie Get Your Gun (1950)
The Barretts of Wimpole Street (1934)
The Barretts of Wimpole Street (1957)
Beau Brummell (1954)
Billy the Kid (1930)
Billy the Kid (1941)
Blossoms in the Dust (1941)
Boys Town (1938)
Carbine Williams (1952)
Conquest (1937)
Deep in My Heart (1954)
Diane (1956)
Edison, The Man (1940)
The Girl in White (1952)
The Gorgeous Hussy (1936)
The Great Caruso (1951)
The Great Waltz (1938)
The Great Ziegfeld (1936)
I Accuse! (1958)
I'll Cry Tomorrow (1955)
Interrupted Melody (1955)
A Lady's Morals (1930)
Love Me or Leave Me (1955)
Lust for Life (1956)
Madame Curie (1943)
The Magnificent Yankee (1950)
Marie Antoinette (1938)
Mata Hari (1932)
Million Dollar Mermaid (1952)
Parnell (1937)
Queen Christina (1933)

Rasputin and the Empress (1932)
Somebody Up There Likes Me (1956)
Song of Love (1947)
The Stratton Story (1949)
Tennessee Johnson (1942)
Three Little Words (1950)
Till the Clouds Roll By (1946)
The Vanishing Virginian (1942)
The Viking (1928)
Viva Villa! (1934)
The Wings of Eagles (1957)
Words and Music (1948)
You Can't Buy Everything (1934)
Young Bess (1952)
Young Tom Edison (1940)

Paramount (31)

Beau James (1957)
The Buccaneer (1938)
The Buccaneer (1958)
The Buster Keaton Story (1957)
Cleopatra (1934)
Dixie (1943)
Fear Strikes Out (1957)
The Five Pennies (1959)
Geronimo (1939)
The Great Moment (1944)
The Great Victor Herbert (1939)
Houdini (1953)
If I Were King (1938)
Incendiary Blonde (1945)
Jesse James (1927)
The Joker Is Wild (1957)
Kit Carson (1928)
Madame Pompadour (1927)
Omar Khayyam (1957)
Our Hearts Were Growing Up (1946)
Our Hearts Were Young and Gay
    (1944)
The Perils of Pauline (1947)
Queen of the Mob (1940)
St. Louis Blues (1958)
The Scarlet Empress (1934)

The Seven Little Foys (1955)
Somebody Loves Me (1952)
The Star Maker (1939)
The Story of Dr. Wassell (1944)
The Ten Commandments (1956)
The Vagabond King (1956)

RKO (14)

Abe Lincoln in Illinois (1940)
Annie Oakley (1935)
Daniel Boone (1936)
The Flying Irishman (1939)
Hans Christian Andersen (1952)
The Iron Major (1943)
Mary of Scotland (1936)
Nurse Edith Cavell (1939)
The Pride of the Yankees (1942)
Queen of Destiny (1938)
Sister Kenny (1946)
The Story of Vernon and Irene Castle
    (1939)
The Toast of New York (1937)
Victoria the Great (1937)

Twentieth Century-Fox/
Twentieth Century (63)

Affairs of Cellini (1934) (distributed
    through UA)
Anastasia (1956)
Anna and the King of Siam (1946)
The Barbarian and the Geisha (1958)
Belle Starr (1941)
Belles on Their Toes (1952)
Beloved Infidel (1959)
The Best Things in Life Are Free
    (1956)
Brigham Young—Frontiersman (1940)
Buffalo Bill (1944)
Captain Eddie (1945)
Cardinal Richelieu (1935) (distributed
    through UA)

Cheaper by the Dozen (1950)
Clive of India (1935) (distributed
   through UA)
The Country Doctor (1936)
The Desert Fox (1951)
Desiree (1954)
The Diary of Anne Frank (1959)
The Dolly Sisters (1945)
Five Fingers (1952)
Five of a Kind (1938)
Follow the Sun (1951)
Frontier Marshal (1939)
The Girl in the Red Velvet Swing
   (1955)
Golden Girl (1951)
The House of Rothschild (1934)
   (distributed through UA)
The I Don't Care Girl (1953)
Irish Eyes Are Smiling (1944)
I Wonder Who's Kissing Her Now
   (1947)
Jesse James (1939)
The King and I (1956)
Lillian Russell (1940)
Little Old New York (1940)
The Loves of Edgar Allen Poe (1942)
A Man Called Peter (1955)
The Mighty Barnum (1934)
My Gal Sal (1942)
Oh, You Beautiful Doll (1949)
The President's Lady (1953)
The Pride of St. Louis (1952)
Prince of Players (1955)
The Prisoner of Shark Island (1936)
The Return of Frank James (1940)
Reunion (1936)
Roger Touhy, Gangster (1944)
A Royal Scandal (1945)
The Song of Bernadette (1943)
Stanley and Livingstone (1939)
Stars and Stripes Forever (1952)
The Story of Alexander Graham Bell
   (1939)
Suez (1938)
The Sullivans (1944)

Swanee River (1939)
The Three Faces of Eve (1957)
Tonight We Sing (1953)
The True Story of Jesse James (1957)
Villa! (1958)
The Virgin Queen (1955)
Viva Zapata! (1952)
Wilson (1944)
With a Song in My Heart (1952)
Young Jesse James (1960)
Young Mr. Lincoln (1939)

United Artists (30)

Abraham Lincoln (1930)
The Adventures of Marco Polo (1938)
Alexander the Great (1956)
Baby Face Nelson (1957)
The Beloved Rogue (1927)
Black Magic (1949)
Captain Kidd (1945)
Catherine the Great (1934)
Davy Crockett, Indian Scout (1950)
Davy Crockett, King of the Wild
   Frontier (1955)
Du Barry, Woman of Passion (1930)
The Fabulous Dorseys (1947)
The Gallant Hours (1960)
The Great Awakening (1941)
The Great Dan Patch (1949)
The Great John L. (1945)
I Want to Live! (1958)
Jack London (1943)
The Joe Louis Story (1953)
Kit Carson (1940)
Moulin Rouge (1952)
The Naked Maja (1959)
Nell Gwyn (1935)
Park Row (1952)
Saint Joan (1957)
A Scandal in Paris (1946)
Sitting Bull (1954)
The Story of G.I. Joe (1945)

That Hamilton Woman (1941)
When the Daltons Rode (1940)

Universal (17)

The Benny Goodman Story (1955)
Chief Crazy Horse (1955)
The Daltons Ride Again (1946)
Damn Citizen (1958)
Diamond Jim (1935)
The Glenn Miller Story (1954)
The Great Imposter (1960)
The Lady from Cheyenne (1941)
Lady Godiva (1955)
The Lawless Breed (1952)
Little Egypt (1951)
Man of a Thousand Faces (1957)
So Goes My Love (1946)
Song of Scheherazade (1947)
Sutter's Gold (1936)
To Hell and Back (1955)
Walk the Proud Land (1956)

Warner Brothers (61)

The Adventures of Mark Twain (1944)
Al Capone (1959)
Alexander Hamilton (1931)
All This and Heaven Too (1940)
Calamity Jane (1953)
The Court-Martial of Billy Mitchell (1955)
The Daughter of Rosie O'Grady (1950)
Devotion (1946)
A Dispatch from Reuters (1940)
Disraeli (1929)
The Divine Lady (1929)
Dr. Ehrlich's Magic Bullet (1940)
Duffy of San Quentin (1954)
Gentleman Jim (1942)
Glorious Betsy (1928)
God Is My Co-Pilot (1945)
The Great Garrick (1937)

The Great Jewel Robber (1950)
Hannibal (1960)
The Helen Morgan Story (1957)
Helen of Troy (1955)
I Am a Fugitive from a Chain Gang (1932)
I'll See You in My Dreams (1951)
The Iron Mistress (1952)
I Was a Communist for the FBI (1951)
Jim Thorpe—All American (1951)
John Paul Jones (1959)
Juarez (1939)
Knute Rockne, All American (1940)
The Lady With Red Hair (1940)
The Left-Handed Gun (1958)
The Life of Emile Zola (1937)
Look for the Silver Lining (1949)
The McConnell Story (1955)
The Mad Empress (1939)
Madame Du Barry (1934)
Mission to Moscow (1943)
My Wild Irish Rose (1947)
Night and Day (1946)
One Foot in Heaven (1941)
Pride of the Marines (1945)
The Prime Minister (1941)
The Private Lives of Elizabeth and Essex (1939)
Rhapsody in Blue (1945)
The Rise and Fall of Legs Diamond (1960)
Roughly Speaking (1945)
The Royal Box (1929)
Sergeant York (1941)
Shine On, Harvest Moon (1944)
So This Is Love (1953)
The Spirit of St. Louis (1957)
The Story of Louis Pasteur (1936)
The Story of Seabiscuit (1949)
The Story of Will Rogers (1952)
Sunrise at Campobello (1960)
Too Much, Too Soon (1958)
Voltaire (1933)
The White Angel (1936)
The Winning Team (1952)

Yankee Doodle Dandy (1943)
Young Man With a Horn (1950)

Allied Artists (4)

The Babe Ruth Story (1948)
The Bob Mathias Story (1954)
Seven Angry Men (1955)
Song of My Heart (1948)

American International (1)

The Bonnie Parker Story (1958)

Monogram (2)

Dillinger (1945)
Young Daniel Boone (1950)

Republic (2)

Daniel Boone, Trail Blazer (1956)
I Dream of Jeannie (1952)

Miscellaneous (5)

I Shot Jesse James (1949) Screen Guild
Prod.
The Jackie Robinson Story (1950) Eagle
Lion Prod.
Keep Punching (1937)
Pretty Boy Floyd (1960) Continental
Distributing
The Return of Jesse James (1950)
Lippert Prod.

■ ■ ■

Appendix D
Biopics by Profession

TABLE D.1
BIOPICS BY PROFESSION, 1927–1960

Profession	1927–1930	1931–1940	1941–1950	1951–1960
Artist	*The Beloved Rogue*	*Affairs of Cellini* *The Barretts of Wimpole Street* *The Great Victor Herbert* *The Great Waltz* *If I Were King* *The Life of Emile Zola* *Swanee River* *Voltaire*	*The Adventures of Mark Twain* *Devotion* *Dixie* *The Great Awakening* *Irish Eyes Are Smiling* *Jack London* *The Loves of Edgar Allen Poe* *My Gal Sal* *My Wild Irish Rose* *Night and Day* *Oh, You Beautiful Doll* *Our Hearts Were Young and Gay* *Our Hearts Were Growing Up* *Rhapsody in Blue* *Song of Love* *Song of My Heart* *Song of Scheherazade* *A Song to Remember*	*The Barretts of Wimpole Street* *Beloved Infidel* *The Best Things in Life Are Free* *Deep in My Heart* *Hans Christian Andersen* *I Dream of Jeannie* *I'll See You in My Dreams* *Lust for Life* *Moulin Rouge* *The Naked Maja* *Omar Khayyam* *Park Row* *St. Louis Blues* *Song Without End* *Stars and Stripes Forever* *The Vagabond King*

The Story of G.I. Joe
Three Little Words
Till the Clouds Roll By
The Vanishing Virginian
Words and Music
Yankee Doodle Dandy

Entertainer

A Lady's Morals
The Royal Box

Annie Oakley
The Great Garrick
The Great Ziegfeld
The Lady with Red Hair
Lillian Russell
The Mighty Barnum
The Star Maker
The Story of Vernon and Irene Castle

Annie Get Your Gun
Black Magic
Buffalo Bill
The Daughter of Rosie O'Grady
The Dolly Sisters
The Fabulous Dorseys
Incendiary Blonde
Is Everybody Happy?
I Wonder Who's Kissing Her Now
Jolson Sings Again
The Jolson Story
Look for the Silver Lining
The Perils of Pauline
Shine On, Harvest Moon

The Actress
The Benny Goodman Story
The Buster Keaton Story
The Eddie Cantor Story
The Eddy Duchin Story
The Five Pennies
The Gene Krupa Story
The Glenn Miller Story
Golden Girl
The Great Caruso
The Helen Morgan Story
Houdini
The I Don't Care Girl
I'll Cry Tomorrow
Interrupted Melody
Jeanne Eagles
The Joker Is Wild
Little Egypt
Love Me or Leave Me
Man of a Thousand Faces
Million Dollar Mermaid

TABLE D.1
BIOPICS BY PROFESSION, 1927–1960 (continued)

Profession	1927–1930	1931–1940	1941–1950	1951–1960
				Prince of Players
				The Seven Little Foys
				So This Is Love
				Somebody Loves Me
				The Story of Will Rogers
				Tonight We Sing
				Too Much, Too Soon
				Valentino
				With a Song in My Heart
				Young Man with a Horn
Government/politics	*Abraham Lincoln*	*Abe Lincoln in Illinois*	*The Magnificent Yankee*	*The Barbarian and the*
	Disraeli	*Alexander Hamilton*	*Mission to Moscow*	*Geisha*
		Cardinal Richelieu	*The Prime Minister*	*Beau James*
		Clive of India	*Tennessee Johnson*	*Damn Citizen*
		Juarez	*Wilson*	*I Accuse!*
		Parnell		*I Was a Communist for*
		Suez		*the FBI*
		Young Mr. Lincoln		*Lady Godiva*
				Seven Angry Men
				Sunrise at Campobello
				Viva Zapata!
				Walk the Proud Land

Outlaw				
Billy the Kid	I Am a Fugitive from a Chain Gang	Belle Starr	Al Capone	
Jesse James	Jesse James	Billy the Kid	Baby Face Nelson	
	The Prisoner of Shark Island	Captain Kidd	The Bonnie Parker Story	
	Queen of the Mob	The Daltons Ride Again	The Great Imposter	
	The Return of Frank James	Dillinger	I Want to Live!	
	Viva Villa!	The Great Jewel Robber	The Law and Billy the Kid	
	When the Daltons Rode	I Shot Jesse James	The Lawless Breed	
		The Return of Jesse James	The Left-Handed Gun	
		Roger Touhy, Gangster	Pretty Boy Floyd	
		A Scandal in Paris	The Rise and Fall of Legs Diamond	
			The True Story of Jesse James	
			Villa!	
			Young Jesse James	

Athlete			
Keep Punching	The Babe Ruth Story	The Bob Mathias Story	
Knute Rockne, All American	Gentleman Jim	Fear Strikes Out	
	The Great Dan Patch	Follow the Sun	
	The Great John L.	Jim Thorpe—All American	
	Harmon of Michigan	The Joe Louis Story	
	The Jackie Robinson Story	The Pride of St. Louis	
	The Pride of the Yankees	Somebody Up There Likes Me	
	The Story of Seabiscuit	The Winning Team	
	The Stratton Story		

TABLE D.1
BIOPICS BY PROFESSION, 1927–1960 (continued)

Profession	1927–1930	1931–1940	1941–1950	1951–1960
Military figure		Geronimo	Captain Eddie God Is My Co-Pilot The Iron Major Pride of the Marines Sergeant York The Sullivans	Alexander the Great Chief Crazy Horse The Court-Martial of Billy Mitchell The Desert Fox Five Fingers The Gallant Hours Hannibal John Paul Jones The McConnell Story Sitting Bull To Hell and Back The Wings of Eagles
Explorer/adventurer	Kit Carson The Viking	The Adventures of Marco Polo The Buccaneer Daniel Boone Kit Carson Stanley and Livingstone Suter's Gold	Davy Crockett, Indian Scout The Return of Daniel Boone Young Daniel Boone	The Buccaneer Calamity Jane Daniel Boone, Trail Blazer Davy Crockett, King of the Wild Frontier The Iron Mistress The Spirit of St. Louis

Royalty	Glorious Betsy	Catherine the Great Cleopatra The Mad Empress Marie Antoinette Mary of Scotland The Private Lives of Elizabeth and Essex Queen Christina Queen of Destiny Rasputin and the Empress The Scarlet Empress Victoria the Great	A Royal Scandal	Anastasia The Virgin Queen Young Bess
Paramour	The Divine Lady Du Barry, Woman of Passion Madame Pompadour	Conquest The Gorgeous Hussy Madame Du Barry Mata Hari Nell Gwyn	That Hamilton Woman	Desiree Diane The Girl in the Red Velvet Swing Helen of Troy The President's Lady
Medical/scientific		The Country Doctor Dr. Ehrlich's Magic Bullet Nurse Edith Cavell The Story of Louis Pasteur The White Angel	The Great Moment Madame Curie Sister Kenny The Story of Dr. Wassell	The Girl in White The Three Faces of Eve

TABLE D.1
BIOPICS BY PROFESSION, 1927–1960 (continued)

Profession	1927–1930	1931–1940	1941–1950	1951–1960
Inventor		A Dispatch from Reuters Edison, The Man Little Old New York The Story of Alexander Graham Bell Young Tom Edison	So Goes My Love	Carbine Williams
Religious figure		Boys Town Brigham Young— Frontiersman	One Foot in Heaven The Song of Bernadette	A Man Called Peter Saint Joan The Ten Commandments

Law enforcement	Duffy of San Quentin Masterson of Kansas The True Story of Lynn Stuart		Frontier Marshal
Business		Cheaper by the Dozen	Diamond Jim The House of Rothschild The Toast of New York You Can't Buy Everything
Education	Belles on Their Toes The King and I	Anna and the King of Siam Biossoms in the Dust	All This and Heaven Too
Other	Beau Brummell The Diary of Anne Frank	The Lady from Cheyenne Roughly Speaking	Five of a Kind The Flying Irishman Reunion

TABLE D.2:
BIOPIC PROFESSIONS BY STUDIO

Profession	TCF	WARNERS	MGM	PAR	UA	Releasing Studio UNIVERSAL	RKO	COLUMBIA	OTHER	TOTAL
Artist	9	9	10	8	7	1	1	2	2	49
Entertainer	11	11	9	9	2	4	2	7	0	55
Outlaw	8	5	3	2	5	3	0	1	5	32
Military figure	3	8	1	1	3	2	1	0	0	19
Government/ politics	7	7	4	1	1	3	1	0	1	24
Athlete	2	5	2	1	3	0	1	1	4	19
Royalty	3	3	4	2	1	0	3	0	0	16
Explorer/adventurer	1	2	1	3	4	1	1	1	2	16
Paramour	3	2	4	1	3	0	0	0	0	13
Medical/scientific	2	3	2	2	0	0	2	0	0	11
Inventor	2	1	3	0	0	1	0	0	0	7
Religious figure	3	1	1	1	1	0	0	0	0	7
Law enforcement	1	2	0	0	0	0	0	2	0	5
Education	3	1	1	0	0	0	0	0	0	5
Business	2	0	1	0	0	1	0	0	0	5
Other	3	1	1	0	0	1	1	0	0	7
Total	63	61	47	31	30	17	14	14	14	291

TABLE D.3:
FEMALE BIOPIC PROFESSIONS

Profession	No. of Cases	% of this Biopic Occupation	% of Female Biopics
Entertainer	26	46.4	29.0
Paramour	16	100.0	17.9
Royalty	15	94.0	16.8
Artist	7	14.2	7.8
Medical/scientific	6	54.0	6.7
Education	5	100.0	5.6
Outlaw	4	12.5	4.5
Religious figure	2	28.5	2.2
Business	1	20.0	1.1
Government/ politics	1	4.0	1.1
Explorer/ adventurer	1	6.3	1.1
Law enforcement	1	20.0	1.1
Other	4	57.0	8.6
Total	89*		100.0

*The number of female biopics includes females who were part of a married couple (The Story of Vernon and Irene Castle), or part of a family (The Dolly Sisters) or Devotion [Brontës]). There were 75 "solo" female biopics.

■ ■ ■

NOTES

Introduction: Clio in Hollywood

1. Katharine Hepburn, herself a star of two biopics, in response to the question of how accurate the actors themselves thought the films were, suggested "I think your common sense really tells you the truth about the amount of research— and if it has been inadequate your visual sense and your hearing find it absurd and careless" (personal communication, October 13, 1989). Yet, a common sense itself shaped by the very forces of cultural construction that are hardly disinterested is not the natural lens it appears to be.

2. A saturation sample of all biopics would consist of 291 films. About half of these films are available on videotape. Appendixes B, C, and D contain lists of all the films cross-indexed by profession and era of production, and by studio.

3. The *Film/Literature Index* has a lengthy section under "biography," but this subject heading refers to print narratives about the people who make movies, and not the movies themselves. Although there are sixteen articles on individual biopics cited in *The New Film Index,* the actual films themselves, compared to other genres, have been largely ignored.

There have been works that deal in part with the biopic. Nick Roddick's *A New Deal in Entertainment: Warner Brothers in the 1930s* (1983) has two chapters that deal with foreign biopics and the studio's representation of American history. Robert Miller's *Star Myths: Show Business Biographies on Film* (1983) looks at popular entertainers and in the coffee table mold, George Fraser's *A Hollywood History of the World: From One Million B.C. to Apocalypse Now* (1988) has some relevant information on the accuracy of biopics, as does Michael Pitts's 1984 filmography on historical films, *Hollywood and American Reality: A Filmography of Over 250 Motion Pictures Depicting U.S. History.*

4. See, for example, Tino Balio (1985), Robert Carringer (1985), and Thomas Schatz (1988) for three recent works that place the meanings of film within the institutional contexts of their production.

5. One of the earliest controversies about the "accuracy" and the "ficticity" of biography concerned Boswell's *Life of Johnson*. When first published, in 1791, it was deemed by no less an authority than the historian Thomas Babingtom Macaulay as a masterwork. Its author was considered the model for his field. Yet, from the 1920s on, with the publication of the voluminous Boswell diaries (the source material for the Johnson biographies), it became apparent that both the chronology of the life, some of the quotes attributed to Johnson, as well as the intimacy of Boswell with the great man, were in serious doubt. The issues surrounding Boswell's history as depicted in the *Life*—the accuracy of reproducing the past versus the author's taking a point of view, the view that biography is a branch of history and not fiction, and making entertainment an incidental value second to accuracy—surround the lives on film as well.

6. In the purposive sample (**PS**) of 100 biopics used for the content analysis, 90 percent of all biopics were prefaced by a written, spoken introduction (in tandem or alone) that asserted the truth status of the narrative that was about to unfold.

7. Emerson echoes the sentiment of his contemporary across the seas, Thomas Carlyle, who, in his lectures "On Heroes, Hero-Worship and the Heroic in History" delivered in 1840 (and published in 1841), articulated the great man thesis of history, suggesting that "in all epochs . . . we shall find the great man to have been the indispensable saviour of his epoch—the lightening without which the fuel would never have burnt."

8. It appears that early on Hollywood recognized that the construct "historical accuracy" detached from the context of the film industry did not exist. Irving Thalberg (quoted in Leab 1990) noted, "if in telling a story, we find it impossible to adhere to historical accuracy in order to get the necessary dramatic effect, we do change it and we do feel it is the right thing to do." As Leab concludes, "Truth, accuracy, and a proper respect for history, then, have been routinely subordinated to the need for dramatic effect and even the whims of filmmakers" (83).

But, as the historian Pierre Sorlin (1990) suggests, it is important to keep in mind not merely the accuracy of a film, but how this version was received by contemporary audiences. To this, I would add the caveat that one must also look at how the film was packaged and sold—ironically or not—by the producing studios.

9. Daniel Leab cites Erik Barnouw on the epistemology particular media impart to history. Barnouw notes that "People who rely . . . on television for their knowledge of the past are dealing with . . . a situation where history is constantly being rewritten by the dominant medium to serve the purposes of the present" (quoted in Leab 1990:80). Barnouw's warnings about the organizational imperatives that shape TV programming hold true for film, magazines, radio, and other mass-based media.

10. Anthropologist Gregory Bateson (1979) and communications researcher Larry Gross (1974), as well as philosopher Ernst Cassirer (in *The Philosophy of Symbolic Forms*) have each noted that material originally encoded in one symbolic mode—gestural, spatial, verbal—is only partly translatable into some other, different symbol system.

11. Early studies of movie attendance patterns noted that children attended more frequently than adults, and young boys went more than young girls. The educational youth market, then, would be a highly valued slice of the mass audience. See "The Payne Fund Studies: The Effects of Movies on Children," in Lowery and De Fleur's *Milestones in Mass Communications Research: Media Effects* (1983).

12. For years, the telephone was called "the Ameche," a reference to Don Ameche, the filmic impersonator of the phone's inventor Alexander Graham Bell. Such popular expressions illuminate the role film representation can play in shaping public perception of history.

13. For a broad cultural reading of what it means to be a star or celebrated person in contemporary Western culture, see Richard Schickel (1985) and Leo Braudy (1986). Some of Braudy's notions are parallel to the ideas advanced here, namely that the state of being celebrated has superseded other kinds of achievement as a social index of worthiness. Obviously Leo Lowenthal (1944), or Walter Lippmann in his 1922 work *Public Opinion,* and Daniel Boorstin (1962), among other writers, have all focused on the metaphorical significance of celebrityhood.

14. If the reader has doubts about the formulation of a producer or head of production like Zanuck or Hal Wallis as significant contributor to a film (other than merely intoning "yes" and "no" when appropriate), the various studio production files for films will create a marked impression that a strong producer was often the main force in producing a project. See, for example, the file at UCLA on *The Dolly Sisters* (1945) (Box FX-PRS-765), where Zanuck dictates, complete with camera angles, the complete and very complicated production number "The Darktown Strutters Ball" that eventually was placed in the film. Conversely, in the same film, Zanuck could also paint with small strokes, as in a comment that a line of dialogue used to refer to contemporary popular heroes cited figures too obscure for today's viewers; "We should get some names which will be more familiar to audiences than are Mayor Gaynor and Christy Matthewson. Probably, 'Everybody from Diamond Jim to Lillian Russell' would sound more familiar to most people." Unconsciously, the two names Zanuck invokes had been the subject of biopics (though not at Fox).

15. Although film studios were well aware that the dead have few rights under American common law, the reputations of the living are not so easily disposed of. A case in point is the MGM film *Rasputin and the Empress* (1932), in which Princess Irina Alexandrovna Yussoupov was shown as the willing sexual partner of the evil monk of the film's title. Alleging that the film libeled her, she sued MGM in a British court, and was awarded substantial damages. In the United

States, a substantial out-of-court settlement (reported, by Daniel Leab [1990], to have been in the neighborhood of $1 million) was reached with the wronged Romanovs.

Such suits may explain why Hollywood preferred their famous to be dead and buried, rather than alive and litigious. See Natalie Zemon Davis's "'Any Resemblance to Persons Living or Dead': Film and the Challenge of Authenticity" (1987).

16. See Kevin Brownlow's *Behind the Mask of Innocence* (1990) for the history of the Evelyn Nesbit story. Nesbit's role as consultant on the Fox film was the last move of a media career that saw her perform as "herself" in vaudeville and silent film versions of her life, with particular attention focused on her role as the love interest in the 1906 murder trial in which her husband Harry Thaw was tried for the murder of architect Stanford White. Nesbit, Thaw, and White are prominent characters, also, in Milos Forman's film of E. L. Doctorow's *Ragtime* (1981).

17. Of course, belief in sampling as a method is itself a kind of presumption of good taste clothed in scientist's garb. However, as we all must wear some costume, the one I chose seems to be the academic self most appropriate for the stated purposes of this work.

18. Richard Dyer, in *Stars* (1979), suggests, similarly, that any image of a film actor is an interaction involving a text and the publicity materials surrounding that text. Thus, the meaning of an image in a film is never only derived from an analyst's analysis of the text alone. Sociologists like Erving Goffman, and earlier forebears, of course, recognized this point about the "constructed" (and for Goffman, reconstructed and fabricated) nature of social behavior, and this perspective of reality as a socially negotiated entity is widely used in studying social interaction.

19. There is nothing in American cinema studies, or any other study of popular culture like the British "Mass Observation" ("M-O") project, a study started in 1937 to collect lay responses to all sorts of popular culture material that made up daily life for the British. See Chaney, 1989:497–499.

20. For an example of recent empirical reception studies applied to literature, see Janice Radway's *Reading the Romance* (1984); for a study of reception of television commercials, see Bernard Timberg and Hal Himmelstein's article "Television Commercials and the Contradictions of Everyday Life: A Follow-up to Himmelstein's Production Study of the Kodak 'America' Commercial" (1989); for research that focuses on culture as a frame for individual and group reception, see Katz and Liebes, "Patterns of Involvement in Television Fiction: A Comparative Analysis" (1986); and also Vic Caldarola's "Reception as Cultural Experience: Visual Mass Media and Reception Practices in Outer Indonesia" (1990) a study of media reception in fundamentalist Muslim Outer Indonesia.

21. Schatz (1988) and others have called attention to the questionable value of only using oral histories in constructing a chronicle of Hollywood that will explain its films. Anecdotal histories—gripping in the telling and listening—often

suffer from what Schatz calls "selective recollection." Similarly, Gabler (1988) notes that the memoirs of writers—often the least powerful creative figures during the studio era—are "history by retribution." Hollywood writers in their writings that recall the production heads of studios finally get a chance to create a history that favors them by writing it themselves. Memoirs and interviews must be balanced with other forms of data, where possible, to avoid becoming part of the public relations machinery that Hollywood put out.

22. See Allen and Gomery's *Film History, Theory, and Practice* (1985), particularly Chapter 2, "Researching Film History" for a good overview on method and other research-oriented issues in the evolution of cinema studies as a discipline.

23. Scholars like Dana Polan would disagree with this mode of characterizing these films, suggesting that the narratives of the studio era were far more contested than my description. Yet, it is my strong suspicion that, at first glance, most of the films in the biopic sample do seem to create a unified facade on these issues. Of course, this does not mean they were either received in this monolithic manner, even if their content suggests it, or that they were marketed with this content in mind.

1. Making History

1. This possibility—of a life valorized in print or on the radio being as artificial as a scripted film—was raised by George Cukor in his *Keeper of the Flame* (1942). Filmed during World War II, the movie was almost a Frankfurt primer on the average citizen's duty to keep a watchful eye on both the media and the great figures created by it. Of course, the mask of artificiality, of the "double life" is a truism of theatrical life (e.g., *A Double Life* [1947]), and, as Goffman described it, everyday life as well. Today, the concept of theatricality of interpersonal performance is more part of the cultural repertoire than it was fifty years ago when Lowenthal's article appeared.

2. Viewers could later compare Davis's two portrayals in film to those of Flora Robson or Florence Eldridge, or, later, to Glenda Jackson's television portrait, and see which one "fits" more comfortably with one's desired image of the queen.

3. While many of the films in the sample try to finesse this issue of their "truth value" by the use of subtle gradations of opening avowals of veracity, other films are more basic. Thus, Fox's *The Sullivans* (1944), the story of five brothers killed in the service of their country, opens with the avowal, "This is a true story." The opposite case can be illustrated by MGM's *The Gorgeous Hussy* (1936), which opens with this convoluted disclaimer: "This story of Peggy Eaton and her times is not presented as a precise account of either—rather, as fiction founded upon historical fact. Except for historically prominent personages, the characters are fictional."

4. These "young" versions are, in essence, homunculi of the later figures. They also enabled a studio to showcase young talent in tandem with older players. Thus, Mickey Rooney, MGM's resident teen, and soon to be a major star, impersonates the youthful Edison (*Young Tom Edison*) until the more mature Spencer Tracy can perform his duties as "the wizard of Menlo Park" in another MGM vehicle, *Edison, The Man*.

5. One of the more unusual examples of the participation of the film biographee is seen in Warners' *Mission to Moscow* (1943). Here, the actual subject of the film, the American ambassador to Moscow Joseph Davies, introduces the film in a lengthy documentary-style, one-camera setup. This introduction both signals the veracity of the subsequent performance by Walter Huston and frames the film as the legitimate and official version of history. Few films have this powerful an imprimatur.

6. For more detail on the shooting of either of the two Jolson biopics, see Herbert Goldman's *Jolson: The Legend Comes to Life* (1988) or Doug McClelland's *From Blackface to Blacklist: Al Jolson, Larry Parks, and 'The Jolson Story'* (1987).

7. The less than exalted Alfred E. Green—who directed Bette Davis's Oscar-winning performance in *Dangerous* (1935)—piloted four biopics, including the enormously successful *Jolson Story*. He also directed the *The Fabulous Dorseys*, *The Jackie Robinson Story,* and *The Eddie Cantor Story* (1953), before ending his career directing for television.

8. Occasionally fame can result in downward, not upward mobility. In *Moulin Rouge* (1952) Henri de Toulouse Lautrec (José Ferrer), a member of the French nobility, "turns his back" on his noble heritage and pursues a career as an artist. This rejection of his presumed "duties" as a member of a privileged family in favor of a struggling artistic life is the cause of conflict with his reactionary father (José Ferrer again in a dual role). Typically, however, conflict arises when people from the previous (lower) social sphere no longer fit into the higher sphere that comes with fame. At times, the famous people themselves do not fit into the sphere their fame has entitled them to inhabit, and the consequences can be either comic (as the Jolson parents demonstrate with their befuddled perceptions of show business) or tragic (the sad case of Diana Barrymore in *Too Much, Too Soon*).

9. Lowenthal felt that fame as a result of a lucky break, or as the windfall of sudden fortune, alienated the individual from a sense of community, and made irrationality, and not hard work, the explanatory factor in life.

10. Adorno and Horkheimer, in their analyses of cartoons, put the issue quite succinctly, noting, "Donald Duck . . . and the unfortunate in real life get their thrashing so that the audience can learn to take their own punishment" (362). Perhaps the less cartoonish biopics create a more masked form of the "take your medicine" philosophy. At any rate, the members of the Frankfurt School were exceptionally gloomy about the prospects of the mass audience under popular culture.

2. Stout-Hearted Men

1. While five of the studios integrated all three functions, three of the majors did not. Columbia had no theater chain, United Artists had no real production facility, and Universal, although integrating all three functions, opted to ignore the large, first-run theaters and concentrate on second-run and smaller houses.

Further, from the mid-1940s on, many independent production companies released through one of the major eight film studios, thus loosening the hold of the concept of "house style" as a style imposed by or characteristic of a studio that maintained total control over a product.

2. See Nick Roddick's *A New Deal in Entertainment* (1983), for the point of view that biopics characterized Warners' output.

3. Schatz (1988) notes that by the mid-1950s, several of the majors (notably Universal) as well as some of the poverty row studios had made the switch from producing "B" films for theatrical release to producing B-style films for TV series. Thus, the rise of TV in the 1950s favored those studios that had always produced quick, short, inexpensive product.

4. Darryl Zanuck, virtually the only studio head who was not an Eastern European immigrant, nevertheless was so intimately associated in his work with that generation of Hollywood's immigrant founding fathers that, as Gabler says, "he had been in Hollywood so long he might have been called a Jewish fellow traveler" (1988:349).

5. Turow (1989:69) rejects this argument that Hollywood producers celluloid America were, in part, "attempts to deal with their ethnicity." Turow says that Gabler "marshals no real support for his argument . . . quotes no speeches, reveals no letters, exposes no other documents which reveal that the studio heads consciously tried to create 'an empire of their own.'" Unfortunately, such high-minded empiricism does not take into consideration that the very kind of personal motivations, perhaps even unconscious motivations, that are part of the pattern of the moguls reinvention of themselves and Hollywood are precisely the kind of material that they would not put into writing. One does not need a Foucault to suggest that the mere absence of a particular written discourse could suggest both its repression by mainstream forces and its power to surface in other, uncensored modes. If one played by such restrictive rules, the absence of Native Americans, or the condescending image of them that has been presented in film, would not be the result of racism, since it is unlikely that producers would put into writing such taboo feelings. See Turow, 1989:67–70.

6. See Austin (1988), Izod (1988), and Jowett (1976) for patterns of movie attendance by age in different eras. See Frith (1981) and Lull (1982) for age as a variable in patterns of leisure.

7. The priorities of making films during wartime, the creation of positive morale on all fronts, elevated all foreign allies to the ranks of heroes. Conversely,

the emphasis on "positive" thinking made the studios even more relentlessly optimistic than before, covering up bad news as well as highlighting the good. Thus, Zanuck had the original dedication to *Buffalo Bill,* "In recognition of the valor and devotion of those Indian warriors who are now in the armed forces of our nation" altered so the viewer would not be reminded "of a situation we would rather not have brought up: our ignoble treatment of the American Indians" (7/13/43, UCLA, Fox Collection, Box FX-PRS-442). To remind the viewers of 1944 that Native Americans were fighting for their country would also force some viewers to ask, given the past treatment of Native Americans by our government, why they should fight at all. See Izod (1988:111–131) for a discussion of how official government policy toward film content shaped movies during wartime. For a compelling, and different, argument of wartime film content, see Polan, 1986.

8. See Doherty, 1988:9 for the detailed context on how Hollywood planned to "exploit" the Castro angle and other Cold War tales. During the World War II "thaw" in Soviet/American relations, Russia was depicted in a modern biopic. Significantly, however, the subject of the film was the *American* ambassador to Moscow, Joseph Davies, whose job, couched in either espionage or religious argot of the word "mission," is both to represent American interests in the Soviet Union and to present the Russian people to filmgoers as worthy of our friendship.

9. The issue of manufacture of these images, these films, of course cuts across any discussion of the images themselves. In this way, none of the films was either directed by a woman or produced by a woman. The images, then, even when allocating a domain to females, is strictly a male-created preserve. One can only speculate about female reception of these images of a world where men have almost complete control over the domain of the symbolic.

3. Night and Day

1. See Brown (1973) for an early account of the organized research efforts, particularly in the art department, for D. W. Griffith's monumental film *Intolerance* (1916).

2. The very choice of the term "bible" used to describe these guides suggests their authoritativeness when it comes to interpreting questions of facts and history in the biopic.

3. Robert Carringer (1985) notes RKO's research department was under the aegis of business, rather than Pandro Berman's creative branch of the studio's organization. Like the research arms of any of the major studios, the extensive files in this department could either be used to re-create, with great accuracy, a specific structure or costume, or could, as was the case with the sets in *Citizen Kane,* be "used evocatively, . . . providing[ing] familiar visual prototypes as a starting point, and the illustrator would improvise the rest" (52).

4. Sometimes obstacles to portraying a biopic life could come from forces outside the producing studio. This occurred with Fox's film on the life of Stephen Foster, *Swanee River*. After Hedda Hopper had suggested, in her column of September 4, 1939, published in *The Washington Post* and other papers carrying her byline, that the film would portray Foster as "inebriated in nearly every scene," letters lamenting this possible denigration of Foster poured into Fox from shocked educators and sundry Stephen Foster societies. After years of "laundering" lives to fit the studio's and the MPPDA's concept of public morality, in this instance, readers at the Breen Office merely cautioned Fox to follow the guidelines used to depict the use of alcohol in any film (Section I, subsection 4, of the Production Code) and, despite proposed boycotts, no changes were made in the film script.

5. This fact of Porter's life—his homosexuality—illustrates the difficulty of doing institutional histories of film based on written material alone. Simply stated, that which can't be discussed or written about ceases to exist as archival data. These "holes" in the language—the refusal to commit to writing about certain practices— parallel similar gaps in the subject matter of the film life. The author is forced to use secondary material and, interestingly, material often not deemed officially appropriate for serious academic study, like Kenneth Anger's hugely entertaining *Hollywood Babylon* (1975). Often only in such nonmainstream media sources can banished or taboo behavior be chronicled at all. Academic standards of proof can be as repressive as the culture they seek to illuminate.

6. One reason researchers were convinced that some semblance to the actual chronology of a life should be maintained was the mail they received from viewers who attended to such perceived factual errors. It was not uncommon for vigilant viewers to write to research departments and point out mistakes that marred their enjoyment of the film, and studios expected mail from "specialists" who, with their trained eyes and ears, would pick out problems average audience members might ignore.

7. For *The Buccaneer*, the effort expended on research was not only prodigious, but had the added cachet of the personal imprimatur of the great De Mille. The souvenir book created for the premiere of the film informs us that "De Mille himself led a research expedition—the only one he has personally conducted—into Louisiana" (Paramount, 1938:20). In the company of a large research staff, and with the assistance of high members of the state government, De Mille and company "cruised 280 miles through the swamps of Louisiana, where the descendants of Lafitte's pirates still live." Their search for historic detail was manifested in authenticity in "costumes, arms, furniture, sets," even to the point of re-creating, from photographs, entire buildings. The book concludes with an extensive list of anachronistic words uncovered by the research team in the course of their search for "accurate" language. This list, an implicit pledge of historical quality control, is an assurance to the viewer that no detail has been spared in bringing them an "accurate" version of history.

8. Zanuck's biopics always contained a dose of romance and comedy to balance out their "serious" themes. The MacGowan Collection at UCLA contains a large number of Zanuck's memos concerning "lightening" the serious plots of *Brigham Young* and *Young Mr. Lincoln.*

For information on Zanuck's ideas on how to film the lives of the less exalted, see Behlmer (1985:7–9) for the December 1932 issue of *The Hollywood Reporter* containing Zanuck's own analysis of the headline-oriented biopics.

9. Ironically, Bell Telephone had played a critical role in destroying Zanuck's partner William Fox. To valorize the man, though, was not the same thing as praising the corporation. In fact, Zanuck made sure that the cinematic inventor, Bell, was devoid of any ignoble capitalist urges.

10. Among the other Fox biopics MacGowan would work on were: *Swanee River, Brigham Young, Young Mr. Lincoln, Belle Starr* (1941), and *Stanley and Livingstone.* In particular, MacGowan's and Zanuck's negotiating skills were nowhere more apparent than in their dealing with the sensitive members of The Church of Latter Day Saints in the making of *Brigham Young.* As they would do with the surviving relatives in *Bell,* Zanuck and MacGowan were able to ensure the cooperation of key personnel from the Mormon community, shrewdly holding the world premieres of both films in the respective backyards of Washington, D.C., and Salt Lake City.

11. See Leff and Simmons's (1990) intriguing history of film censorship, for Joy's history at the MPPDA and later at Fox.

12. Later in Zanuck's career, this philosophy, the "rooting interest," became almost a fixation. His memos of the late 1940s and early 1950s are filled with references to and analyses of his past biopic triumphs and what had made them work. In a sense, many of Zanuck's later biopic projects are remakes of several basic plots that had earlier worked for him, and to which he urged writers, time and again, to attend. See chapters four and five for fuller discussions of intertextuality and biography.

13. Bell's granddaughter, Mrs. Gilbert Grovesnor, was married to the head of the prestigious National Geographic Society, of which her grandfather was a charter member. The family, in addition to possessing great wealth, were cultural and social icons of the Washington, D.C., scene. Such people should, at all costs, be accommodated, for their participation would have great value in the publicity campaign for the film.

14. Thomas Elsaesser (1986:26) makes a similar point about the function of trials and other public gatherings in the Muni/Dieterle cycle of Warner's biopics. He feels such presentations by the biopic figure "can come to stand for the democratic process itself." See Chapter five, "Configuring a Life" for a fuller discussion of the function of trials in biopics.

15. Wallis and director William Dieterle still managed to slip in several shots that the Breen Office, by its own standards, should have caught, particularly the

early sequences where Du Barry's bare feet are kissed by her ardent admirers, and fondled by the king.

16. Breen explicitly congratulated Mayer for his clean pictures, as contrasted to the questionable taste of a Wallis or a Zanuck.

17. See Muriel Cantor's 1971 study, *The Hollywood TV Producer,* on how the television producer's concept of the audience member shapes his role as a producer. Cantor conceptualizes the producer as a surrogate for the taste of the audience member, though such a feel is based on little first-hand contact. This view of "the audience" in turn shapes the producer's options on what is acceptable television content for "average" viewers. I presume a similar model could be applied to the film producer.

18. See, for example, Thomas 1967 or Crowther, 1960. See also some of the ghost-written autobiographies of the early founders of the film industry, particularly Adolph Zukor's 1953 work *The Public Is Never Wrong* or Jack Warner's extremely entertaining *My First Hundred Years in Hollywood* (1965).

4. Reel Life

1. I deem *The Lady with Red Hair* typical after analyzing the 100 films in the purposive sample, not before. Here, typical means the film contains a significant number of structural affinities with other biopics. It does not suggest that the acting, or mise-en-scène, or direction is like other films; only that the way the life on film has been constructed is.

2. J. A. Burrow, in *The Ages of Man: A Study in Medieval Writing and Thought,* suggests that the frame of life's stages can be seen as "established norms . . . to which individual life histories will more or less closely conform" (1986:1). Thus, these stages "purport to explain why the course of human life runs as it does," and in a sense are normative guides for constructing lives and comparing them to one another.

3. In the seven cases where the biographee plays him or herself, the film life often includes younger actors portraying the great figure in youth, cutting at some point to the real person. We see this in *The Fabulous Dorseys* and *To Hell and Back,* but we see the opposite tack—the real person playing him or herself—in *The Bob Mathias Story,* in which the film starts *in medias res.*

4. Samuel Goldwyn, for example, had lifelong feuds—and equally long business dealings—with Louis B. Mayer and Jesse Lasky. Darryl Zanuck, first nurtured by the Warners, later felt betrayed by them, leaving their employ to found his own company. Harry Cohn engaged in a lifelong love/hate relation with almost every person who worked for him, and many who did not. Thus, the pattern of engagement and alienation is a common thread in the narratives of the moguls.

5. A number of writers—William Ivens (1953), Ian Watt (1957)—have made

the point that a particular medium (prints, novels, photographs) described a vernacular life long before other arts took up this praxis. Thus, dating the democratization of fiction from the eighteenth century may not be completely accurate.

6. The workings of fame are not limited to the species *Homo sapiens*. Two films about famous animals throw into the relief the mechanisms that explain the role of various explanatory factors in fame. In *The Story of Seabiscuit,* the fact that Man O'War is Seabiscuit's father convinces Sean (Barry Fitzgerald) his faithful, wily trainer that, despite his small stature and against the judgments of all conventional horse trainers, the horse is a winner. What we have in the saga of Seabiscuit is a tale no different from a Dieterle biopic at Warners. Sean holds an opinion that runs against popular wisdom. Even after the horse repeatedly fails to win a race, he maintains his faith in his beloved horse. And, just as Pasteur, Zola, and others have their sudden moments of Archimidean discovery after repeated failure, so too there is a moment in the life of the horse where Sean realizes why the racer has not been winning. After Sean detects the slight flaw in "The Biscuit's" character (he is too sociable around other horses), he corrects this through retraining, and genes win out. The horse's life is a procession of triumph and profit, culminating with a last shot in the film in which the ultimate accolade, the same one given to the cinematic Lincoln, is accorded the horse; it is immortalized in a public sculpture, though the Seabiscuit art is sited at Santa Anita rather than the nation's capital.

7. A number of films finesse the death issue, presenting it in disguised or tempered forms. *Devotion, The Sullivans,* and *The Adventures of Mark Twain* contain scenes in which the deceased famous appear as benevolent ghosts, fondly smiling down upon loved ones left behind. Other films, like *Young Mr. Lincoln,* while not actually showing the death of the leading figure, allude strongly to it by closing the film with a monumental (commemorative) sculpture, or plaque. We find this ending in *Pride of the Yankees, The Babe Ruth Story, Man of a Thousand Faces, The Story of Seabiscuit, The Great Caruso,* and *The Winning Team,* to name several examples.

8. While the occasionally eccentric family does appear, often their eccentricity is limited to minor "business" and not morals. The Gilbreths of *Cheaper by the Dozen,* although progressive (and even somewhat peculiar) when it comes to ideas like education, efficiency, and hygiene, are reactionary in other spheres. Led by ascerbic Clifton Webb (as father Frank) and patient Myrna Loy (as mother Lily), one of the most memorable scenes in the movie focuses on the humiliation of a representative of Planned Parenthood who has mistakenly been steered to the twelve-child Gilbreth household. After listening patiently to the reasonable pitch of an unmarried spinsterish representative (Mildred Dunnock), Frank, fairly bursting his buttons, whistles, and all twelve children of the proud polygenitors descend upon the hapless Planned Parenthood lady. Single woman is routed, and the tradition of family carries the day.

9. In particular, entertainers, both male and female, are often resisted by their

families because the career places them outside a "normal" community established by the family. Class boundaries do not seem to matter much here, as both wealthy parents (Dorothy, the future Mrs. Caruso) and poor (Chauncey Olcott) reject the theater as a threat to established patterns that have dominated their family for years. Most families, then, promulgate a conservative preservation of tradition, meaning they resist most innovations. Only families "born in a trunk," like the Cohans, the Keatons (*The Buster Keaton Story*), or the Foys (*The Seven Little Foys*), embrace the theater as a continuation of family tradition and not a threat to it.

10. The correspondence between Fox and the Mormon Church is fascinating, as each side, while pretending not to, cautiously makes suggestions about how the life should be built. At one point, Laurence Olivier was considered for the part of Brigham Young that went to Dean Jagger. See the MacGowan Collection at UCLA for these materials.

11. Biopics of composers and writers are particularly good examples of linking romance as motivation to the actions that made the artist famous. Cole Porter, Cohan, Chopin, Elizabeth Barrett Browning, Robert Schumann, the Brontë sisters, and even the Dolly sisters are all shown creating characteristic artwork that was motivated specifically by the love of a heterosexual partner, often a spouse. The biopic thus suggests that history is made through romance, particularly the brand heterosexuals favor.

12. Griselda Pollock's analysis (1980) of different biographical discourses constructed about the life of Vincent Van Gogh is an example of how artistic genius is linked with outsiderness. In fact, Pollock goes one step beyond this formulation, arguing that popular mediations of Van Gogh's life suggested that outsiderness is not merely a symptom of artistic genius, but a confirmation of it.

13. Brennan and Cooper were an exceptional, male-male "star pairing," and they played their respective roles of down-to-earth observer (Brennan) and the great man who is not aware of his greatness (Cooper) in at least five films.

14. Chance, of course, is a kind of causality that differs in the contours of its predictability and its random distribution in a population. It can also be presented, like rational causality, neatly and obviously (as in *A Song to Remember* where the chance meeting of Chopin and Liszt saves the former's career), or be sprung upon the viewer by surprise.

15. Divine inspiration as a type of motivation for career is, obviously, common in biopics of people who feel they have been called to serve some faith. Thus, in *A Man Called Peter*, Peter Marshall, despairing of his life, is saved by an unseen presence in the form of a divine voice that saves him from falling over a cliff on a fog-shrouded Scottish evening. *The Song of Bernadette* and *Saint Joan*, *Brigham Young* and *The Ten Commandments* are also biographies in which the leading figures enter their vocation after the direct intervention of God. Other than these holy figures, divine intervention is a rare explanation in the biopic, though the hand of God is frequently, and piously, cited, by biopic parents or elders.

16. The poem reads: "If Nancy Hanks/Came Back as a Ghost/Seeking News/ Of What She Loved Most/She'd Ask First/'Where's My Son? /What's Happened To Abe? /What's He Done?' "

"'You Wouldn't Know/About My Son? /Did He Grow Tall? /Did He Have Fun? /Did He Learn to Read? /Did He Get to Town? /Do You Know His Name? / Did He Get On?' "

17. Not only is the film motivated by the questions posed by Lincoln's own mother, but the point of view of the surrogate mother—Abigail Clay—can be said to frame the entire film.

18. Such a mystical device was used in a contemporaneous Lincoln film, RKO's *Abe Lincoln in Illinois*. There, Lincoln returns to his boyhood home in New Salem only to find it abandoned save for the ghosts of significant figures from his past (his mother, Ann Rutledge). The ghosts are only too willing to advise him, and it is his beloved mother's quoting of the scriptures that convinces him to seize his destiny as a public figure.

19. Because of the reflexive way fame is constructed, the expectation is increased in the biopic; one out of every three films is about the process of entertainment itself, in which staged routines ritualistically and pleasurably punctuate the narrative.

20. One of the earliest silent movie stars, ironically, was opera diva Geraldine Farrar. Signed to a Lasky Company contract by Samuel Goldwyn when he was still known as Goldfish, she scored an enormous triumph in her 1915 film record of one of her greatest operatic roles, *Carmen*. Later stars—among them Lily Pons, Grace Moore, Lawrence Tibbet, and Ezio Pinza—would use sound film to increase their audiences. Farrar, a charismatic raven-haired singer, was able to do it without.

21. A number of writers, notably Thomas Schatz, have noted that while other studios "retooled" their images, MGM continued to parley the same musical formula in biography. See Schatz, 1988: 447.

22. In contrast to the life of the not-so-famous Tanguay, RKO executives felt that the very familiarity of Annie Oakley's life would be the hook that attracted most people, whether the narrative had music (as did MGM's *Annie Get Your Gun*) or not. See the RKO memo of December 14, 1945, at the RKO Collection at UCLA, Annie Oakley File

5. Configuring a Life

1. From Sandburg (1926), Ford appropriated several bits of verbatim dialogue, as in the Lincoln/Buck confrontation where Lincoln challenges Buck to "wet his horns" and prove that he's the "biggest buck in the lick" (p. 40), and the complaint of the two farmers Hawthorne and Woolridge (p. 94).

2. It is possible that framing Ann Rutledge as Lincoln's lost love—a histori-

cally dubious fact—was suggested by the graveyard meditation on this romance contained in the popular *Spoon River Anthology* of Edgar Lee Masters, published in 1915. But it is also possible, as Charles Affron has suggested (1982:177), that graveyard meditations are very much characteristic of the John Ford canon: *My Darling Clementine* (1946) and *She Wore a Yellow Ribbon* (1949) contain scenes similar to the graveyard soliloquy in *Young Mr. Lincoln*.

3. At the trial, Lincoln's common sense and loyalty to the defendants' mother allows him to triumph over the more sophisticated legal maneuvers of his opponent Felder and Felder's advisor, Stephen Douglas. Trotti had been working on some version of a Lincoln biography since 1938, and in notes accompanying a script called "Lincoln Trial Story," dated January 1, 1938, Trotti wrote that "this story is based, in part, on a murder trial which I covered as a newspaper man." When he realized that Lincoln, the attorney, could be used as a figure in an invented but dramatically telling trial scene, he constructed the life through the filter of his own experience. As Trotti told Zanuck, "The story, therefore, has some historical basis, although the characters and incidents used, with the exception of Lincoln, Douglas and Mary Todd, are fictional" (UCLA, Fox Collection, Box FX-PRS-785).

4. The scale of biography could, of course, be diminutive as well as large. A series published in the 1940s and aimed at the lucrative children's market—"Living Biographies"—typically condensed a life into twenty pages.

5. Justin Kaplan's biography of Mark Twain opens when its subject is thirty-one, and his life of Walt Whitman begins when the poet is sixty. "Since Kaplan's breakthrough, it has become a common biographical device to start somewhere in the middle" (Graves, 1991:71). The print biography, then, has to some extent adopted the strategy of opening a biographical narrative *in medias res.*

6. Bordwell, Staiger, and Thompson (1985:42) note that the flashback is a relatively rare device in sound film. In their (mislabeled) "unbiased sample" of 100 films, the flashback occurs in twenty films, only five of which are from the sound era. The biopic is thus characterized by its relatively frequent use of a device that is rare in the total body of films.

7. Montage did become a staple of signifying practices in the classical period, and directors like Slavko Vorkapich became specialists in directing self-contained montage sequences that were embedded in feature-length narrative works. While montage is a common element in many films of the period 1927–1960, it is almost essential to the biopic's concept of teleology and predetermination.

8. Montage can also be used systematically to eliminate key episodes in a life that need to be part of the plot, but are too unpleasant to dwell on. Jubilee Jim Fisk's disastrous manipulation of the bullion market in *The Toast of New York* is glossed over in a brief montage. The human suffering caused by his greed is elided into a montage of food shortages and unemployment that occupies twenty seconds or so in the film. Montage at least suggests events exist.

9. The trial is, of course, neither a site nor a device unique to the biopic, for it is found in musicals (*Gentlemen Prefer Blondes* [1953], westerns (*The Westerner* [1940]), as well as being a staple of crime and detective films. But in the biopic, the trial often has a specific function; it is typically used to sum up the message of a life and a film rather than to build suspense.

10. Dana Polan cites Mikhail Bakhtin's notion that trials "are a historically central element in the development of narrative: not only does a trial link narrative to the juridical and ideological interests of a society . . . the trial possesses a certain specific narrative power—an assured source of narrative resolution, a way to disambiguate narrative complexity through the univocal decision of an authoritative law" (1986:21).

11. Films about athletes suggest that all sports are full of compelling moments where the performer must triumph, or fail; in a way, this view of athletic competition is true. *The Winning Team,* where Grover Cleveland Alexander battles alcoholism and the New York Yankees, or *The Bob Mathias Story,* where the Olympic auditions, literally called trials, test his mettle, are but two examples of athletes having to perform challenges that go beyond merely doing well.

12. In *The Story of Alexander Graham Bell,* Bell's wife Mabel writes a love note on which the absent-minded inventor scribbles the eventual proof of his telephone patent; in *Doctor Ehrlich's Magic Bullet,* Ehrlich's wife inadvertently heats one of his slides, leading to the process of discovery of the treatment for syphilis.

13. Public trials can validate deeply personal feelings, permanently sealing private matters with a public judgment. We see this in *Song of Love,* in which, at a trial for the guardianship of the young Clara Weick (in love with penniless Robert Schumann) Liszt wins over the court (and the opposition of Clara's father) by praising the genius of Robert, and forecasting (inaccurately) his bright financial future.

14. See Behlmer, 1985:178–184, for material on the Cohan/Cagney input into *Yankee Doodle Dandy.*

15. The actor need not be established to "whitewash" the nature of the famous. Many sources suggest that Al Jolson was an unbearable egotist, whose genius as a performer did not carry over into his personal life. When casting the part in *The Jolson Story,* Columbia used a relatively minor actor, Larry Parks. However, Jolson occupied so high a position in show business pantheon and in the household gods of Columbia head Harry Cohn that, despite the number of more realistic films being made of musical performers at the same time *Jolson* was in production, Cohn opted for the revered artist treatment of the life. Parks's good-natured performance—for which he received an Academy Award nomination for the prize that went that year to Fredric March for *The Best Years of Our Lives*—suggested Jolson was in the thrall of a humanitarian dybbuk who propelled him to please the audience, leaving little else for his wife "Julie Benson."

16. Sometimes the association of a star with a certain kind of film and character can prove to be an overwhelming barrier across which even the biggest performers cannot leap. Preview cards for *Parnell* suggest that one of the reasons the

film flopped—critically and commercially—was while audience members could accept Myrna Loy as Katie O'Shea, they could not accept action man Gable as serious statesman Charles Parnell. Thus, an anonymous respondent at a preview in Santa Anna in May 1937 noted "The leading people are always fine—but this is not their kind of picture" (USC, John Stahl Collection, *Parnell* folder). Although the costumes may have been a dry run for his role as Rhett Butler in *Gone With the Wind* (1939), the public found him inappropriately cast as the Irish statesman involved in a scandalous divorce trial.

17. Sometimes, genetics failing, extremely creative makeup could convince the audience that the actor "was" the character. We see this gambit in *Man of a Thousand Faces,* where publicity avers James Cagney wore over twenty different makeups in portraying actor Lon Chaney, and in *Moulin Rouge,* the biopic of the painter Toulouse-Lautrec, where Jose Ferrer, through makeup and contortion, impersonates the stunted physique of the great artist. On the other hand, too much makeup could obscure the comfortable recognition of a star, as the disagreement between producer Hal Wallis and makeup artist Perc Westmore over Paul Muni's makeup for *The Life of Emile Zola* suggests. As Wallis noted, "My feeling is I would rather take Muni as he is and make him up for the character so far as hair and beard is concerned and still retain the impression for the audience that Paul Muni is playing the part than I would to try to reproduce Zola exactly and so disguise Muni and make over his facial characteristics as to lose the Muni personality" (in Behlmer, 1985:37–38).

18. Actors not physically similar (Douglas to van Gogh) could be, studio promotion reminds us, linked by blood. Thus RKO claimed Katharine Hepburn was a relative of *Mary of Scotland.* Further, the performer could have been "trained" by the biographee him or herself, as a review in *Variety* on August 20, 1952, claimed was the case with Blossom Seeley's coaching of irrepressible Betty Hutton, and as the film *Jolson Sings Again* falsely intimated.

19. An actor's type of star image need not be owned by that person, but could even be used by other actors in creating a character for a biopic. In writing the script for the RKO headliner *The Flying Irishman,* the scene between Douglas "Wrong Way" Corrigan and a stubborn airport inspector was based not on Corrigan's own dictated recollections, "Notes on What Corrigan Thought of His Family and the People Who Made an Impression on His Life" (which the studio owned). Instead, in yet another demonstration of the power of intertextuality in shaping a biopic life, the writers of the film were told to think of well-known screen pairings as the motivation for the scene: "The characterization between Douglas and the Inspector should be along the lines of a Pat O'Brien and a Jimmy Cagney—they fight between themselves—because of different points of view" (UCLA, RKO Collection, story conference of September 19, 1938). Similarly, Zanuck's comments in the margin of an October 15, 1934, draft of *Cardinal Richelieu* suggests that the writers portray Louis XIII's attitude toward a character in terms of a recent acclaimed screen portrayal: "he's Laughtoning her."

20. So powerful are certain assumptions that, at times, conscious, largely controlled promotions are unnecessary. Garbo's well-known distaste for public-ity—itself, a kind of publicity—became part of the discourses of her movies and the publicity for them. MGM's promotion for *Queen Christina* did not have to hype, as Fox did for *Young Mr. Lincoln,* "Garbo as You've Never Seen Her," be-cause precisely the opposite case was true. The film played upon well-known public assumptions about the enigmatic Swedish star and the affinity of these constructions with the MGM images of the Swedish monarch. Since Greta Garbo's promotion, by MGM, had centered on her "exotic," aloof nature, her appearance in *Queen Christina,* along with the man she was earlier rumored to have been in love with, John Gilbert, creates a connection between image and life that is a powerful one. Earlier, witnessing their silent rapture in *Love* (1927), the publicity call, "See Garbo and Gilbert in *Love*" had been changed from the earlier, more daring title, proclaiming "See Garbo and Gilbert in *Heat!*" The public went to the movies to see fiction masquerading as documentary, as offscreen lovers embrace, enacting a drama that has been closely tailored to parallel the real-life publicity fabrication of it. Garbo's persona—the woman who gives up all for love—thus shaped the narra-tives of her two other biopics, *Mata Hari* (1932) and *Conquest* (1937). Had MGM starred her in *Madame Curie,* a property acquired for her but given, instead, to Greer Garson, the life of the Nobel Laureate would have taken on a different slant.

21. See Lehmann-Haupt 1990:C-16.

22. In a contradiction typical of Hollywood, the subjects of the very films that show how resistant are the entertainment establishments, are themselves, im-mune to the laws they help to break. Although enduring the regular cycles of suc-cess and failure, the fact that Jolson, Keaton, and Schumann are the subjects of films exempts them from any short-term cycles, and assures them exemption as "permanent" household gods of entertainment.

23. Recent arguments, such as those presented by a number of authors in Balio, 1991, suggest that the relationship between film and television was more likely intertwined than subordinated. However, I am not arguing here that one me-dium came to dominate the others in simplistic terms. Rather, I suggest that televi-sion came to be seen as the prime forum for the expression of public ideas in a way film once was. In many ways, film benefited from the arrival of television, as stu-dios were used to produce short, serial-like fare for TV, and later, as TV became a market for the studio's own vast film libraries. But, in the long run, the arrival of television diminished film as a vehicle for the expression of public culture.

6. The Frame Shrinks

1. Biopics continued to be made post-1960. For example, in the decade of 1961–1970, there were a number of high-grossing biopics: *Patton* at 27 million;

Funny Girl at 24.9 million, and *Lawrence of Arabia* (1962) grossed 16.9 million. In the period of 1971–1980, only *Coal Miner's Daughter,* in 1980, managed to break into the top fifty grossing films of the decade, and the years 1981–1986 saw only two biopics, *Gandhi* (1982) and *Out of Africa* (1985), rank at numbers 72 and 26, respectively, for the period between 1980 and 1986. Contrast these figures with the decade 1941–1950, where twelve of the top seventy-five grossing films were biopics, and *Sergeant York,* in 1941, was the top-grossing film of the year, and one senses the ebb and flow of popularity of the genre as a staple in the film repertoire. The biopic is thus a characteristic of the culture of the studio period, and not the post-studio era. For the record, 1971 marked the first time that independent productions exceeded studio releases. But the power of the studios as integrated motion picture corporations had been on the decline since the mid-1940s.

2. Prior to made-for-TV movies (first aired in 1966), TV had a long history of presenting biography or key episodes from the life of the famous. Shows like *You Are There* (CBS, 1953–1957) re-created individual events from history (the Gettysburg Address, the Hindenburg disaster). Hosted by newsman Walter Cronkite, the show opened with the assurance that "All things are as they were then . . . ." Other "anthology" shows, like *The Philco Television Playhouse,* presented small versions of history, like the re-creation of the famous 1925 Floyd Collins cave-in. Some of these shows—like *You Are There*—originated on radio (where John Charles Daly was the host). Other shows were undoubtedly shaped by movie and theatrical versions of the great life.

3. Lowery and De Fleur (1983:268) note that by 1959, 88 percent of the homes in the United States had television sets. Only a little more than ten years earlier, in 1948, there had been 100,000 sets in the entire country. The growth of television surpassed, in rapidity, the growth of radio and other earlier "new" technologies as a common item in the American home.

4. As Douglas Gomery observed, "TV-movie production schedules were so swift they could 'scoop' theatrical fare. Some made-for-TV movies had completed their second runs before their more famous theatrical cousins had come to town" (1987:207).

5. The theme of sexuality and difference, so popular on talk shows, is echoed in "dignified" TV discourse by the Renée Richards story, *Second Serve* (1986), in which Vanessa Redgrave gives an eerie and powerful impersonation of Richard Raskin (called "Radley" in the film), the (male) New Jersey opthalmologist smitten with tennis and determined to excel in this sport as a woman. To achieve both these goals, he undergoes a sex-change operation, playing tennis as Renée Richards.

6. See Postman (1985), for a jeremiad against TV's pollution of cultural content by its entertainment component. Unfortunately, Postman joins the chorus of people (Allen Bloom and E. D. Hirsch to name two) who blame "declining" standards of literacy on the influence of TV as a medium. None of these writers—who give little evidence of actually watching, on a regular basis, the shows they

denounce—seems to understand that TV represents a continuity, and not a change, in media's role in populist education. In the nineteenth century for every "refined" article in *The Atlantic Monthly,* there were innumerable articles in the more colorful *Police Gazette;* for every Henry James observation of American mores, there were ten Horatio Alger volumes sold.

7. In fact, several subgenres unique to TV—drug recovery tales, plane crash tales, women battling illness and false imprisonment in mental institutions—seem to have been solidified by the made-for-TV movie, which, demographics suggest, are watched by a largely—though not exclusively—female audience.

8. Studies by Gerbner and Gross (1976) and the *Surgeon General's Report on Television and Social Behavior* in 1971 suggested much of TV watching is ritualistic; viewers elect to "watch TV" as something to do during a certain period of time, or for a certain duration, as opposed to deciding to watch a specific program on TV.

9. See Browne, 1984: 585–599. VCRs may have disrupted the link between viewer behavior and network scheduling, as time-shifting enables viewers to record a program presented at one "natural" time for viewing at some unnatural future date. Viewers can even speed by commercials during these shows—"zap" them—thus further disrupting the grand plan of some network supertext.

10. While film is certainly affected by timeliness, television's speed of production (compared to film) and its unique comparative format (all the networks are directly competing in the same markets) give salience to short-lived temporal variables as programming markers in a way that film seldom has to cope with. Such considerations—the power of the sweeps period, competition in one's time slot—virtually define a level of programming and production strategy.

11. There is a tradition of Hollywood studio's "exploiting" a current cultural trend to appeal to a particular demographic group at nearly the moment such a trend is in vogue. See Doherty (1988) for an analysis of how changing leisure patterns of American teenagers helped create and sustain a genre of film, the teenpic, that was made to appeal to current, rapidly changing teen tastes in music and other spheres.

In the film sample used in this study, this recency phenomenon occurred several times, notably in the cases where celebrities, particularly athletes, portrayed themselves. See the discussion of the "headliner" biopic in Chapter three, "Night and Day," and Chapter four, "Reel Life."

12. For example, Universal was concerned that *Sutter's Gold* (1936) would have its value lowered by a proposed competing MGM film about the gold rush, *The Tide of the Empire.* MGM assured Carl Laemmle, Sr., that their portrayal was comic, and would in no way lessen his investment. See the *Sutter's Gold* file at the MPPDA Collection at the Academy of Motion Picture Arts and Sciences Library.

13. In the realm of nonbiographical docudrama, viewers could relive the story of the Israeli rescue attempt at Entebbe. ABC once again got there first, airing *Victory at Entebbe* on December 13, 1976, while NBC aired their version of history, *Raid on Entebbe,* on January 9, 1977.

14. In certain instances, given the expanded horizons of news opened up by satellites, cable, and other parts of the new communications technologies, fame has become more transient, more divisible than ever. The half-life of a celebrity—with rare exceptions—seems to have shrunk in inverse relation with the increased number of arenas of electronically induced fame. Yesterday's sensational news story is, ten years later, merely fodder for an expanded cable repertoire. Jessica Hahn passes from a minor figure in an ongoing morality tale, to a centerfold in *Playboy*, a figure of interest to readers of *People* and *Us*, a supporting player in the Bakker biopic *Fall from Grace* (1990), and, finally, the husky voice behind one of those 900 telephone numbers; viewers on TV are invited to call Jessica (for upwards of $10 per call) and hear her version of the story seen and read in different incarnations.

15. Sterling and Kittross (1990) note that the change, in the early 1970s, in the syndication rules increased the number of non-network-produced programs. Thus, television stars—like Farrah Fawcett—could head their own production companies, and articulate an image of fame that reflected well upon their image. The change in the syndication rule may have attracted small screen stars to the genre by giving them control over their image in biography they might not have enjoyed prior to the change.

16. The potential of extending the narrative possibilities via the mini-series does not mean this has necessarily been the case. Rather, the mini-series seems to be a more bloated (but less luxurious-looking) relative of the blockbuster movie. Series like *Roots* (1977), which in some content areas broadened the subject matter of TV, are the exceptions to the predictable *Lonesome Dove* (1990) and *Winds of War* (1989) that characterize the mini-series.

17. It is no coincidence that these lesser-known figures valorized on TV are impersonated by stars of a smaller magnitude than those who illuminated fame during the studio era. Television has spawned a whole generation of stars who, try as the might, are only stars on TV (Elizabeth Montgomery, Leslie Ann Warren, Richard Chamberlain, Jane Seymour, Jaclyn Smith, and Ann Gillian, to name a few). It seems somehow apt that, having known them through the more intimate mode of television, that they portray modern, everyday folk rather than great figures from some remote past.

18. Further, the everyday famous, in merely trying to do something they are prohibited from doing by their alleged handicap, become the subject for TV immortality. Thus, within two weeks of each other, CBS (*No Other Love*, April 23, 1979) and ABC (*Like Normal People*, April 13, 1979) both featured the tale of the same retarded couple who threw their community into an uproar when the announced a desire to do the most "normal" thing one aspires to on TV—get married.

19. An intriguing issue here is to what extent the smaller frame of cultural fame suggested by TV is a function of the lesser star power of its performers? Is it that Elizabeth Montgomery is not capable of rendering grand figures from history, in the manner of Bette Davis, or is the smaller, more intimate viewing context of

TV suggestive of a miniature of fame, a scaled-down version of the big screen figures and their doings?

The data for TV, of course, are not as conclusive as those for film since they cover only a ten-year period from the inception of the made-for-TV biopic (1971) until 1980.

20. One thinks of a recent exception to this, David Lynch's 1980 biopic of John Merrick, *The Elephant Man*. But fame defined through suffering or disformity is the terrain of television, not film.

21. Here, of course, is an angle at which TV and the tabloids part company. One of the greatest characteristics of the tabloids' picturing of the fame of the already famous is the degree they are made to suffer. On TV, the suffering of the already famous is held to a minimum, distributing this trait to the more "normal" people in the population while they enjoy the fruits of their fame.

22. Thus, ABC's *All Together Now* (February 5, 1975), the saga of the Lindsay family, shows four orphaned children who, in their desire to remain intact even when orphaned, take issue with society's official definition of family: they can be a family, together, without the benefit of parents.

23. One of the operating assumptions in shaping the famous TV female as a victim is that it affords a "good cry" to the genre's predominantly female audience. Nick Browne (1984:594–595) suggests that the audience for made-for-TV movies is predominantly female, and films—and even certain genres—are scheduled on nights when "traditionally" the audience has a male or female cast. The linkage between women and the victim biography (which further validates the powerlessness of women at the hands of their male perpetrators) is a connection to the tradition of associating genre to gender that has its cinematic roots in the so-called "woman's picture," and its literary roots back even further.

24. In fairness to television, issues of women's rights—though rarely the rights of other minorities like gays, lesbians, and people of color—have been discussed in the forum of the biopic, in films like *Roe v. Wade* (NBC, May 15, 1989), or *Portrait of a Rebel: Margaret Sanger* (CBS, April 22, 1980), or *Sgt. Matlovich and the Air Force* (syndicated, August 21, 1978). But the primary locus of fame on TV, for women, is as a suffering figure whose acceptance of her fate is presumably coded by viewers as heroism.

25. George Gerbner (1976) would suggest that such a view of the world, as a place of overwhelming violence and illness, creates anxiety in heavy viewers, not complacency. Taking an opposite view to Gerbner, Fiske and Hartley (1987) suggest that TV narrates or articulates our worst-case scenarios for us, providing a safe release for the monstrous anxieties that might remain private and not public. Thus, illness and violence tales merely make public private fears.

26. While the antiquated label "paramour" may have disappeared from vocabulary of the made-for-TV biopic, the woman who loses everything for love, and is defined by her love, is a staple of television fiction.

27. Liebert, Sprafkin, and Davidson (1982:161) cite Dallas Smythe's 1954 study "Reality as Presented by Television," in which the demographics of national origin are remarkably similar to those of Hollywood during the studio era. If anything, these data on the worlds of TV and film, though hardly exhaustive of all films or TV programs, suggest a consistent world view at least in regard to what part of the world is fit to be viewed.

28. Statements such as these—that Dieterle-style biopics are out of synch with today's audiences—are obviously not empirically proven by any audience data I have here, but are suggested by the shifts in the content of the films themselves. However, a recent study by Kubey and Csikszentmihalyi (1990) suggests most people use TV to *avoid* negative affective states. That is, most people seem to desire escape from boredom, or avoidance of serious topics when they watch TV. For a summary of their findings, see (1990:171–180).

Appendix A

1. Even while purporting to "open up the canon," by including overlooked films in a study, scholars should be aware that they mean opening up the mainstream commercial canon that has survived. Specifically, I refer to the elimination, in most film studies, of ethnic and minority cinemas that emerged as attempts to combat the images of groups cultivated by the major film corporations. Often the films made by these companies are not reported because they have not survived, or have yet to surface in archives. The history of Hollywood, and any conclusions about the cultural impact made by Hollywood on audiences, then, is the history of corporations that became successful by ignoring and marginalizing "minority" groups.

Films like *Keep Punching,* the 1937 biopic about boxing champion Henry Armstrong, are hard to chart because they were produced by a small independent companies, denied distribution into the major theater chains, and have not survived except as examples of "alternative" film practice. My list of films then is unintentionally biased toward the mainstream, and its definition of the audience being addressed with their appropriate rhetoric of fame.

2. I am not adhering to a knee-jerk brand of positivism disguised as empiricism in my own privileging of sampling as a method of data collection. Sampling—in all its forms—is one step in a multivalent research process that, in a search for a context in which to place a body of films, should include many orders of data. Perhaps a large sample, systematically selected—e.g., all biographical films released by major studios in the period 1927–1960—is still, as the logician Korzybski noted, an incomplete structure. The complete context in which to place films might be an environment in which comparisons could be made to all films and all

mediated material used by a particular community. If making and understanding film are social acts, should not the unit of analysis be the very community whose commonality holds semantic processes or interpretive communities together? This is a daunting ethnographic task, and to the best of my knowledge it has yet to be done, though the work of communications researcher Sol Worth was moving in this direction at the time of his death in 1977.

REFERENCES

Adorno, Theodor and Max Horkheimer. 1944. "The Culture Industry: Enlightenment as Mass Deception." In *Dialectic of Enlightenment,* pp. 349–383. New
York: Seabury.

Affron, Charles. 1982. *Cinema and Sentiment.* Chicago: University of Chicago
Press.

Allen, Robert. 1980. *Vaudeville and Film 1895–1915: A Study in Media Interaction.* New York: Arno Press.

——— and Douglas Gomery. 1985. *Film History, Theory, and Practice.* New
York: Alfred A. Knopf.

*American Film Institute Catalog of Motion Pictures Produced in the US; Feature
Films, 1921–1930.* 1971. New York: Bowker.

Anderson, Christopher. 1986. "Jesse James, the Bourgeois Bandit: The Transformation of a Popular Hero." *Cinema Journal* 26, no. 1 (Fall), 43–64.

Anger, Kenneth. 1975. *Hollywood Babylon.* San Francisco: Straight Arrow Books.

Auerbach, Erich. 1953. *Mimesis: The Representation of Reality in Western Literature.* Translated by William Trask. Princeton: Princeton University Press.

Austin, Bruce. 1988. *Immediate Seating: A Look at Movie Audiences.* Belmont,
Calif.: Wadsworth Publishing Co.

Balio, Tino, ed. 1985. *The American Film Industry.* Madison: University of Wis-
consin Press.

———, ed. 1991. *Hollywood in the Age of Television.* New York: Harper Collins
Academic.

Bateson, Gregory. 1972. *Steps to an Ecology of Mind.* San Francisco: Chandler
Press.

———. 1979. *Mind and Nature: A Necessary Unity.* New York: Bantam Books.

Baxandall, Michael. 1985. *Patterns of Intention: On the Historical Explanation of Pictures*. New Haven: Yale University Press.

Behlmer, Rudy. 1985. *Inside Warner Brothers: 1935–1951*. New York: Simon and Schuster.

Berg, A. Scott. 1989. *Goldwyn: A Biography*. New York: Ballantine Books.

Bergan, Ronald. 1986. *The United Artists Story*. London: Octopus Books.

Berger, Peter L. and Thomas Luckman. 1967. *The Social Construction of Reality: A Treatise in the Sociology of Knowledge*. New York: Anchor Books.

Bergman, Andrew. 1971. *We're in the Money: Depression America and Its Films*. New York: Harper.

Bergreen, Lawrence. 1990. *As Thousands Cheer: The Life of Irving Berlin*. New York: Viking.

Berube, Alan. 1990. *Coming Out Under Fire: The History of Gay Men and Women in World War Two*. New York: The Free Press.

Bobo, Jacqueline and Ellen Seiter. 1991. "Black Feminism and Media Criticism: The Women of Brewster Place." *Screen* 32, no. 3 (Fall).

Boorstin, Daniel. 1962. *The Image: A Guide to Pseudo-Events in America*. New York: Atheneum.

Bordwell, David, Janet Staiger, and Kirstin Thompson. 1985. *The Classical Hollywood Cinema: Film Style and Mode of Production to 1960*. New York: Columbia University Press.

Braudy, Leo. 1986. *The Frenzy of Renown: Fame and Its History*. New York: Oxford University Press.

Brown, Karl. 1973. *Adventures with D. W. Griffith*. Edited by Kevin Brownlow. New York: Farrar, Straus and Giroux.

Browne, Nick. 1984. "The Political Economy of the Television (Super) Text." In *Television: The Critical View*, ed. Horace Newcomb, pp. 585–599. 4th ed. New York: Oxford University Press.

Brownlow, Kevin. 1968. *The Parade's Gone By*. New York: Alfred A. Knopf.

———. 1990. *Behind the Mask of Innocence*. New York: Alfred A. Knopf.

Burrow, J. A. 1986. *The Ages of Man: A Study in Medieval Writing*. Oxford: Clarendon Press.

Caldarola, Victor. 1990. "Reception as Cultural Experience: Visual Mass Media and Reception Practices in Outer Indonesia." Ph.D. dissertation, University of Pennsylvania.

Cantor, Muriel. 1971. *The Hollywood TV Producer: His Work and His Audience*. New York: Basic Books.

Carringer, Robert L. 1985. *The Making of Citizen Kane*. Berkeley and Los Angeles: University of California Press.

Chaney, David. 1989. "Mass Observation." In *International Encyclopedia of Communications*, vol. 2, pp. 497–499. New York: Oxford University Press.

Crowther, Bosley. 1960. *Hollywood Rajah: The Life and Times of Louis B. Mayer.* New York: Holt, Rinehart and Winston.

Curtis, James C. 1978. "Clio's Dilemma: To Be a Muse or to Be Amusing." In *Material Culture and the Study of American Life,* ed. Ian M. G. Quimby, pp. 201–218. New York: W. W. Norton.

Custen, George F. 1982. "Talking about Film." In *Film/Culture: Explorations of Cinema in Its Social Contexts,* ed. Sari Thomas, pp. 237–246. Metuchen, N. J.: Scarecrow Press.

———. 1986. "Hollywood and the Production of Culture." *Journal of Communication* 35 (Spring), 123–132.

Davis, Natalie Zemon. 1987. "'Any Resemblance to Persons Living or Dead': Film and the Challenge of Authenticity." *The Yale Review* 76, no. 4 (Summer), 457–480.

Denby, David. 1990. "Emile and Louis and Mikhail and Vaclav." *Premiere* 3, no. 12 (August), 34–35.

Dershowitz, Alan M. 1990. "Reversal of Image: Watching Someone Playing Yourself." *The New York Times,* October 14, sec. H, pp. 15, 17

Doherty, Thomas. 1988. *Teenagers & Teenpics: The Juvenalization of American Movies in the 1950s.* Boston: Unwin-Hyman.

Doty, Alexander. 1990. "The Cabinet of Lucy Ricardo: Lucille Ball's Star Image." *Cinema Journal* 29, no. 4 (Summer), 3–22.

Douglas, Kirk. 1988. *The Ragman's Son.* New York: Simon and Schuster.

Dyer, Richard. 1979. *Stars.* London: BFI Publishing.

———. 1986. *Heavenly Bodies: Film Stars and Society.* New York: St. Martin's Press.

Eames, John Douglas. 1975. *The MGM Story: The Complete History of Fifty Roaring Years.* London: Octopus Books.

———. 1985. *The Paramount Story.* London: Octopus Books.

Elsaesser, Thomas. 1986. "Film History as Social History: The Dieterle/Warner Brothers Bio-Pic." *Wide Angle* 8, no. 2, 15–31.

Eng, Ian. 1985. *Watching Dallas: Soap Opera and the Melodramatic Imagination.* New York: Methuen.

Feuer, Jane. 1982. *The Hollywood Musical.* London: Macmillan.

Finler, Joel W. 1988. *The Hollywood Story.* New York: Crown.

Fiske, John and John Hartley. 1987. "Bardic Television." In *Television: The Critical View,* ed. Horace Newcomb, pp. 600–612. 4th ed. New York: Oxford University Press.

Flinn, Tom. 1975. "William Dieterle: The Plutarch of Hollywood." *Velvet Light Trap,* no. 15 (Fall).

Fraser, George MacDonald. 1988. *A Hollywood History of the World: From One Million B.C. to Apocalypse Now.* New York: Fawcett Columbine.

Freeman, Joseph. 1941. "Biographical Films." *Theatre Arts Monthly* (December).

Frith, Simon. 1981. *Sound Effects: Youth, Leisure, and the Politics of Rock and Roll.* New York: Pantheon.

Gabler, Neal. 1988. *An Empire of Their Own: How the Jews Invented Hollywood.* New York: Crown.

Gaines, Jane and Charlotte Herzog, eds. 1990. *Fabrications: Costume and the Female Body.* New York: Routledge.

Gay, Peter. 1988. *Sigmund Freud: A Life for Our Time.* New York: Doubleday.

Gerbner, George. 1958. "The Social Role of the Confession Magazine." *Social Problems* (Summer).

Gerbner, George and Larry Gross. 1976. "Living with Television: The Violence Profile." *Journal of Communication* 26, no. 2 (Spring), 176–199.

Goffman, Erving. 1974. *Frame Analysis: An Essay on the Organization of Experience.* New York: Harper.

Goldman, Herbert. 1988. *Jolson: The Legend Comes to Life.* New York: Oxford University Press.

Gomery, Douglas. 1986. *The Hollywood Studio System.* New York: St. Martin's Press.

———. 1987. "*Brian's Song:* Television, Hollywood, and the Evolution of the Movie Made for Television." In *Television: The Critical View,* ed. Horace Newcomb, pp. 197–220. 4th ed. New York: Oxford University Press.

Graves, Ralph. 1991. "The 'Pope' Who Is Revising Our Bible of Sayings." *Smithsonian* (August), 68–77.

Gross, Larry P. 1974. "Modes of Communication and the Acquisition of Symbolic Competence." In *Media and Symbols: The Forms of Expression, Communication and Education.* Seventy-third Yearbook of the National Society for the Study of Education. Edited by Donald Olsen, pp. 56–80. Chicago: University of Chicago Press .

Gussow, Mel. 1971. *Don't Say Yes Until I Finish Talking: A Biography of Darryl F. Zanuck.* New York: Doubleday.

Hall, Stuart. 1980. "Encoding/Decoding." *Culture, Media, Language,* ed. Stuart Hall. London: Hutchinson.

Hanson, Cynthia A. 1988. "The Hollywood Musical Biopic and the Regressive Performer." *Wide Angle* 10, no. 2, 15–23.

Hepburn, Katharine. 1989. Letter, Katharine Hepburn to author, October 13, 1989.

Hirschhorn, Clive. 1979. *The Warner Brothers Story.* London: Octopus Books.

———. 1983. *The Universal Story.* London: Octopus Books.

———. 1989. *The Columbia Story.* London: Octopus Books.

Holroyd, Michael. 1971. *Lytton Strachey: A Biography.* New York: Holt, Rinehart and Winston.

Hurst, Richard Maurice. 1979. *Republic Studios.* Metuchen, N.J.: Scarecrow Press.

Ivens, William, Jr. 1953. *Prints and Visual Communication*. Cambridge, Mass.: M.I.T. Press.

Izod, John. 1988. *Hollywood and the Box Office, 1895–1986*. New York: Columbia University Press.

Jarvie, I. C. 1978. "Seeing Through Movies." *Philosophy of Social Science* 8, 374–397.

Jewell, Richard and Vernon Harbin. 1982. *The RKO Story*. New York: Arlington House.

Jordan, H. T. 1935. "Bad History." *Cincinnati Times-Star,* May 5, 1935.

Joseph, Robert. 1940. "William Dieterle Gets Hollywood's New Ideas" *Coast Magazine* 3, No. 1 (January), 6–9.

Jowett, Garth. 1976. *Film, the Democratic Art: A Social History of the American Film*. Boston: Little, Brown.

———. 1990. "Mass Media, History and the Development of Communications Research." In *Image as Artifact: The Historical Analysis of Film and Television,* ed. John E. O'Connor. Malabar, Fla.: Robert E. Krieger Publishing Co.

Katz, Elihu and Tamar Liebes. 1986. "Patterns of Involvement in Television Fiction: A Comparative Analysis." *European Journal of Communication* 1, no. 2 (June), 151–171.

Kubey, Robert and Mihaly Csikszentmihalyi. 1990. *Television and the Quality of Life: How Viewing Shapes Everyday Experience*. Hillsdale, N.J.: Lawrence Erlbaum Associates.

Larkin, Rochelle. 1975. *Hail Columbia*. New Rochelle, N.Y.: Arlington House.

Leab, Daniel. 1990. "The Moving Image as Interpreter of History—Telling the Dancer from the Dance." In *Image as Artifact: The Historical Analysis of Film and Television,* ed. John E. O'Connor, pp. 69–95. Malabar, Fla.: Robert E. Krieger.

Leff, Leonard J. and Jerold Simmons. 1990. *The Dame in the Kimono: Hollywood, Censorship, and the Production Code, from the 1920s to the 1960s*. New York: Grove Weidenfeld.

Lehmann-Haupt, Christopher. 1990. "How Ronald Reagan Overcame Doubts and Became President," *The New York Times,* November 5, 1990, C-16.

Liebert, Robert M., Joyce N. Sprafkin, and Emily S. Davidson. 1982. *The Early Window: Effects of Television on Children and Youth*. New York: Pergamon Press.

Loews International, Inc. 1938. *Campaign Book for Marie Antoinette*.

———. 1940. *Campaign Book for Edison the Man*. New York.

———. 1943. *West Coast Premiere Book for Madame Curie*. Los Angeles.

Lowenthal, Leo. 1944. "Biographies in Popular Magazines." In *Radio Research: 1942–1943,* ed. Paul Lazarsfeld and Frank Stanton. New York: Duell, Sloan and Pearce.

Lowery, Shearon and Melvin S. De Fleur. 1983. *Milestones in Mass Communications Research: Media Effects*. New York: Longman.

Lull, James. 1982. "Popular Music: Resistance to New Wave." *Journal of Communication* (Winter), 121–131.

McLelland, Doug. 1987. *From Blackface to Blacklist: Al Jolson, Larry Parks, and 'The Jolson Story'*. Metuchen, N.J.: Scarecrow Press.

McLuhan, Marshall. 1964. *Understanding Media: The Extensions of Man*. New York: McGraw-Hill.

Maltin, Leonard. 1991. *Leonard Maltin's TV Movies and Video Guide*. New York: Signet.

Manchester, William, 1983. *The Last Lion: Winston Spencer Churchill*. New York: Dell.

Marc, David. 1985. *Demographic Vistas*. Philadelphia: University of Pennsylvania Press.

Mast, Gerald. 1987. *Can't Help Singin': The American Musical on Stage and Screen*. New York: Overlook Press.

Mead, Margaret and Rhoda Metraux, eds. 1953. *The Study of Culture at a Distance*. Chicago: University of Chicago Press.

Meyer, Leonard. 1956. *Emotion and Meaning in Music*. Chicago: University of Chicago Press.

Miller, Robert. 1983. *Star Myths: Show Business Biographies on Film*. Metuchen, N.J.: Scarecrow Press.

Milliken, Carl. 1940. "Information Please." *The Warners Club News* (June).

Mordden, Ethan. 1988. *The Hollywood Studios: House Style in the Golden Age of the Studios*. New York: Alfred A. Knopf.

Morley, David. 1980. *The Nationwide Audience: Structure and Decoding*. London: BFI Books.

O'Connor, John E. 1988a. "History in Images/Images in History: Reflections on the Importance of Film and Television Study for an Understanding of the Past." *American Historical Review* 93, no. 5 (December), 1200–1207.

———. 1988b. "A Reaffirmation of American Ideals: Drums Along the Mohawk (1939)." In *American History/American Film*, ed. John E. O'Connor, pp. 97–120. New York: Frederick Ungar.

O'Connor, John J. 1990. "The Small Screen Has Its Shining Moments." *The New York Times*, July 9, 1990, H-27.

Okuda, Ted. 1987. *The Monogram Checklist*. Jefferson, N.C.: McFarland.

Paramount Films, Inc. 1938. *Campaign Book for The Buccaneer*. New York.

Pitts, Michael. 1984. *Hollywood and American Reality: A Filmography of Over 250 Motion Pictures Depicting U.S. History*. Jefferson, N.C.: McFarland.

Polan, Dana. 1986. *Power and Paranoia: History, Narrative, and the American Cinema, 1940–1950*. New York: Columbia University Press.

Polanyi, Michael. 1967. *The Tacit Dimension.* New York: Doubleday.

Pollock, Griselda. 1980. "Artists Mythologies and Media Genius, Madness and Art History." *Screen* 21, no. 3, 57–96.

Postman, Neil. 1985. *Amusing Ourselves to Death.* New York: Bantam Books.

Powdermaker, Hortense. 1950. *Hollywood the Dream Factory: An Anthropologist Looks at the Movies.* Boston: Little, Brown.

Radway, Janice. 1984. *Reading the Romance: Women, Patriarchy, and Popular Literature.* Chapel Hill: University of North Carolina Press.

Roddick, Nick. 1983. *A New Deal in Entertainment: Warner Brothers in the 1930s.* London: BFI.

Rosenstone, Robert. 1988. "History in Images/History in Words: Reflections on the Possibility of Really Putting History Onto Film." *American Historical Review* 93, no. 5 (December), 1173–1185.

Sandburg, Carl. 1926. *Abraham Lincoln: The Prairie Years, 1809–1861.* New York: Dell Publishing Co.

Schatz, Thomas. 1988. *The Genius of the System.* New York: Pantheon.

Schickel, Richard. 1985. *Intimate Strangers: The Culture of Celebrity.* New York: Doubleday.

Schwartz, Charles. 1977. *Cole Porter: A Biography.* New York: Dial Press.

Shohat, Ella. 1990. "Ethnicities-in-Relation: Towards a Multicultural Reading of American Cinema." In *Ethnicity and the American Cinema,* ed. Lester Friedman. Urbana: University of Illinois Press .

Smythe, Dallas. 1954. "Reality as Presented by Television." *Public Opinion Quarterly* 18, 143–156.

Sorlin, Pierre. 1990. "Historical Films as Tools for Historians." In *Image as Artifact: The Historical Analysis of Film and Television,* ed. John O'Connor. Malabar, Fla.: Robert E. Friedman Publishing.

Starr, Kevin. 1985. *Inventing the Dream: California Through the Progressive Era.* New York: Oxford University Press.

Sterling, Christopher H. and John M. Kittross. 1990. *Stay Tuned: A Concise History of American Broadcasting.* 2d ed. Belmont, Calif.: Wadsworth Publishing Co.

Surgeon General's Scientific Advisory Committee on Television and Social Behavior. 1971. *Television and Growing Up: The Impact of Televised Violence.* Report to the Surgeon General, United States Public Health Service. Washington, D.C.: U.S. Government Printing Office.

Thomas, Bob. 1967. *King Cohn: The Life and Times of Harry Cohn.* New York: G. P. Putnam's Sons.

Thomas, Tony and Aubrey Solomon. 1979. *The Films of Twentieth Century-Fox.* Seacaucus, N.J.: Citadel Press.

Timberg, Bernard and Hal Himmelstein. 1989. "Television Commercials and the

Contradictions of Everyday Life: A Follow-up to Himmelstein's Production Study of the Kodak 'America' Commercial." *Journal of Film and Video* 41, no. 3 (Fall), 67–79.

Turow, Joseph. 1989. "Routes and Roots." *The Journal of Communication* 39, no. 4 (Autumn), 67–70.

Wallace, Anthony F. C. 1970. *Culture and Personality.* 2nd ed. New York: Random House.

Warner, Jack, with Doug Jennings. 1965. *My First Hundred Years in Hollywood.* New York: Random House.

Watt, Ian. 1957. *The Rise of the Novel.* Berkeley and Los Angeles: University of California Press.

White, Hayden. 1978. *Tropics of Discourse.* Baltimore: Johns Hopkins University Press.

————. 1988. "Historiography and Historiophoty." *American Historical Review* 93, no. 5 (December), 1193–1199.

Worth, Sol. 1981. *Studying Visual Communication.* Edited by Larry Gross. Philadelphia: University of Pennsylvania Press.

Zukor, Adolph, with Dale Kramer. 1953. *The Public Is Never Wrong: The Autobiography of Adolph Zukor.* New York: G. P. Putnam's Sons.

Index

Abe Lincoln in Illinois (John Cromwell, 1940), 59, 163, 272n18
Abel, Michael, 171, 173
Abraham Lincoln (D. W. Griffith, 1930), 150
Actress, The (George Cukor, 1953), 52, 65, 156–157, 157f
Adler, Augusta, 112
Adorno, Theodor, 33, 50, 232. *See also* Frankfurt School
Adventures of Marco Polo, The (Archie Mayo, 1938), 64, 89, 99
Adventures of Mark Twain, The (Irving Rapper, 1944), 150, 210
Alexander, Grover Cleveland, 274n11
Alexander Hamilton (John Adolfi, 1931), 61, 76
Alexander's Ragtime Band (Henry King, 1938), 135, 172
All About Eve (Joseph L. Mankiewicz, 1950), 105
All This and Heaven Too (Anatole Litvak, 1940), 64, 112, 115, 142, 194f
All Together Now (TV movie, Randal Kleiser, 1975), 280n22
Allen, Woody, 54
Allgood, Sara, 79
Allied Artists, 80
Allyson, June, 202

Ameche, Don, 63, 129, 134f, 135, 261n12
Anderson, Maxwell, 105
Anne Boleyn (Ernst Lubitsch, 1920), 5, 101
Anna and the King of Siam (John Cromwell, 1946), 92, 153
Annie Get Your Gun (George Sidney, 1950), 45, 64
Aristotle, 150
Arliss, George, 30, 50, 60–61, 62f, 63f, 71, 76, 83, 84, 195, 205; as representative biopic actor, 60–63
Armstrong, Henry, 85
Armstrong, Louis, 207
Arnold, Edward, 77
As You Like It (William Shakespeare), 150
Assassination of Trotsky, The (Joseph Losey, 1972), 100–101
Astaire, Fred, 86
Auerbach, Erich, 207

Babe (TV movie, Buzz Kulik, 1975), 228
Babe Ruth Story, The (Roy Del Ruth, 1948), 57f, 72, 164, 217
Bachelor Father (TV series, ABC, CBS, NBC, 1957–1962), 227

Ball of Fire (Howard Hawks, 1941), 115

Bancroft, Anne, 98

Bankhead, Talullah, 99

Barbarian and the Geisha, The (John Huston, 1958), 99, 185

Barnouw, Erik, 260n9

Barnum, P. T., 59

Barrows, Sydney Biddle, 217

Barrymore, Diana, 9

Barrymore, John, 46f, 47

Battle of Manila Bay, The (Blackton and Smith, 1898), 5

Baxandall, Michael, 25

Beau James (Melville Shavelson, 1957), 47, 141

Beck, Jean, 112

Becket (Peter Glenville, 1964), 171

Belasco, David, 126, 149

Bell, Alexander Graham, 131–139, 192

Bell Telephone, 130, 133, 137f

Beery, Wallace, 59, 120

Bendix, William, 56, 57f

Benet, Rosemary, 167

Benjamin, Walter, 33, 207. *See also* Frankfurt School

Bergner, Elizabeth, 99

Bernhardt, Sarah, 5

Billy the Kid (William Bonney), 53, 79

biopic
—accuracy of, 9–12, 34–44, 110, 128, 129, 139
—causality in, 149, 165–168, 178, 186, 271n14, 271n15
—changes in, 29, 50–51, 84–86, 90, 119–121, 142–143, 169–175, 196–197, 207, 211–213
—censorship and, 110, 139–142, 169–171, 189
—community and, 72–74, 85–86, 127–128, 156, 187–188, 192; on TV, 215
—construction of the self in, 25–26, 151–156, 168–169, 175, 182, 230–231, 263n1; on TV, 215
—death in, 153
—defined, 5–7
—democracy and, 127–128, 175, 192, 210
—differentiated from other genres, 60–67, 112, 128, 148–149
—ethnicity and, 77–78, 121, 155, 174
—entertainers and, 149, 195–196, 205–208; and innovation, 208–211; on TV, 222
—family and, 68–69, 152–158
—formal characteristics of, 51–60, 177, 182–186, 206–211
—friends and, 69–71, 101, 159–165
—fame and, 34, 169, 215; on TV, 222
—gender and, 12, 66, 102–107, 157–158, 160–161, 166; in made-for-TV movies, 278n7
—house style and, 80–90
—ideology and, 16–18, 22, 71–74, 75, 78, 101–102, 113, 205, 207; on TV ideology, 217–225
—innovation and resistance in, 191–192, 208–211
—intertextuality and, 111, 142–147, 149, 172, 174–175; sources of, 178–182
—introductory titles and, 51–56, 167–168
—legal considerations and, 22–23, 110, 124–127, 261–262n15
—made-for-TV, 130, 212–213, 214–232
—message of, 175–176, 189, 211–212
—narrative construction and, 148–156; big break, 206–208
—nationality and, 77–78, 90–102
—origins of, 5–7
—producers and, 4–5, 20–22, 47–48, 50, 92–96, 99–101, 111, 118–119, 132, 142, 145–147, 151–152, 169–175, 206
—professions and, 88–90
—public history and, 2–4, 12–16,

113, 190, 205, 212; on TV, 214–215, 232, 277–278n6
—and relationships to other historical texts, 8–12, 146, 177, 195–196
—research for, 34–45, 60, 110–147, 124–139, 267n7
—romance in, 159–161, 175, 274n12
—sexual minorities and, 121–124, 216, 267n5
—social class and, 78–79
—stars and, 4, 18, 22, 34, 44–48, 59–60, 120–121, 135, 172, 181, 193–202, 262n18, 264n4, 274–275nn15–20; availability of as determinants of, 195–197; star/genre formulations in, 202–205
—and studio mode of production, 29, 47–50, 80–90, 110, 120–121, 195; disintegration of, 214
—talent and, 168–169
—time frame represented in, 93–95
—truth-telling function of, 51–60, 183, 263–264n3
Black Fury (Michael Curtiz, 1935), 8
Blackton, J. Stuart, and Albert E. Smith, 5
Blossoms in the Dust (Mervyn LeRoy, 1941), 147, 166, 185, 188, 189f, 202, 203f
Bob Mathias Story, The (Francis D. Lyon, 1954), 55, 86, 269n3, 274n11
Bolivar, Simón, 101
Bonnie Parker Story, The (William Witney, 1958), 27
Boone, Daniel, 185
Boorstin, Daniel, 25, 220
Boys Town (Norman Taurog, 1938), 65, 82, 138
Brady Bunch, The (TV series, ABC, 1969–1974), 227
Brahms, Johannes, 96, 209
Brando, Marlon, 101

Braudy, Leo, 6, 25, 28, 111, 220, 223
Breen, Joseph, 139, 140
Breen Office, *see* Production Code Administration
Brennan, Walter, 162, 166, 271n13
Brian's Song (TV movie, Buzz Kulik, 1970), 228
Brice, Fanny, 59
Brigham Young—Frontiersman (Henry Hathaway, 1940), 159, 161, 187
Brown, John, 59
Brown v. the Board of Education of Topeka, Kansas, 98
Browne, Nick, 218
Buccaneer, The (C. B. De Mille, 1938), 44, 77, 128, 267n7
Buchowetski, Dimitri, 5
Buck, Jules, 171, 173
Buckner, Robert, 160
Buffalo Bill (William Wellman, 1944), 52, 144, 145f, 163, 265–266n8
Buntline, Ned, 163
Buñuel, Luis, 54
Burns, Ken, 16
Burton, Richard, 100
Buster Keaton Story, The (Sidney Sheldon, 1957), 170, 271n9

Cagney, James, 3, 59, 64, 65f, 86, 154f, 193, 275n17, 275n19
Cagney, William, 160–161
Calamity Jane (David Butler, 1953), 64
Callas, Maria, 8
Capaletti, John, 230
Capra, Frank, 120
Capture of the Biddle Brothers, The (1902), 6
Carbine Williams (Richard Thorpe, 1952), 64, 183
Cardinal Richelieu (Rowland V. Lee, 1935), 19, 36, 61, 71, 114, 129, 144, 275n19
Carlotta, empress of Mexico, 194
Carnegie, Andrew, 33, 77
Carnegie, Hattie, 33

Carter, Caroline (Mrs. Leslie), 125–127, 149–150
Caruso, Enrico, 48, 73, 90, 209
Castro, Fidel, 101
Catherine the Great, empress of Russia, 79
Chamberlain, Richard, 279n19
Chambers, Karen, 227
Chaney, Lon, 71, 94, 153, 163, 209, 224, 275n17
Charles and Diana: A Royal Love Story (TV movie, James Goldstone, 1982), 219
Che! (Richard Fleischer, 1969), 100
Cheaper by the Dozen (Walter Lang, 1950), 131, 155–156, 270n8
Chief Crazy Horse (George Sherman, 1955), 98
Chopin, Frédéric, 97, 153, 163, 164
Christina, queen of Sweden, 201f
Christopher Columbus (TV movie, David Macdonald, 1949), 215
Churchill, Winston, 152, 183
Citizen Kane (Orson Welles, 1941), 21
Civil War, The (TV documentary, Ken Burns, 1990), 16
Cleopatra, 7
Cleopatra (C. B. De Mille, 1934), 92
Clive of India (Richard Boleslawski, 1935), 92
Clooney, Rosemary, 223, 230, 231
Clum, John, 98
Coal Miner's Daughter (Michael Apted, 1980), 276–277n1
Coburn, Charles, 72, 77
Cohan, George M., 59, 71, 73, 86, 152, 182–183, 193
Cohn, Harry, 58, 78, 147, 206, 269n4
Colbert, Claudette, 144
Collier, Constance, 45, 163
Collins, Eddie, 160
Columbia, 80, 84
Compton, Betty, 141
Connolly, Maureen, 228
Conquest (Clarence Brown, 1937), 276n20

Consent Decree, *see Paramount Decree*
content analysis, coding categories explained, 236–239
Cooper, Gary, 56, 64, 89, 117f, 120, 162, 271n13
Corbett, James J., 56, 60, 73, 86
Corrigan, Douglas "Wrong Way," 55, 58, 130, 176
Cosby Show, The (TV series, NBC, 1984–1992), 227
Country Doctor, The (1936), 81
Courageous Mr. Penn (Lance Comfort, 1941), 101
Court-Martial of Billy Mitchell, The (Otto Preminger, 1955), 64, 116–118, 117f, 142
Crabtree, Lotte, 87, 196
Crews, Laura Hope, 126
Cuba (Richard Lester, 1979), 101
Cukor, George, 67
Cummings, Jack, 85
Curie, Eve, 41–42
Curie, Marie, 16, 19, 41f, 196
Custer, George Armstrong, 205

Dailey, Dan, 200–201
Daniel Boone (David Howard, 1936), 27, 185
Danton (Dimitri Buchowetski, 1920), 5
Darnell, Linda, 159
Davies, Joseph, 100f
Davis, Bette, 7, 30, 34, 59, 64–65, 105, 113, 121, 193–194, 194f, 205, 231, 279n17
Day, Dennis, 87
Day, Doris, 64, 65f, 86, 195
Dean, Dizzy, 207
Death of a Centerfold: The Dorothy Stratten Story (TV movie, Gabrielle Beaumont, 1981), 227
Dietz, Howard, 89
Demerest, William, 69, 164
De Mille, Cecil B., 44, 128
Dempsey, Jack, 162
de Rezske, Jean, 73

Desert Fox, The (Henry Hathaway, 1951), 183
Desportes, Henriette, 194
Devil and Miss Jones, The (Sam Wood, 1941), 77
Devotion (Curtis Bernhardt, 1946), 37, 103, 226
Diamond Jim (Edward Sutherland, 1935), 77, 152
Dieterle, William, 2, 13, 66–67, 210; *A Dispatch from Reuters*, 13, 14f, 67, 211; *Dr. Ehrlich's Magic Bullet*, 67, 72, 184, 140–142, 190; *Juarez*, 44, 62, 67, 98; *The Life of Emile Zola*, 3, 62, 67, 83, 275n17; *Madame Du Barry*, 52, 140; *The Story of Louis Pasteur*, 27, 62, 67, 72, 83; *Tennessee Johnson*, 13, 15f, 67; *Omar Khayyam*, 67; *The White Angel*, 67
Dietrich, Marlene, 99
Diff'rent Strokes (TV series, NBC, 1978–1987), 227
Dillinger (Max Nosseck, 1945), 84
Dionne quintuplets, 176
Disney, Walt, 95
Disney Studios, 84
Dispatch from Reuters, A (William Dieterle, 1940), 13, 14f, 67, 211
Disraeli (Alfred E. Green, 1929), 60–61, 62f, 71, 144
Dr. Ehrlich's Magic Bullet (William Dieterle, 1940), 67, 72, 184; censorship struggle over, 140–142, 190
Dolly Sisters, The (Irving Cummings, 1945), 47, 103, 105, 143, 172, 199, 261n14
Donath, Ludwig, 68, 70
Donna Reed Show, The (TV series, ABC, 1958–1966), 227
Doors, The (Oliver Stone, 1991), 2
Douglas, Kirk, 197–198, 198f, 199
Douglas, Stephen, 273n3
Drums Along the Mohawk (John Ford, 1939), 111, 144
Du Barry, Jeanne Bécu, comtesse, 96
Duchin, Eddy, 163

Dunnock, Mildred, 270n8
Durbin, Deanna, 85
Duryea, Dan, 162
Dyer, Richard, 194–195

Eagels, Jeanne, 94
East of Eden (Elia Kazan, 1955), 118
Ebenstein, Morris, 126
Edel, Leon, 182
Edison, Thomas Alva, 19, 43, 44
Edison, The Man (Clarence Brown, 1940), 19, 20f, 22, 43, 62, 65, 185
Ehrlich, Paul, 96–97, 140, 153, 192, 211
Eight Is Enough (TV series, ABC, 1977–1982), 227
Eldridge, Florence, 35, 35f
Elephant Man, The (David Lynch, 1980), 280n20
Elizabeth I, queen of England, 34–35, 35f, 182, 194
Emerson, Ralph Waldo, 1, 8, 260n7
Etting, Ruth, 65f, 86, 106, 195
Execution of Mary Queen of Scots, The (Edison, 1895), 5

Fabulous Dorseys, The (Alfred E. Green, 1947), 55, 86, 226, 269n3
Fall from Grace (TV movie, 1990), 279n14
Family Affair (TV series, CBS, 1966–1971), 227
Farrar, Geraldine, 272n20
Fawcett, Farrah, 279n15
Fear Strikes Out (Robert Mulligan, 1957), 170
Ferrer, Jose, 275n17
film: reception and, 26, 107–109, 263n23, 266n9; and socialization, 26, 33–34
Fisher, Fred, 48–50, 202
Five of a Kind (H. Leeds, 1938), 226
Five Pennies, The (Melville Shavelson, 1959), 76, 207
Flanagan, Father, 146
flashbacks, 182–184, 273n6
Fliess, Wilhelm, 151

Flying Irishman, The (Leigh Jason, 1939), 55, 130, 275n19
Flynn, Errol, 7, 46f, 46–47, 56, 60, 205
Follow the Sun (Sidney Lanfield, 1951), 37
Fonda, Henry, 45, 65, 144, 153, 181f
Ford, Francis, 160
Ford, Henry, 32, 43, 77
Ford, John, 51, 67, 153, 160
Foy, Eddie, 59
Foy, Eddie, Jr., 59
France, Anatole, 211
Frankfurt School, 16, 32–34
Franklin, Sidney, 40
Fraser, George, 259n3
Freed, Arthur, 85, 171
Freud, Sigmund, 151
Frick, Henry Clay, 77
Friese-Greene, William, 74
Froman, Jane, 71, 163, 224
Funny Girl (William Wyler, 1968), 29, 59, 276–277n1
Funny Lady (Herbert Ross, 1975), 59

Gable, Clark, 155, 195
Gallant Hours, The (Robert Montgomery, 1960), 65
Gance, Abel, 5
Gandhi (Richard Attenborough, 1982), 276–277n1
Garbo, Greta, 104f, 195, 200f, 276n20
Garfield, John, 53
Garland, Judy, 45, 87
Garson, Greer, 30, 40f, 43, 188, 189f, 195, 202, 203f, 276n20
Gay, Peter, 184
Gaynor, Mitzi, 47, 87, 196
Geertz, Clifford, 25
Gehrig, Lou, 56, 73, 162, 211
Gene Krupa Story, The (Don Weis, 1959), 170
Gentleman Jim (Raoul Walsh, 1942), 60, 73
Gentlemen Prefer Blondes (Howard Hawks, 1953), 274n9

George, Hetta, 112
Gerbner, George, 16, 77
Geronimo (Paul H. Sloan, 1939), 98
Gibbon, Edward, 146, 182
Gibson, Mel, 6
Gilbert, John, 104f, 276n20
Gilbreth, Frank, 155, 192
Gillian, Ann, 231, 279n19
Girl in the Red Velvet Swing, The (Richard Fleischer, 1955), 22, 107
Girl in White, The (John Sturges, 1952), 105
Gladney, Emma, 166, 185, 188, 192
Glenn Miller Story, The (Anthony Mann, 1954), 64, 90
Golden Girl (Lloyd Bacon, 1951), 47, 86, 196–197, 200–201
Goldwyn, Samuel, 21, 56, 78, 147, 269n4, 272n20
Gone With the Wind (Victor Fleming, 1939), 16
Gordon, Ruth Brown, 156
Gorgeous Hussy, The (Clarence Brown, 1936), 107
Grable, Betty, 47, 199
Grace Kelly (TV movie, Anthony Page, 1983), 219
Gramsci, Antonio, 189f, 190, 210
Grand Amour de Beethoven, Un (Abel Gance, 1936), 5
Grant, Cary, 119, 125f, 199
Grapes of Wrath, The (John Ford, 1940), 181
Graziano, Rocky, 55, 60, 163
Great Awakening, The (a k a *New Wine*) (1941), 27
Great Caruso, The (Richard Thorpe, 1951), 56, 67, 73, 90, 128, 150, 165, 187
Great Dan Patch, The (Joseph M. Newman, 1949), 103
Great Ziegfeld, The (Robert Z. Leonard, 1936), 59, 84, 119, 185
Greek Tycoon, The (J. Lee Thompson, 1978), 8
Greenwood, Charlotte, 48–50, 49f
Gross, Larry, 261n10

Guinan, Texas, 50, 63
Gunfighter, The (Henry King, 1950), 87
Guyana Tragedy: The Story of Jim Jones (TV movie, William A. Graham, 1980), 220

Hahn, Jessica, 279n14
Hammerstein, Oscar, 171
Harmon of Michigan (Charles Barton, 1941), 55, 84
Harris, Roy, 129, 131–135
Harris, Townshend, 99
Haver, June, 48–50, 49f, 199, 202, 203
Hays, Will, 97, 140. *See also* Production Code Administration
Hayward, Susan, 55, 63, 66, 71
Held, Anna, 59
Henry VIII, king of England, 182
Hepburn, Katharine, 27, 44, 48, 71, 87, 105, 193, 202, 259n1
Herndon, Billy (Lincoln's law partner), 163
Hilton, James, 42
Hitchcock, Alfred, 21, 101
Hogan, Ben, 85, 86
Holm, Celeste, 105
Holmes, Oliver Wendell, 54, 184
Holroyd, Michael, 184
Homer, 9
Hope, Bob, 59, 120
Hopkins, Miriam, 113, 125, 127f
Horkheimer, Max, 33
Houdini (George Marshall, 1953), 187
House of Rothschild (Alfred L. Werker, 1934), 61, 71, 129
How the West Was Won (John Ford, Henry Hathaway, George Marshall, 1963), 59
Howard, Joe, 18, 58, 143
Hudson, Rock, 223
Hudson's Bay (Irving Pichel, 1940), 131
Hutton, Betty, 45, 47, 50, 56, 63–64, 86, 202

I Am a Fugitive from a Chain Gang (Mervyn LeRoy, 1932), 62
I Don't Care Girl, The (Lloyd Bacon, 1953), 47, 171–175, 174f
I Dream of Jeannie (Allen Dwan, 1952), 84
I Want to Live! (Robert Wise, 1958), 27, 55, 63
I Wonder Who's Kissing Her Now (a k a *Hello My Baby*) (Lloyd Bacon, 1947), 11, 18, 20, 47, 58, 179; production of, 143–144
Iliad, The (Homer), 9
I'll Cry Tomorrow (Daniel Mann, 1955), 55, 63, 105, 170
I'll See You in My Dreams (Michael Curtiz, 1951), 64
In Old Chicago (Henry King, 1938), 111, 131, 172
Incendiary Blonde (George Marshall, 1945), 63, 64
Indiana Jones and the Temple of Doom (Steven Spielberg, 1984), 221
Interrupted Melody (Curtis Bernhardt, 1955), 68, 104, 168, 208
Irish Eyes Are Smiling (Gregory Ratoff, 1944), 143
Iron Duke, The (1934), 61
Is Everybody Happy? (Charles Barton, 1943), 55
Iturbi, José, 57

Jack London (Alfred Santell, 1943), 64, 179, 207
Jackie Robinson Story, The (Alfred E. Green, 1950), 55, 98
Jagger, Dean, 271n10
James, Henry, 182
Jarvie, Ian, 11
Jesse James (Henry King, 1939), 65, 129, 181
Jessel, George, 18, 20, 47, 87, 143, 171–175; *The I Don't Care Girl*, 174f, 197
Jim Thorpe—All American (Michael Curtiz, 1951), 98

Joe Louis Story, The (Robert Gordon, 1953), 9
John Paul Jones (John Farrow, 1959), 64
Johnson, Julian, 132
Johnson, Samuel, 1, 260n5
Joker Is Wild, The (Charles Vidor, 1957), 58, 199
Jolson, Al, 58, 71, 75, 192
Jolson Story, The (Alfred E. Green, 1946), 58, 68, 75, 84, 144, 147
Jones, Rev. Jim, 220
Joplin, Janice, 8
Jowett, Garth, 4
Joy, Col. Jason, 131, 137–139
Juárez, Benito, 2, 99
Juarez (William Dieterle, 1939), 44, 62, 67, 98

Kaye, Danny, 78
Keaton, Buster, 94, 162, 209
Keaton, Diane, 6
Keep Punching (1937), 85, 98
Kennedy, Jacqueline, 8
Kennedys of Massachusetts, The (TV mini-series, 1989), 221
Kenny, Sister Elizabeth, 103, 166, 192
Kern, Jerome, 171, 196
King and I, The (Walter Lang, 1956), 92
Kirsten, Dorothy, 57
Knute Rockne, All American (Lloyd Bacon, 1940), 85
Korda, Alexander, 5
Kreuts, Harold, 224

Lacan, Jacques, 77, 107–108
Lady with Red Hair, The (Curtis Bernhardt, 1940), 113, 125–127, 127f, 142, 149–150, 235, 269n1
Lady's Morals, A (Sidney Franklin, 1930), 59, 120
Lafitte, Jean, 44, 77
Land Without Bread (Luis Buñuel, 1932), 54
Lanza, Mario, 48, 57, 90

Lasky, Jesse, 269n4, 272n20
Laughton, Charles, 59
Lawrence, Gertrude, 29
Lawrence, Marjorie, 68, 71, 104, 168, 208, 211
Lawrence of Arabia (David Lean, 1962), 276–277n1
Leab, Daniel, 260n8, 260n9
Leave It to Beaver (TV series, CBS, ABC, 1957–1963), 227
Le Flore, Ron, 230
Left-Handed Gun, The (Arthur Penn, 1958), 53
Lester, Richard, 101
Lewis, Joe E., 199
Liberace (TV movie, Billy Hale, 1988), 219
Liberace: Behind the Music (TV movie, David Green, 1988), 219
Life of Emile Zola, The (William Dieterle, 1937), 3, 62, 64f, 67, 83, 275n17
Lifeboat (Alfred Hitchcock, 1944), 21
Like Normal People (TV movie, Harvey Hart, 1979), 279n18
Lillian Russell (Irving Cummings, 1940), 65
Lincoln, Abraham, 199
Lincoln, Mary Todd, 168, 273n3
Lind, Jenny, 48, 120
Lindbergh, Charles, 50
Lippman, Walter, 1
Lissauer, Herman, 112, 115, 124, 127
Little Mo (TV movie, Daniel Haller, 1978), 228
Livingstone, David, 98, 187
Liszt, Franz, 70, 209
Lloyds of London (Henry King, 1936), 38, 131
Locke, Sondra, 231
Lonesome Dove (TV mini-series, 1990), 279n16
Longest Night, The (TV movie, Jack Smight, 1972), 227
Look for the Silver Lining (David Butler, 1949), 172

Loos, Anita, 188
Loren, Sophia, 231
Losey, Joseph, 100
Love (Edmund Goulding, 1927), 276n20
Love Me or Leave Me (Charles Vidor, 1955), 64, 65f, 86, 105
Lowenthal, Leo, "Biographies in Popular Magazines," 6, 25, 32–34, 69, 84, 85, 155, 164, 169, 179, 206, 212, 264n9
Loy, Myrna, 202, 270n8
Lubitsch, Ernst, 5
Lukács, Georg, 23
Lund, John, 45
Lust for Life (Vincente Minnelli, 1956), 146, 150, 197–199, 198f

McClure, Jessica, 217, 223
McCrae, Joel, 145f
McDermid, Finlay, 97
MacGowan, Kenneth, 38, 129–139, 167
Madame Curie (Mervyn LeRoy, 1943), 17, 40–42, 40–41f, 72, 107, 179, 184, 195, 276n20; star pairings in, 202, 204f
Madame Du Barry (Ernst Lubitsch, 1919), 5, 101
Madame Du Barry (William Dieterle, 1934), 52, 140
Madison, Dolley, 77
Mae West (TV movie, Lee Philips, 1982), 230
Magic Box, The (John Boulting, 1951), 74
Magnificent Doll, The (Frank Borzage, 1946), 77
Magnificent Yankee, The (John Sturges, 1950), 54, 185
Maltz, Albert, 53
Man Called Peter, A (Henry Koster, 1955), 165, 166, 207, 228, 271n15
Man of a Thousand Faces (Joseph Pevney, 1957), 65, 154f, 163, 275n17

Manchester, William, 183
Mandell, Danny, 56
Mankiewicz, Herman, 172
Mann, Delbert, 55
March, Fredric, 27, 87
Marie Antoinette, 96
Marie Antoinette (W. S. Van Dyke II, 1938), 38, 39f
Marshall, Peter, 165, 166, 207, 271n15
Martin, Mary, 196f
Mary, Queen of Scots, 193
Mary of Scotland (John Ford, 1936), 105
Massey, Raymond, 59, 199, 205
Mata Hari (George Fitzmaurice, 1932), 276n20
Mathias, Bob, 86
Maxin, Hiram, 63
Mayer, Louis B., 50, 100, 142, 147, 206, 269n4
Mead, Margaret, 11, 24
Meet John Doe (Frank Capra, 1941), 77
Meet Me in St. Louis (Vincente Minnelli, 1944), 111, 171
Merman, Ethel, 124
Merrick, John, 280n20
methodology, 235–239
Metro-Goldwyn-Mayer (MGM), 80, 84–86, 89–90
Mighty Barnum, The (Walter Lang, 1934), 27, 59
Miller, Marilyn, 172
Miller, Mark Crispin, 200, 222
Milliken, Carl, Jr., 114, 116
Minnelli, Vincente, 67, 171
Miracle, The (Roberto Rossellini, 1950), 170
Miracle of Morgan's Creek, The (Preston Sturges, 1944), 45
Mission to Moscow (Michael Curtiz, 1943), 19, 100f
montage, 182, 184–186, 273n7, 273n8
Montgomery, Elizabeth, 231, 279n17, 279n18
Moore, Grace, 48, 50, 120, 272n20

Morgan, Frank, 69
Mother Wore Tights (Walter Lang, 1947), 131
Motion Picture Producers and Distributers of America (MPPDA), 23, 37, 139–142, 189
Molière (Abel Gance, 1909), 5
Monogram, 80
Moulin Rouge (John Huston, 1952), 275n17
Mrs. Miniver (William Wyler, 1942), 43
Mulvey, Laura, 108
Muni, Paul, 2, 3, 8, 30, 61–63, 64f, 69, 83, 146, 163, 195, 275n17
Murphy, Audie, 54, 56, 58, 98
My Blue Heaven (Henry Koster, 1950), 197
My Darling Clementine (John Ford, 1946), 273n2
My Four Years in Germany (1918), 6
My Gal Sal (Irving Cummings, 1942), 143
My Mother the Car (TV series, NBC, 1965–1966), 227
My Three Sons (TV series, ABC, CBS, 1960–1972), 227
My Wild Irish Rose (David Butler, 1947), 53, 73, 76, 79, 217

Napoleon (Abel Gance, 1927), 5
Neal, Patricia, 227, 230
Nesbit, Evelyn, 22
Nichols, Red, 76, 207
"Night and Day" (Cole Porter), 86–87, 142
Night and Day (Michael Curtiz, 1946), 17, 196f; censorship and, 119–125, 125f; research for, 36, 119–125, 128
Nixon, Richard, 1–2
No Other Love (TV movie, Richard Pearce, 1979), 279n18
Novotna, Jarmila, 57

O'Brien, Pat, 275n19
O'Connor, John E., 7, 16

O'Connor, Una, 96
Odyssey, The (Homer), 9
Oh, You Beautiful Doll (John Stahl, 1949), 47–50, 49f, 127, 202
O'Hara, Maureen, 145f
Olcott, Chauncey, 73, 76, 79
Olivier, Laurence, 271n10
Omar Khayyam (William Dieterle, 1957), 67
Onassis, Aristotle, 8
Ordeal of Bill Carney, The (TV movie, Jerry London, 1981), 226
Osmond, Marie, 231
Out of Africa (Sidney Pollack, 1985), 276–277n1
Owen, Reginald, 52
Ox-Bow Incident, The (William Wellman, 1943), 131

Paramount Decree (*United States v. Paramount Pictures, et al.*, 334 U.S. 131, 1948), 141, 170
Paramount, 80, 84, 86, 141
Parker, Bonnie, 162
Parnell (John Stahl, 1937), 36, 153, 274–275n16
Parsons, Louella, 141
Pasternak, Joseph, 85
Pasteur, Louis, 2, 160, 192, 211
Patricia Neal Story, The (TV movie, Anthony Harvey, 1981), 227–228
Patton (Franklin Schaffner, 1970), 1–2, 276n1
Payne Fund Studies, 261n11
Peck, Gregory, 87
Perils of Pauline, The (George Marshall, 1947), 45, 56, 64, 163
Peter der Grosse (Dimitri Buchowetski, 1922), 5
Photoplay Studies, 13
Pidgeon, Walter, 202, 203f
Piersall, Jimmy, 162
Pierson, Louise Randall, 42f, 53
Pinza, Ezio, 272n20
Pliny, 146
Plutarch, 9
Pons, Lily, 272n20

Porter, Cole, 17, 86, 119, 121–122, 147, 199
Porter, Linda Lee, 121–122
Powell, William, 202
Power, Tyrone, 129, 135, 138, 159
Preminger, Otto, 117f
President's Lady, The (Henry Levin, 1953), 63, 107
Pride of St. Louis, The (Harmon Jones, 1952), 150, 207
Pride of the Marines (Delmar Daves, 1945), 53–54
Pride of the Yankees, The (Sam Wood, 1942), 27, 51, 56, 65, 68, 162–163, 165, 217, 228
Private Life of Helen of Troy, The (Alexander Korda, 1927), 5
Private Life of Henry VIII (Alexander Korda, 1933), 5, 59
Private Lives of Elizabeth and Essex, The (Michael Curtiz, 1939), 7, 59
Production Code Administration (PCA), 118, 122, 130, 131, 135, 139–142, 170, 189–190
Provine, Dorothy, 27

Quayle, Dan, 205
Queen Christina (Rouben Mamoulian, 1933), 104f, 200f, 276n20
Queen Elizabeth (1912), 5

Radio-Keith-Orpheum (RKO), 80, 83–84, 87, 107, 266n3
Raging Bull (Martin Scorsese, 1980), 69
Raid on Entebbe (TV movie, Irvin Kershner, 1977), 278n13
Rainer, Luise, 59
Rains, Claude, 126
Rambeau, Marjorie, 163
Rasputin and the Empress (Richard Boleslawsky, 1932), 261–262n15
Reagan, Ronald, 32, 205
Redford, Robert, 205
Republic, 80
Return of Frank James, The (Fritz Lang, 1940), 65

Reunion (Norman Taurog, 1936), 226
Reuter, Julius, 96, 192, 210, 211
Rhetoric (Aristotle), 150
Richards, Renée, 216
Ritter, Thelma, 71
Rivers, Joan, 216
Robertson, Dale, 201
Robocop (Paul Verhoeven, 1987), 221
Rockne, Knute, 85, 160
Rogers, Ginger, 86
Rogers, Will, 123
Rommel, General Erwin, 183
Roosevelt, Franklin, 182
Roots (TV mini-series, 1977), 16, 279n16
Rose, The (Mark Rydell, 1979), 8
Rosie: The Rosemary Clooney Story (TV movie, Jackie Cooper, 1982), 231
Rossellini, Roberto, 170
Roth, Lillian, 55, 106, 185
Roughly Speaking (Michael Curtiz, 1945), 43f, 53
Royal Romance of Charles and Diana, The (TV movie, Peter Levin, 1982), 219
Rubinstein, Artur, 69
Ruman, Sig, 190
Russell, Lillian, 76, 79
Russell, Rosalind, 43f, 191f
Ruth, George Herman ("Babe"), 56, 57f, 58, 72, 73, 85, 153, 162
Rutledge, Ann, 180, 272n18
Ryan, Leo (congressman), 220

St. Louis Blues (Allen Reisner, 1958), 98
Sakall, S. Z. ("Cuddles"), 48–50, 49f, 96
Saldanas, Theresa, 231
Salome, 7
sampling, and film studies, 22–23, 27–28, 261–262n21; sample explained, 235–237, 281n1, 281n2
Sand, George, 86, 164
Sandburg, Carl, 180

Sante Fe Trail (Michael Curtiz, 1940), 59

Saussure, Ferdinand de, 77

Scanlon, Billy, 73

Schaffner, Franklin, 1

Schatz, Thomas, 20, 260n4

Schmidt, Al, 53–54

Schubert, Franz, 27, 96

Schumann, Clara, 48, 71, 96, 209

Schumann, Robert, 71, 209

Second Serve (TV movie, Anthony Page, 1986), 216

Sergeant York (Howard Hawks, 1941), 65, 165–166, 276–277n1

Seven Angry Men (Charles Marquis Warren, 1955), 59

Seven Little Foys, The (Melville Shavelson, 1955), 59, 226, 271n9

Seymour, Jane, 279n19

Shakespeare, William, 150

Sharif, Omar, 100

She Wore a Yellow Ribbon (John Ford, 1949), 273n2

Shemanski, Mike, 8

Sherwood, Robert, 59

Shine On, Harvest Moon (David Butler, 1944), 53, 103

Show Boat (Kern and Hammerstein, 1927), 171

Shurlock, Geoffrey, 37, 141

Siegel, Don, 115

Simmons, Jean, 157f

Sinatra, Frank, 101, 199

Sister Kenny (Dudley Nichols, 1946), 19, 72, 107, 136, 147, 150, 190–192, 191f, 210, 211

Sitting Bull (Sidney Salkow, 1954), 98

Sloane, Everett, 60, 163

Smith, Alexis, 87, 119, 125f

Smith, C. Aubrey, 96

Smith, Jaclyn, 279n19

Smith, Roger, 154f

Snead, Sam, 58

So Goes My Love (Frank Ryan, 1946), 63

Somebody Loves Me (Irving S. Brecher, 1952), 64

Somebody Up There Likes Me (Robert Wise, 1956), 55, 60, 69, 163

Something for Joey (TV movie, Lou Antonio, 1977), 230

Song of Love (Clarence Brown, 1947), 71, 86

Song to Remember, A (Charles Vidor, 1945), 57, 62, 68–69, 70, 74, 86, 97

Song Without End (Charles Vidor, 1960), 70

Sperling, Milton, 116–118, 117f

Spirit of St. Louis, The (Billy Wilder, 1957), 65

Stanley, Henry, 98, 187

Stanley and Livingstone (Henry King, 1939), 34, 65, 72, 92, 98, 187

Stanwyck, Barbara, 45

Star! (Robert Wise, 1968), 29

Stars and Stripes Forever (Henry Koster, 1952), 131

Stevens, George, 120

Stevens, Mark, 202, 203

Stewart, James, 50, 64–65, 89, 120

Story of Alexander Graham Bell, The (Irving Cummings, 1939), 19, 63, 65, 81, 111, 134f, 150, 181, 181f, 187; construction of, 129–139

Story of Dr. Wassell, The (C. B. De Mille, 1944), 65

Story of Louis Pasteur, The (William Dieterle, 1936), 27, 62, 67, 72, 83

Story of Seabiscuit, The (David Butler, 1949), 103, 270n6

Story of Vernon and Irene Castle, The (H. C. Potter, 1939), 86, 103, 184

Strachey, Lytton, 7, 23, 146

Stratten, Dorothy, 227

Stratton, Monty, 50

Stratton Story, The (Sam Wood, 1949), 51, 64, 90

Strauss, Johann, 96

Streisand, Barbra, 59

Suez (Allen Dwan, 1938), 111, 129, 139

Sullivan, John L., 73, 86

Sullivans, The (Lloyd Bacon, 1944), 185, 217, 226

Sutter's Gold (James Cruze, 1936), 278n12

Swanee River (Sidney Lanfield, 1939), 63, 143

Sweet Dreams (Karel Reisz, 1985), 2

Tanguay, Eva, 171–175, 174f

television biopic: cable TV and, 220–221; construction of fame, 29–30, 223; differs from film biopic, 29–30, 130, 176, 212–213, 217–225, 278n10, 278n11; entertainers and, 222, 229–231; everyday famous vs. elite famous in, 214, 216–217, 221–225, 228; evolution of, 215–216, 276n2; family and, 226–227; gender and, 225–228, 280n23; intertextuality and, 216–217, 220, 230–231, 280n21; minorities and, 226, 280n24; professions and, 228–229; reception of, 215, 218–221, 222; stars and, 222; times and place of, 231; timeliness of, 219; victimization of biographee in, 223–228

Temple, Shirley, 226

Ten Commandments, The (C. B. De Mille, 1956), 92

Tennessee Johnson (William Dieterle, 1942), 13, 15f, 67

Terry Fox Story, The (TV movie, Ralph Thomas, 1983), 224

That Hamilton Woman (Alexander Korda, 1941), 107

Thebom, Blanche, 57

Tibbet, Lawrence, 272n20

Tin Pan Alley (Walter Lang, 1940), 143

To Hell and Back (Jesse Hibbs, 1955), 55–56, 269n3

To Race the Wind (TV movie, Walter Grauman, 1980), 224

Toast of New York, The (Rowland V. Lee, 1937), 77, 273n8

Tonight We Sing (Mitchell Leisen, 1953), 47

Too Much, Too Soon (Art Napolean, 1958), 46, 46f

Topaz (Alfred Hitchcock, 1969), 101

Toscanini, Arturo, 69

Toulouse-Lautrec, Henri de, 275n17

Tracy, Spencer, 20f, 22, 43–44, 65, 157f, 202, 205

trials, functions of in biopics, 136–137, 150, 181, 186–192, 274n9, 274n10

Trotti, Lamar, 19, 131, 135, 139, 167, 180, 181; congruence with Zanuck's ideas on biopic, 136–137

Truffaut, François, 2, 26

Tucker, Sophie, 58

Twain, Mark, 184

Twentieth Century Films, 129

Twentieth Century-Fox, 80, 83–87, 172, 196–197

United Artists, 80, 84, 89

Universal, 80, 84–85

Untouchables, The (TV series, ABC, 1959–1963), 84

Valentino, Rudolph, 94

Van Gogh, Vincent, 146, 192, 197–199

Victory at Entebbe (TV movie, Marvin J. Chomsky, 1976), 278n13

Villa, Pancho, 99

Villa! (James B. Clark, 1958), 98

Virgin Queen, The (Henry Koster, 1955), 59

Viva Villa! (Jack Conway, 1934), 98

Viva Zapata! (Elia Kazan, 1952), 98

Voltaire (John G. Adolfi, 1933), 61, 63f

Vorkapich, Slavko, 273n7

Wald, Jerry, 101

Walk the Proud Land (Jesse Hibbs, 1956), 98

Walker, Mayor James J., 141

Walker, Robert, 86
Walking Through Fire (TV movie, Robert Day, 1979), 228
Wallis, Hal, 21, 116, 121, 123, 140, 142, 160–161, 206, 275n17
Walsh, Raoul, 67
Warhol, Andy, 175
Warner, Harry, 100
Warner, Jack, 119, 205
Warner Brothers, 60, 67, 80, 83, 86, 87, 89, 112, 121, 126
Warren, Leslie Ann, 279n19
Wayne, John, 99, 197
Webb, Clifton, 270n8
Wellman, William, 52
West, Mae, 230
Western Union, 130, 135, 139
Westerner, The (William Wyler, 1940), 274n9
Westmore, Perc, 275n17
White, Hayden, 7, 9, 11, 25, 79, 177
White, Pearl, 45, 94, 163
White, Ryan, 217
White Angel, The (William Dieterle, 1936), 67
Whitmore, James, 163
Wilde, Cornell, 163
Wilde, Oscar, 32
Wilder, Billy, 67
Wilson (Henry King, 1944), 11, 97, 131
Winds of War, The (TV mini-series, 1989), 279n16
Winning Team, The (Lewis Seiler, 1952), 64, 217, 274n11
Wise, Robert, 55
Wister, Owen, 54
With a Song in My Heart (Walter Lang, 1952), 63, 71, 105, 131, 163, 224
Words and Music (Norman Taurog, 1948), 169–170
Wordsworth, William, 150
Worth, Sol, 282n2
Wyler, William, 67

Yankee Doodle Dandy (Michael Curtiz, 1942), 3, 59, 65, 78, 127, 153, 160–161, 165, 182–183, 210, 217
York, Alvin, 54
You Can't Buy Everything (1934), 77
Young, Brigham, 159
Young Bess (George Sidney, 1953), 51, 59, 165, 182
Young Daniel Boone (Reginald LeBorg, 1950), 51
Young Jesse James (William Claxton, 1960), 51
Young Man With a Horn (Michael Curtiz, 1950), 64
Young Mr. Lincoln (John Ford, 1939), 19, 51, 65, 135–136, 153, 167–168, 184; as an example of intertextual mediation, 180–182
Young Tom Edison (Norman Taurog, 1940), 51

Zaharias, Babe Didrickson, 228
Zanuck, Darryl F., 61, 116, 147, 164, 177, 206, 275n19; concept of the biopic, 50, 82, 97, 111, 129–130, 161, 171–175, 197, 202; intertextuality of his films, 142–147; on poetic license in biopics, 37–38, 128, 138–139, 160; as producer, 20–21, 129–139 (*The Story of Alexander Graham Bell*), 159–160 (*Brigham Young*), 167–168, 171–175, 180–182, 261n14 (*Young Mr. Lincoln*), 171–175 (*The I Don't Care Girl*), 196–197, 200–202 (*Golden Girl*); on "rooting interest" in biopic, 18–21, 132–137, 162, 173–174; vaudeville biopics, 47–50, 85, 87
Zapata, Emiliano, 99
Zelig (Woody Allen, 1983), 54
Ziegfeld, Florenz, 160
Zola, Emile, 2, 96, 146, 160, 211